American Culture in the 1920s

Twentieth-Century American Culture
Series Editor: Martin Halliwell, *Professor of American Studies, University of Leicester*

This series provides accessible but challenging studies of American culture in the twentieth century. Each title covers a specific decade and offers a clear overview of its dominant cultural forms and influential texts, discussing their historical impact and cultural legacy. Collectively the series reframes the notion of 'decade studies' through the prism of cultural production and rethinks the ways in which decades are usually periodised. Broad contextual approaches to the particular decade are combined with focused case studies, dealing with themes of modernity, commerce, freedom, power, resistance, community, race, class, gender, sexuality, internationalism, technology, war and popular culture.

American Culture in the 1910s
Mark Whalan

American Culture in the 1920s
Susan Currell

American Culture in the 1930s
David Eldridge

American Culture in the 1940s
Jacqueline Foertsch

American Culture in the 1950s
Martin Halliwell

American Culture in the 1960s
Sharon Monteith

American Culture in the 1970s
Will Kaufman

American Culture in the 1980s
Graham Thompson

American Culture in the 1990s
Colin Harrison

American Culture in the 1920s

Susan Currell

Edinburgh University Press

In memory of Vivien Hart

© Susan Currell, 2009

Edinburgh University Press Ltd
22 George Square, Edinburgh
www.euppublishing.com

Typeset in 11/13 pt Stempel Garamond by
Servis Filmsetting Ltd, Stockport, Cheshire, and
printed and bound in Great Britain by
CPI Antony Rowe, Chippenham and Eastbourne

A CIP record for this book is available from the British Library

ISBN 978 0 7486 2521 5 (hardback)
ISBN 978 0 7486 2522 2 (paperback)

Published with the support of the Edinburgh University Scholarly Publishing Initiatives Fund

Arts & Humanities
Research Council

Contents

Figures

Case Studies

Acknowledgements

I would like to thank the University of Sussex and the Arts and Humanities Research Council of Great Britain for funding the research leave that made this book possible. Thanks also to series editor Martin Halliwell for his patient encouragement and unstinting support, and also to Nicola Ramsey and staff at Edinburgh University Press. I am grateful to my colleagues and friends at the University of Sussex who supported this research and helped me at various stages, either by honouring my leave, taking over my teaching or giving constructive advice. Thanks also to Berit Potter at the Whitney Museum of American Art, and Judy Lopez at the O'Keeffe Museum. My other thanks go to all the friends and family who enquired after my progress and the numerous enthusiasts who have taken time to make documents, music and films from the 1920s available over the internet.

My greatest debt is to Warren Pleece, who has done more to support the writing of this book than I can begin to describe. I dedicate this book to you and our amazing sons, Frank and Georgy Pleece: your gracious tolerance and generosity towards this book has been truly humbling.

Chronology of 1920s American Culture

Date	Events	Criticism	Literature
1920	Republican Warren G. Harding elected. Women granted national franchise. Prohibition of alcohol begins. 4,000 suspected communists and radicals arrested, including Nicolo Sacco and Bartolomeo Vanzetti. Marcus Garvey's First International Convention of the Negro Peoples of the World. Deaths of Hollywood actresses Olive Thomas and Virginia Rappe.	George Santayana, *Character and Opinion in the United States* Thomas Stearns Eliot, *The Sacred Wood* Van Wyck Brooks, *The Ordeal of Mark Twain* Lothrop Stoddard, *The Rising Tide of Color* Sigmund Freud, *Beyond the Pleasure Principle* John Dewey, *Reconstruction in Philosophy* First tabloid newspaper, *New York Daily News*, published	F. Scott Fitzgerald, *This Side of Paradise* and *Flappers and Philosophers* Ezra Pound, *Hugh Selwyn Mauberley* Edward Bok, *The Americanization of Edward Bok* Carl Sandburg, *Smoke and Steel* Sinclair Lewis, *Main Street* Edith Wharton, *The Age of Innocence* Zane Grey, *The Man of the Forest*
1921	Emergency Immigration Act creates selective immigration quotas. Einstein arrives in New York. American Birth Control League founded. Lie detector invented. First Miss America contest held.	Little magazines *The Double Dealer* and *Broom* founded Sigmund Freud, *Group Psychology and the Analysis of the Ego* Anne Shaw Faulkner, 'Does Jazz Put the Sin in Syncopation?'	John Dos Passos, *Three Soldiers* Sherwood Anderson, *The Triumph of the Egg* Booth Tarkington, *Alice Adams* Ben Hecht, *Erik Dorn* Dorothy Canfield, *The Brimming Cup*

Performance	Film	Music and Radio	Art and Design
Eugene O'Neill, *The Emperor Jones* Zona Gale, *Miss Lulu Bett* Martha Graham dances in 'Xochitl'	*Why Change Your Wife?* (Cecil B. DeMille) *The Flapper* (Alan Crosland) *Within Our Gates* and *The Brute* (Oscar Micheaux)	Mamie Smith records 'Crazy Blues' Paul Whiteman records 'Whispering' and 'Japanese Sandman' George Antheil's *Symphony no. 1* Radio Corporation of America (RCA) founded First licensed radio broadcast from KDKA in Pittsburgh Presidential election results announced on radio	Edward Steichen's *Time/Space Continuum* Joseph Stella, *The Voice of the City of New York Interpreted* (1920–22) Charles Sheeler, *Church Street El*
Eubie Blake and Noble Sissle, 'Shuffle Along' John Alden Carpenter, 'Krazy Kat' Fletcher Henderson begins at the Roseland Ballroom	*The Kid* (Charles Chaplin) *The Four Horsemen of the Apocalypse* (Rex Ingram) *The Affairs of Anatol* (Cecil B. DeMille) *Never Weaken* (Harold Lloyd) *Manhatta* (Paul Strand and Charles Sheeler) Clara Bow wins 'The Fame and Fortune Contest'	Jack Dempsey beats Georges Carpentier in the first boxing match broadcast on radio First radio coverage of the World Series broadcast by WJZ Van and Schenck, 'Ain't We Got Fun?' Irving Berlin, 'All by Myself' and 'Say it with Music'	Ralph Steiner, *Typewriter Keys* Charles Demuth, *Incense of a New Church* and *Business* Stuart Davis, *Bull Durham* and *Lucky Strike*

Date	Events	Criticism	Literature
1922	Wage cuts cause 600,000 coal miners and 400,000 railroad workers to strike. Aimee Semple McPherson becomes first female radio evangelist. Tutankhamen's Tomb discovered by British archaeologist Howard Carter. Vitamins D and E discovered. Copies of James Joyce's banned *Ulysses* destroyed by US Post Office.	*Secession* (to 1924) and *The Fugitive* (to 1925) founded Harold Stearns (ed.), *Civilization In the United States* William Fielding Ogburn, *Social Change with Respect to Culture and Original Nature* Walter Lippman, *Public Opinion* Margaret Sanger, *The Pivot of Civilization* John Dewey, 'The American Intellectual Frontier' *Reader's Digest* begins	T. S. Eliot, *The Waste Land* James Weldon Johnson, *The Book of American Negro Poetry* Sinclair Lewis, *Babbitt* F. Scott Fitzgerald, *The Beautiful and the Damned* and *Tales of the Jazz Age* T. S. Stribling, *Birthright* Claude Mckay, 'The White House' Harry Leon Wilson, *Merton of the Movies*
1923	President Harding dies; Calvin Coolidge assumes presidency. Teapot Dome scandal emerges. First birth control clinic opens in New York. Tax cut from 50 to 40 per cent for the rich. Émile Coué makes his first tour of the US.	First issue of *Time* published *Opportunity: A Journal of Negro Life* first published Marcus Garvey, *The Philosophy and Opinions of Marcus Garvey* D. H. Lawrence, *Studies in Classic American Literature* Upton Sinclair, *The Goose-Step*	Jean Toomer, *Cane* William Carlos Williams, *Spring and All* and *The Great American Novel* Wallace Stevens, *Harmonium* Waldo Frank, *Holiday* Langston Hughes, 'The Weary Blues' Gertrude Atherton, *Black Oxen*

Performance	Film	Music and Radio	Art and Design
Eugene O'Neill, *The Hairy Ape* George White's musical revue 'Scandals of 1922'	*Nanook of the North* (Robert Flaherty) Will Hays becomes Director of the Motion Picture Producers and Distributors of America (MPPDA) Grauman's Egyptian Theater opens in Los Angeles	Louis Armstrong moves to Chicago Duke Ellington moves to New York with 'The Washingtonians' George Anteil, *Jazz Sonata* and *Death of the Machines* First pre-assembled radios go on sale Fiddlin' John Carson first plays on Atlanta's WSB	Paul Strand's *Double Akeley* Charles Sheeler, *Skyscraper* and *Offices* Gerald Murphy, *Engine Room* Ralph Steiner, *Always Camels* John Howells and Raymond Hood win the Chicago Tribune Tower competition.
Elmer Rice's *The Adding Machine* Musical revue 'Runnin Wild' introduces 'The Charleston' to mainstream America Alma Cummings wins the first American dance marathon	Harold Lloyd in *Safety Last* *Flaming Youth* (John Francis Dillon) *The Covered Wagon* (James Cruz) *The Ten Commandments* (Cecil B. DeMille) First 16mm camera produced	Bessie Smith records 'Downhearted Blues' and 'Gulf Coast Blues' Billy Jones' 'Yes, We Have No Bananas' a hit song King Oliver's Creole Jazz Band, 'Chimes Blues' Bix Beiderbecke forms the Wolverines The A&P Gypsies becomes the first band created by a radio sponsor	George Bellows, *Between Rounds* Charles Sheeler, *Bucks County Barn* Paul Outerbridge, *Jello Mold in Dish* Man Ray, *Object to be Destroyed* Louis Lozowick, *Pittsburgh, Chicago* and *Cleveland*

Date	Events	Criticism	Literature
1924	Richard Loeb and Nathan Leopold found guilty of murdering Bobby Franks. National Origins Act increases immigration restrictions. *Buck* v. *Bell* makes forcible sterilisation constitutional. Ku Klux Klan reaches height of popularity with 5 million supporters. Senate votes to bar all Japanese immigrants to the US. J. Edgar Hoover becomes head of the Bureau of Investigation. Hitler publishes *Mein Kampf*.	H. L. Mencken and George Nathan begin *The American Mercury* *Saturday Review of Literature* founded W. E. B. Du Bois, *The Gift of Black Folk* Ford Madox Ford founds *The Transatlantic Review* Gilbert Seldes, *The Seven Lively Arts* Lulu Hunt Peters' *Diet and Health* becomes non-fiction bestseller	Edna Ferber, *So Big* John Crowe Ransom, *Chills and Fever* Marianne Moore, *Observations* Julia Peterkin, *Green Thursday* Walter White, *The Fire in the Flint*
1925	John Scopes convicted of teaching the theory of evolution. KKK rally 40,000 in Washington DC. Electrical condenser microphone introduced. Pickwick Club in Boston collapses.	Irving Babbitt, *Democracy and Leadership* Bruce Barton, *The Man Nobody Knows* Frederic Thrasher, *The City* *The New Yorker* first published Alain Locke (ed.), *The New Negro* Marita Bonner, 'On Being Young, a Woman, and Colored'	F. Scott Fitzgerald, *The Great Gatsby* John Dos Passos, *Manhattan Transfer* Sherwood Anderson, *Dark Laughter* Willa Cather, *The Professor's House* Ernest Hemingway, *In Our Time* Gertrude Stein, *The Making of Americans* William Carlos Williams, *In the American Grain* Theodore Dreiser, *An American Tragedy* T. S Eliot, *Poems 1909–1925* Ellen Glasgow, *Barren Ground*

Performance	Film	Music and Radio	Art and Design
Maxwell Anderson and Laurence Stallings, *What Price Glory?* Eugene O'Neill, *Desire Under the Elms* Paul Whiteman's first 'Experiment in Modern Music' Flagpole sitting fad begins	*The Thief of Bagdad* (Raoul Walsh) *The Iron Horse* (John Ford) *Manhandled* (Allan Dwan) *Greed* (Erich Von Stroheim)	Al Jolson, 'California, Here I Come' Photographs transmitted by wireless between London and New York National conventions of the Republican and Democratic parties broadcast nationally for the first time	George Bellows, *Dempsey and Firpo* Gerald Murphy, *Odol* and *Razor* Paul Rosenfeld, *Port of New York: Essays* American Radiator Building completed Georgia O'Keeffe, *Dark Abstraction* Debut of *Little Orphan Annie* comic strip
'The Coconuts' starring the Marx Brothers with songs by Irving Berlin John Alden Carpenter, *Skyscrapers* Paul Whiteman's 'Second Experiment in Modern Music'	*The Gold Rush* (Charles Chaplin) *The Big Parade* (King Vidor) *The Phantom of the Opera* (Rupert Julian)	Louis Armstrong and Bessie Smith record 'St Louis Blues' Bessie Smith records 'Lonesome Desert Blues' George Anteil, *Jazz Symphony* Louis Gruenberg, *Jazzberries* and *The Daniel Jazz* Warner Brothers begin radio broadcasting from KFWB in Los Angeles	*Exposition Internationale des Arts Décoratifs et Industriels Modernes* in Paris Georgia O'Keeffe and Alfred Stieglitz move to the Shelton Hotel Georgia O'Keeffe, *New York with Moon* Aaron Douglas, *Invincible Music: The Spirit of Africa* Man Ray, *Clock Wheels* Arthur Dove, *Miss Woolworth*

Date	Events	Criticism	Literature
1926	Tax cuts from 40 to 20 per cent for the wealthy. Great Miami Hurricane causes $100 million damage and ends land boom. Gertrude Ederle swims the English Channel. Rudolph Valentino and Harry Houdini die prematurely. Vitamin B1 discovered.	Langston Hughes, 'The Negro Artist and the Racial Mountain' Langston Hughes, Zora Neale Hurston, Wallace Thurman, Aaron Douglas, Bruce Nugent, Gwendolyn Bennett and John P. Davis publish *Fire!!* H. L. Mencken, *Notes on Democracy* *New Masses* magazine founded Book-of-the-Month Club founded	Ernest Hemingway, *The Sun Also Rises* Langston Hughes, *The Weary Blues* Carl Van Vechten, *Nigger Heaven* William Faulkner, *Soldiers' Pay* Hart Crane, *White Buildings* Elizabeth Madox Roberts, *The Time of Man* Frances Newman, *The Hard-Boiled Virgin* Anita Loos, *Gentlemen Prefer Blondes*
1927	Charles Lindbergh flies non-stop from New York to Paris. Sacco and Vanzetti executed. Henry Ford's production line opens at the River Rouge factory. First long-range television signal transmitted from Washington DC to New York. Babe Ruth hits his 60th home run of the season (a record unbroken until 1961).	Charles Beard, *The Rise of American Civilization* Vernon L. Parrington, *Main Currents in American Thought* Judge Ben B. Lindsay and Wainwright Evans, *The Companionate Marriage* Joseph Wood Krutch, 'The Modern Temper'	Sinclair Lewis, *Elmer Gantry* Langston Hughes, *Fine Clothes to the Jew* Willa Cather, *Death Comes for the Archbishop* Ernest Hemingway, *Men Without Women* James Weldon Johnson, *God's Trombones: Seven Negro Sermons in Verse* Elizabeth Madox Robert, *My Heart and Flesh* Thorton Wilder, *The Bridge of San Luis Rey*

Performance	Film	Music and Radio	Art and Design
Eugene O'Neill, *The Great God Brown* The Savoy Ballroom opens in Harlem Mae West, *Sex* Paul Green, *In Abraham's Bosom*	*Don Juan* (Alan Crosland) *What Price Glory?* (Raoul Walsh) *The Son of the Sheik* (George Fitzmaurice) *The Black Pirate* (Albert Parker) *Ella Cinders* (Alfred Green) *Moana* (Robert Flaherty)	Louis Armstrong records 'Heebie Jeebies' William Grant Still, *Levee Land* National Broadcasting Company (NBC) founded Jelly Roll Morton, 'Black Bottom Stomp' Vincent Lopez, 'Always'	Harmon Foundation holds first annual art exhibition of Negro Art Archibald John Motley Jr, *Cocktails* Chrysler Building started Georgia O'Keeffe, *City Night* Edward Hopper, *Sunday*
e.e. cummings, *Him* Jerome Kern and Oscar Hammerstein, *Show Boat* George Anteil, *Ballet Mécanique* and *Jazz Symphony* performed in Carnegie Hall James Price Johnson, *Yamekraw*	*The Jazz Singer* (Alan Crosland) *Sunrise* (F. W. Murnau) *Underworld* (Josef Von Sternberg) *IT* (Clarence Badger) *Flesh and the Devil* (Clarence Brown) Buster Keaton stars in *The General* (Clyde Bruckman) The Roxy opens in New York	Duke Ellington begins at the Cotton Club Victoria Spivey, 'T. B. Blues' Irving Berlin, 'Blue Skies' Duke Ellington, 'Black and Tan Fantasy' NBC links fifty stations across twenty-four states for an all-day live transmission of the Lindbergh medal award listened to by thirty million people Radio Act regulates the radio industry	*Machine Art* exhibition in New York Charles Sheeler photographs Ford's River Rouge factory Georgia O'Keeffe, *The Radiator Building – Night, New York* Arthur Dove, *George Gershwin – Rhapsody in Blue part I and II* Edward Hopper, *Automat* and *The Drug Store*

Date	Events	Criticism	Literature
1928	Republican Herbert Hoover defeats Al Smith in a landslide election for the presidency. Ruth Snyder's execution pictured on front page of the *New York Daily News*. Alexander Fleming discovers penicillin. Vitamin C discovered. Great Okeechobee Hurricane, Florida, causes 2,500 deaths.	Margaret Mead, *Coming of Age in Samoa* Zora Neale Hurston, 'How It Feels to Be Colored Me' Franz Boas, *Anthropology and Modern Life* *American Literature* journal started	Allen Tate, *Mr Pope and Other Poems* Claude McKay, *Home to Harlem* Djuna Barnes, *The Ladies Almanack* Nella Larsen, *Quicksand* Jessie Fauset, *Plum Bun: A Novel Without a Moral* Upton Sinclair, *Boston* Vina Delmar, *Bad Girl*
1929	First coast-to-coast airline created. The stock market crashes in late October; twenty-nine million shares sold in five days. Gastonia Strike. St Valentine's Day Massacre kills six gangsters and a bystander.	Walter White, *Rope and Faggot: A Biography of Judge Lynch* Robert and Helen Lynd, *Middletown* John Dewey, *The Quest for Certainty* Joseph Wood Krutch, *The Modern Temper* James Truslow Adams, *Our Business Civilization: Some Aspects of American Culture*	Ernest Hemingway, *A Farewell to Arms* Wallace Thurman, *The Blacker the Berry* Thomas Wolfe, *Look Homeward Angel* William Faulkner, *Sartoris* and *The Sound and the Fury* Agnes Smedley, *Daughter of Earth* Nella Larsen, *Passing* Dashiell Hammet, *Red Harvest*

Performance	Film	Music and Radio	Art and Design
Sophie Treadwell, *Machinal* Eugene O'Neill, *Strange Interlude* Martha Graham performs *Immigrant: Steerage, Strike* George Gershwin's *An American in Paris* premiers at Carnegie Hall The Marx Brothers star in *Animal Crackers*	*The Crowd* (King Vidor) *Our Dancing Daughters* (Harry Beaumont) *The Wedding March* (Erich Von Stroheim) *Speedy* (Harold Lloyd) Walt Disney produces first Mickey Mouse cartoon, *Plane Crazy*, followed by his first sound animation *Steamboat Willie*	Louis Armstrong, 'West End Blues' Ruth Etting, 'Love Me or Leave Me' Helen Kane, 'I Wanna Be Loved By You' Will Rogers Program broadcast to millions on NBC First car radios manufactured	Demuth, *I Saw the Figure 5* Margaret Bourke-White, *Niagara Falls Generators* Edward Hopper, *Manhattan Bridge Loop* and *Night Windows* Charles Sheeler, *River Rouge Industrial Plant* Buckminster Fuller introduces his Dymaxion House
Elmer Rice, *The Subway: A Play in Nine Scenes* Eugene O'Neill, *Dynamo*	*Black and Tan* starring Duke Ellington *St. Louis Blues* starring Bessie Smith *Hallelujah* (King Vidor) *The Broadway Melody* (Harry Beaumont)	Fats Waller and Louis Armstrong, 'Aint Misbehavin' The Rounders and The Brox Sisters, 'Singing in the Rain' Bessie Smith, 'Wasted Life Blues' *Amos 'n' Andy* radio show first broadcast on NBC	Alexander Calder, *Circus* Charles Sheeler, *Upper Deck* Thomas Hart Benton, *Georgia Cotton Pickers* Museum of Modern Art founded Hugh Ferris publishes the *Metropolis of Tomorrow*

The Intellectual Context

In his reflection on the decade in 1931, the writer F. Scott Fitzgerald described the 1920s as 'the ten-year period that, as if reluctant to die outmoded in its bed, leaped to a spectacular death in October, 1929, [which] began about the time of the May Day riots in 1919'.[1] Patterns in culture never begin and end quite so clearly, but the 1920s are neatly encased within two major events – the end of World War I and the Wall Street Crash – that give distinctive boundaries to those years. These two events consolidated, accelerated and confirmed intellectual responses to modernity that had begun much earlier and continued well beyond the 1920s. Despite this, ideas about culture and society operate in relationship with the political and social environment of the time, making it possible to describe the culture of the 1920s as distinct as well as part of longer-term trends. The introduction of new mass communications, notably radio programming and sound on film, the unprecedented prominence of racial and nativist ideologies in public culture, the popularisation of psychoanalysis, female suffrage and the prohibition of alcohol rendered the decade clearly different from others that had come before. Ideas about these social, technological and scientific changes emerged in the philosophies and ideologies that developed over the period; this book examines the part that those ideas, both old and new, played in the cultural productions of the 1920s.

The rejection of tradition and the celebration of the new was a pervasive cultural theme beneath Fitzgerald's comment that the 1920s refused to die 'outmoded' and 'old'. Historians have identified this tension between progress and tradition as a central paradox underlying American history and culture.[2] Although not exclusive to it, the decade after the Great War until the onset of the Great Depression highlighted this tension more clearly than any other decade. While often characterised as an era of apolitical individualism, an era of business culture, hedonism and political retreat, the period can more accurately be seen as an era of cultural renaissance created from the very ambivalence, the irresolvable tensions, over ideas about the past and the possibilities of the future.

This combination of despair and possibility was highlighted by an iconoclastic autobiographical work that received a Pulitzer Prize in 1919: *The Education of Henry Adams*. The book charted Adams' struggle to reconcile traditional ideas with the transformations of modernity, examining his 'unlearning' of thought in the face of technological and cultural change.[3] In the aftermath of World War I, Adams' confusion and disorientation resonated with the rapidly changing intellectual and social environment in which Americans found themselves. With the cessation of hostilities, the old rules that cohered society no longer applied – some attempted to find (and enforce) new rules, and others worked to embrace and shape a new experimental culture without fixed rules. The schism that these ideas revealed made culture a furious battleground where ideological commitments were developed in a crucible of uncertainty and change.

Cultural Decline

What was clear was that the end of the war presented America with a host of new problems to address. The pre-war experimentalism in culture had relied on a booming optimism about the future and progress, but the war exposed the bankruptcy of such idealism. Economist Thorstein Veblen claimed that America had 'gone into moral and industrial eclipse', while revisionist histories quickly dismantled the illusion that either peace or democracy had been successfully restored by the peace treaty.[4] Theologian Reinhold Niebuhr stated in his diary in 1923 that '[g]radually the whole horrible truth about the war is being revealed. Every new book destroys some further illusion'.[5] Poets and writers expressed their disillusion and the intellectual impasse it caused in their work: in *Gerontion* (1920), T. S. Eliot expressed the 'Thoughts of a dry brain in a dry season', asking 'After such knowledge, what forgiveness?' In his poem *Hugh Selwyn Mauberley* (1920), Ezra Pound expressed the collapse of ideals and trust in democracy that rocked intellectual discourse for the decade, writing of soldiers who had 'walked eye-deep in hell/ believing in old men's lies, then unbelieving/ came home, home to a lie,/ home to many deceits', having wasted their youth, 'For an old bitch gone in the teeth,/ For a botched civilization'. To Pound, civilisation died alongside soldiers, fighting 'For two gross of broken statues,/ For a few thousand battered books'.[6]

Few intellectuals could see any hope in the political or economic establishment and the old ideals of freedom and democracy appeared to be in shreds. The battle for world democracy had entailed a sharp curtailment of individual freedoms for Americans: the Bolshevik revolution in Russia in 1917 had led authorities to suppress domestic radicalism for fear of similar turmoil, and legislation such as the Espionage Act of 1917 and the Sedition Act of 1918 prevented open criticism of or opposition to the political establishment. Yet the end of the war only unearthed further class and race tensions as the rising cost of living and mass immigration led to huge waves of strikes, protests and race riots. For African Americans the first few years of 'peace' were the most violent in their history since slavery had ended, with over twenty-five race riots across the country causing hundreds of deaths and thousands of injuries. African American soldiers' experience of vicious attacks, lynching (at least 456 people were killed by lynch mobs between 1918 and 1927) and race riots in the 'Red Summer' of 1919 highlighted the absurdity of their wartime fight for American democracy.[7]

Those who questioned democracy were increasingly considered dangerous to postwar stability and order. In 1919 Attorney General A. Mitchell Palmer – a former liberal and advocate of women's suffrage and child labour laws – sanctioned violent 'Palmer raids' on union members, communists, anarchists and other radicals as industrial and social unrest literally exploded around the country. Celebrated anti-communist investigator J. Edgar Hoover began his career in the Department of Justice during the Palmer Raids, later becoming head of the FBI in 1924. Intellectuals, scientists, feminists and civil libertarians were all scrutinised for anti-American sentiments and the investigation of radical activities as criminal ones persisted under Hoover's leadership for the next four decades. The 1920 arrest of two Italian-born anarchists, Nicola Sacco and Bartolomeo Vanzetti, symbolised the extent of the oppression by the political establishment. Although arrested and tried for robbery and murder, the case appeared a witch-hunt by an extremist establishment rather than a fair criminal investigation. The case became a cause célèbre among intellectuals and artists, and their execution in 1927 became a symbol of civil and political repression throughout the decade and into the 1930s.

While the Red Panic of 1919 subsided, the restoration of faith in democracy took far longer. The inadequacies of the Treaty of Versailles alongside America's military interventions in Russia and Latin America in the early 1920s created an overwhelming sense of continuing world and domestic instability. Even though the rest of the country was experiencing an economic downturn, 42,000 new millionaires had emerged from wartime business profits, exacerbating class tension and resentment.[8] In 1919, when Democrat President Woodrow Wilson suffered a stroke, the country appeared debilitated by chaos and conflict. In a pre-election speech in 1920, Republican Presidential candidate Warren G. Harding offered an appealing vision of returning stability and calm to the nation: 'America's present need is not heroics, but healing; not nostrums, but normalcy; not revolution, but restoration; not agitation, but adjustment'.[9]

Despite this, 'normalcy' and 'adjustment' did not mean a return to pre-war ideals or traditions, but a huge expansion in business freedom and capitalist acquisition that unwove the progressive reforms and ideals of the previous two decades. The election of Harding in 1920 marked the true beginning of the business era, most notably with the appointment of Andrew Mellon, a wealthy businessman, as Secretary of the Treasury. Mellon cut business and income tax and halved federal spending over the decade. While much of Europe rebuilt itself or experienced severe depressions and social turmoil, from 1922 economic activity boomed in the United States; having expanded industrial production during the war, it increased peacetime production to an unprecedented degree. As a result America became the most productive and prosperous nation in the world.

This rise of business culture, with its associated materialism and anti-intellectualism – and later corruption – heralded a new detachment from politics for the intellectual and artist: 'These rulers of America, as they were called in magazine articles, showed little interest in books or ideas'.[10] Fitzgerald claimed that '[t]he events of 1919 left us cynical rather than revolutionary . . . [i]t was characteristic of the Jazz Age that it had no interest in politics at all'.[11] He summarised the intellectual retreat from politics as part weariness from 'Great Causes' and part greed in the postwar boom, claiming that artists and the intelligentsia sold out when 'we began to have our slices of the national cake'.[12] The idealism of the war diminished into financial gain as Fitzgerald suggested that 'maybe we had gone to war for J. P. Morgan's loans after all'.[13] For some of the 'lost generation' of writers, cultural retreat from this philistine world of business existed only in Europe.

Machine Culture

The boom in business was fuelled by progress in new technologies and methods of mass production, which caused further anxieties over human culture. Calvin Coolidge's statement that 'the man who builds a factory builds a temple' only served to underline that business had become the new national religion.[14] Like Henry Adams, many believed that new scientific ideas had overthrown governing philosophies, and even modernists expressed ambivalence about what this meant for the future. Lewis Mumford, a moderniser and city planner, claimed that American culture had become narrower because 'business, technology, and science not merely occupied their legitimate place but took to themselves all that had hitherto belonged to art, religion and poetry'.[15] To Mumford, this 'sinister world' needed replacement with the synthesis, not separation, of art and science, based upon a 'criticism of the past and the rejection of stereotyped interests and actions'.[16] Modernisers such as Mumford called for a new reinterpretation of culture, one that was practical and scientific but also spiritual and creative.

Mumford's optimism for the new scientific future was glaringly absent from the criticism of the past that prevailed in much of the intellectual pessimism of the decade, in which intellectuals saw themselves as besieged defenders of culture against a tide of philistinism. This, however, did not mean a retreat into the past: in the collection of essays *Civilization In the United States* (1922), Harold Stearns claimed the past to be irrelevant: 'We have no heritages or traditions with which to cling except those that have already withered in our hands and turned to dust'. Yet the present offered few compensations: 'the most moving and pathetic fact in the social life of America today is emotional and aesthetic starvation' characterised by the spiritual poverty of a regimented, shallow, materialistic industrial society.[17] These anxieties reflected ubiquitous concerns over the changing notion of 'the human' in relation to science and the machine during the early twentieth century – and Henry Ford's methods of mass production and welfare capitalism became the prime cultural metaphor of the shallow, regimented age.

Fordism and Culture

In 1900 there were 8,000 automobiles in the United States; by 1926 there were twenty million. Henry Ford was at the forefront of a manufacturing revolution and his methods became synonymous with modernity through-out the world. By 1920 half of the cars in the world were Model T Fords.[18] In 1914 Ford's Highland Park Factory alone produced 240,700 Model Ts; by 1923 this number had risen to 2,055,300.[19] Ford's production methods were premised on two central ideas: the assembly line and the uniformity of a product. Ford then linked efficient production to workers' wages by introducing the legendary five-dollar, eight-hour day in 1914.[20] The pay-off for the increase in wages and lower working hours was that workers had to submit to greater control over their non-working lives as well as in the work-place. The Ford Sociological Department, created to administer the five-dollar wage, sent field agents into the community to visit workers at home to make sure that they were living sober and moral lives before their wages could be raised. Thus, the activities of workers outside of work became directly connected to their income and the profits of the company.

Ford's empire consisted of towns, factories, hospitals and schools dedi-cated to the purpose of maintaining the smooth running and profitability of his business. Owning rubber plantations, hydroelectric dams, and steel, iron, coal and forestry works ensured the supply of raw materials. His own-ership of railroads and shipyards ensured effective transportation of those materials. Over the 1920s, gangsters aiming to control the distribution of alcohol emulated Ford's method of 'vertical integration' as the perfect business model.

Ford's lesser known activities, however, indicated that he was as inter-ested in streamlining workers as streamlining the industry for vast profit: running welfare programmes, hospitals, schools and colleges ensured a supply of healthy, trained and rationalised productive bodies. Along with this, his activities in radio programming, publishing and education over the 1920s illustrated the extent to which Ford aimed not just to produce goods, but to control the production of workers themselves.

This increased surveillance and control, along with an apparent mechani-sation of the worker's mind and body, was noted by the Italian political the-orist and activist Antonio Gramsci, in his now famous essay 'Americanism and Fordism', written from prison in 1929.[21] Gramsci saw that Henry Ford's system was not just a smoothly running factory but had become an ideol-ogy uniquely associated with 'Americanism' itself. Gramsci claimed that, in America, 'rationalization has determined the need to elaborate a new type of man suited to the new type of work and productive process', and that the concern of industrialists with the leisure-time behaviour of their workers indicated a new form of psychological, sexual and social conformity, which appeared to originate with the worker himself in the form of self-control.

Concerns over the humanity of these types of production methods are reflected in the aesthetics and cultural debates of the period. As indicated by Gramsci, the increasing dominance of mass-produced culture went hand in hand with the emergence of a culture of increased social control, mechanisation and conformity.

Ford was not only 'producing' workers: the flip side of mass production was mass consumption. The growth of middle-class America – made up increasingly of people living in suburban houses, commuting, socialising and shopping using automobiles – fuelled intellectual concerns over the disappearance of 'authentic' culture into one that was mass produced, created to distract and depoliticise the consumer. Lewis Mumford's reaction to the mechanisation of culture was thus not unusual: 'The movies, the White Ways, and the Coney Islands, which almost every American city boasts in some form or other, are means of giving a jaded and throttled people the sensations of living without the direct experience of life – a sort of spiritual masturbation. In short, we have had the alternative of humanizing the industrial city or de-humanizing the population. So far we have de-humanized the population'.[22]

In 1927 Henry Ford's production line switched to the River Rouge factory, the largest manufacturing facility in the world. Abandoning the Model T for the Model A, the switch also signified Ford's capitulation to consumer fashion and the culture of abundance, while the appearance of this futuristic plant, designed by architect Albert Kahn and photographed by precisionist artist Charles Sheeler, paradoxically coincided with Ford's increasing nostalgia and obsession with a lost past; in 1929 Ford opened Greenfield Village, a museum dedicated to reassembling the rapidly disappearing past.[23]

Despite this, the mechanisation of culture held a fascination that became central to a variety of cultural outputs. Recognising the new cultural force of the machine in 1922, photographer Paul Strand described the relationship between machine and society as a modern Trinity: 'God the Machine, Materialistic Empiricism the Son, and Science the Holy Ghost'.[24] Writers, artists and intellectuals engaged both pessimistically and exuberantly with the resulting 'machine aesthetics' of the new machine age.

As America emerged as the foremost economic, political and cultural power, American culture took on a new importance, not only for Americans but for the rest of the world. Fitzgerald claimed '[w]e were the most powerful nation. Who could tell us any longer what was fashionable and what was fun?'[25] In addition to exporting raw and finished goods, wrote Malcolm Cowley, the United States now exported 'cultural goods, hot and sweet jazz bands, financial experts, movies and political ideals'.[26] The recovery of society and democracy appeared intertwined with the rebuilding of national cultural values on a new world stage, yet there was no consensus on the shape that this new culture should take. As Mumford noted, cultural pessimism was paralysing intellectual thought, dispelling the founding drive, the 'will-to-utopia', in wider American society. 'Looking around at our contemporaries who have survived the war, it is fairly evident that most of them are in the first stage of panic and despair,' he wrote, arguing for a 'utopia of reconstruction' on which to base new ideals and society.[27]

The Science of Culture

Despite a deeply ingrained pessimism, intellectual activity over the period did produce a vibrant culture of ideas and perceptions that appeared to liberate society from outmoded and outworn beliefs and behaviours. To America's foremost philosopher, John Dewey, postwar reconstruction depended upon 'reconstruction in philosophy' that would rebuild national culture and revive democracy.[28] Dewey believed that '[c]onceptions of possibility, progress, free movement and infinitely diversified opportunity have been suggested by modern science', but that society was afflicted by 'the heritage of the immutable . . . ordered and systematized' that lay 'like a dead weight upon the emotions, paralyzing religion and distorting art'.[29] Overthrowing the past, then, was a political act of revivifying democracy.

Born in 1859, Dewey was influenced by the philosopher William James' turn to pragmatism as a solution to contemporary problems of democracy, knowledge and education. His belief in the holistic connection between science and art, experience and reality, the individual and community provided a counterpoint to the despair and nihilism that permeated cultural tensions in the decade. Rather than return to the security of tradition, however, Dewey believed that the philosopher and intellectual had a public role 'to assist in [the] clarification and redirection of men's thoughts' and 'to free experience from routine and from caprice'. Dewey argued for social stability based not on tradition or dogmatic belief, but on intelligent and rational responses to the needs of social progress in the present: 'we rely on precedent as authority only to our own undoing', he argued.[30]

Pragmatism was often perceived simply as an instrumental philosophy of action rather than ideas; Dewey, however, saw it as a method of creating action 'informed with vision, imagination, reflection'; a method relevant for solving modern conflicts and confusion in which culture was central.[31] Eschewing dogma and a priori belief – notably the nationalistic dogmas which had led to the war in Europe – Dewey claimed that the new world position of America demanded a new philosophy which showed faith 'in the power of intelligence to imagine a future which is the projection of the desirable in the present, and to invent the instrumentalities of its realization'.[32] Dewey offered a salve to the tensions in society between the past and future. Over the 1920s his ideas permeated into discussions over politics, education, community and society. Most notably, the 1920s marked the popularisation of the ideas of pragmatism more widely than ever before.[33]

Dewey also believed that it was in the popularisation and ethical application of scientific knowledge that democracy could be sustained. Dewey's ideas undercut the pessimism of the 1920s by arguing that democracy in mass society was not only possible but likely, with the rapid increase of mass communication and education. His writings indicated that mass society was not inherently in decay. Despite this, Dewey's ideas did not offer the stability of belief that many needed. To Dewey 'truth' was relative, mutable and based upon untested outcomes; for him it was 'the quest for certainty' that harmed society and hampered social progress. Few, however, celebrated uncertainty with quite the same passion.[34]

Reassessing American Culture: Social Science

Dewey's pragmatism influenced a new approach to gathering, analysing and applying information within the social sciences.[35] The 1920s marked a new era for the social sciences with the formation of the Chicago School of sociology and the work of urban sociologists Robert Park and Ernest Burgess from around 1918. Robert Park had been a student of both Dewey at Michigan, and William James at Harvard. The University of Chicago sociologists and their students were deeply influenced by empirical methodology coming out of the sciences, believing in investigation through personal experience, firsthand observations and interviewing methods combined with empirical data. Their researches aimed to describe reality in a new way that had a big impact on other forms of cultural and literary production.

The social scientists of the 1920s developed new techniques and observations that were based on empirical evidence rather than applying a priori theories to a range of situations. Their research marked a shift towards collaborative and interdisciplinary work, which combined several disciplines such as sociology, the political sciences, psychology, anthropology, statistics and economics. Further to this, the Chicago School sociologists became distinctive in the way that they incorporated a variety of evidence-based cultural documents into their studies, assembling their studies using personal documents such as diaries and letters, intensive field observations based on months spent participating in a community (sometimes even in disguise or under-cover), documentary sources such as newspaper articles, photographs or court records alongside the use of statistical techniques, and social and environmental mapping. These new methods aimed to illustrate a more truthful experience of the subject under investigation from a variety of angles, embellished at times with diaries or letters, and at others with journalistic commentary from the researcher.

The desire to access a truthful experience of the subject under study meant using a variety of scientific methods. Biologist Jacques Loeb's study of ant society, for example, informed Robert Park's analysis of the city. Likewise, William Ogburn insisted on the importance of psychology and psychoanalysis to sociology in order to know the 'etiology of our own desires and the mechanisms of their behavior'.[36] The influence of Freudian thought on sociology enabled sociologists like Burgess to develop their ideas about group and social psychology and explore new arenas like social psychiatry in later years.

The methods of the Chicago School attempted to portray a reality that was multilayered and relative rather than the singular vision of the moralistic reformer of previous decades, heralding new ideas about communication and the construction of reality. This new research undermined the universalism upon which certainty and sta-bility relied. Anthropologists like Margaret Mead examined culture as a relative rather than fixed phenomenon, thus counteracting the prevailing trend of evolutionary determinism sanctioned by cultural pessimists such as Lothrop Stoddard (discussed below). Mead's study of Polynesian culture, *Coming of Age in Samoa* (1928), popularised the idea of cultural relativism by showing that all cultures had equal validity, and shocked many by showing a 'primitive' culture as happier and more stable because less sexually repressed than more 'civilised' American society. A new investigation of American cultural pluralism evolved in the wake of such anthropological studies made abroad.

In the 1920s American social scientists also turned their attention from the study of 'foreign' cultures to their own, beginning with the investigation of immigrant or migrant culture in the urban environment – *The Polish Peasant in Europe and America* (1918), *Old World Traits Transplanted* (1921), *The Negro in Chicago* (1922), *The Neighborhood* (1923), *The City* (1925), *The Gang* (1927) and *The Ghetto* (1928) – followed by research into the middle classes in the suburban setting such as *Middletown* (1929).[37] To many, these investigations indicated that social problems were caused by maladjustment to culture. The disparity between social and technological developments and human capacity to keep up with and adapt to cultural change became a central concern of sociologists such as William Ogburn, who invented the term 'cultural lag' to describe the problem. Ogburn's conceit not only influenced intellectual thought but became central to popular ideas about modern living and self-improvement. The increasing speed of social change led to a flurry of investigations that attempted to remap the social and cultural landscape of America.[38]

The Culture of Science

Dewey's ideal of a democracy of well-informed and educated citizens was counteracted by the concern that corporations and private business entrepreneurs now exercised a new domination over intellectual life, as the relationship between academia, intellectuals and big business actually merged more than ever. The huge growth and popularisation of social science research was assisted by increased research funding by American millionaire philanthropists. Carnegie and Rockefeller had begun their foundations in the progressive era, but huge numbers of research-based studies were sponsored by a variety of philanthropic endeavours, among them the Brookings Institution and the Pollak Foundation for Economic Research. If the research of the social scientists and psychoanalysts were to make effective material changes to the shape of modern culture, then the sponsorship of rich philanthropists and corporations was vital to this project.[39] Likewise, the newly formed public relations and advertising agencies during this period recognised the potential commercial use of social science research and the new ideas of social psychology, a relationship highlighted in 1924, when a leading exponent of the Behaviourist school of psychology, John B. Watson, became vice-president of the country's leading advertising agency, J. Walter Thompson.[40]

While the social sciences started to use scientific research methods in a more systematic way, the shift came alongside a new dissemination of science in popular culture. In 1921 Einstein's arrival in New York created a media sensation, followed by numerous attempts to popularise and explain his theories, including the animated movie *The Einstein Theory of Relativity* (1923) that showed how '[o]ne by one, Einstein sweeps away every accepted notion'.[41] The year 1921 also saw the founding of the Science Service in Washington DC, a science news syndicate which aimed to make all of the latest theories and discoveries accessible and freely available to ordinary Americans.[42] As a consequence, the discovery of vitamins, calories, new hormones such as insulin, and medical cures such as penicillin became integrated into popular knowledge for the first time. Edwin Emery Slosson of the newly formed Columbia school of Journalism ran 'Easy Lessons in Einstein' for his journalism students and by 1927 the Science Service had ventured into radio broadcasting with 'Science News of the Week' being syndicated to 22 stations by 1929.[43] A proliferation of popular-science magazines and bestsellers added to this expansion of scientific knowledge, impacting on all aspects of culture, from art and poetry to self-help and fashion. From streamlined design to physical health, progress and modernity appeared to depend on a more scientific approach to life.

Culture as Therapy

The huge popularisation of one particular field of science appeared to threaten traditional culture more than any other: psychoanalysis. Freud first visited America in 1909 and his newly translated work had permeated into intellectual circles of radical writers, who used Freud as a way of challenging tradition and conservatism. However, it wasn't until the 1920s that Freud 'became epidemic in America'.[44] Just as Einstein's theory had revealed the deception of surface appearance, Freud's indicated that beneath the appearance of normality lay unseen unconscious drives: both revealed that there were unseen forces behind the movements of the natural and social world.

To many, the Great War confirmed Freud's theories about the irrational and brutal beneath the veneer of civilised society, revealing the dangerous possibilities of the primal instincts in human nature. Not only had the war exposed the fragility of modern democracy, it had generated and revealed the existence of widespread psychological disorders that had been previously undetected or undiagnosed: 'America is by way of being something of a psychiatrical clinic,' claimed Veblen in 1922.[45] Psychiatric treatment of shell-shocked soldiers illustrated the usefulness of Freud's theories for treating the traumatised and the neurotic – ideas that became extended to the peacetime adjustment of Americans to the new conditions of modernity. To many intellectuals, their disillusion with received values and institutions was justified in the discoveries of psychoanalysis, a field that counteracted the pessimism it created by offering a new path to social progress. In many ways the tension between the past and future progress within American society was represented in the neurotic individual, trapped in the past and unable to progress to 'normalcy' until psychoanalysis unlocked the door to a more stable future. As Freud noted in 1927, progress in psychoanalysis (and culture more generally) relied on a tension between the past and the present, where 'the present . . . must have become the past – before it can yield points of vantage from which to judge the future'.[46]

By the 1920s intellectual interpretations of American history were being amended by Freud's theories. In his negative appraisal of the state of American culture in 1922, Harold Stearns employed the Oedipal complex to describe the poor state of American culture: 'America is a very young country . . . [w]e have not sufficiently grown up but that we must still cling to our father and mother'.[47] The critic Waldo Frank in *Our American* (1919) also analysed contemporary problems as a result of 'repression on a national scale'.[48] Frank interpreted the postwar psychic imbalance as an effect of the centuries of Puritan and pioneer repressions. Materialism and the drive for success had replaced the natural instincts, they argued. Only in the rediscovery of the far reaches of human consciousness, through art, literature and poetry, and a rejection of the past, would it be possible to cure the neurotic industrial monster that America had become. In this way the past was cast as 'disease' with culture as the cure.

By the start of the 1920s such ideas about the individual and society were being circulated in the mass media outside of elite and intellectual circles, even appearing in the more conservative echelons of *Good Housekeeping* magazine.[49] In 1920 one writer claimed that it was 'hard to pick up a newspaper or a magazine without finding psychoanalytic terms', and by 1925 another writer was calling Freud the 'Columbus of the Subconscious' and the 'God of psychoanalysis'.[50]

This widespread use of psychoanalysis was not unproblematic. The discipline itself experienced crisis with the appearance in the 1920s of a 'new' psychoanalytic psychology, 'an eclectic mix of Adler, Jung and Freud'.[51] The huge popularisation of Freudian ideas in the mass media resulted in a lack of orthodoxy that appeared to be exploiting public interest in the new trend rather than assisting progression. The popular overuse of Freudian theory led to dilution, misinterpretation and downright quackery, developments that in turn became an object of satire for writers and artists.[52] As Alfred Kuttner noted in 1922, the nation's embrace of Freudianism in the 1920s exhibited 'the most extravagant development of the so-called "wild" psychoanalysis'.[53] The adaptation of Freud to new market and social conditions took on a variety of guises; from the appearance of the first popular magazine on psychology in 1923 came a torrent of popular literature on the new psychology, including books, magazine articles and newspaper columns.[54] Like Einstein, Sigmund Freud became a household figure, and made the first of five appearances on the cover of *Time* magazine on 27 October 1924.

The public profile of psychoanalysis was raised further in 1924 when four psychoanalysts gave expert testimony in the notorious Loeb–Leopold murder trial. William Randolph Hearst even sent a public invitation to Freud to testify on behalf of the defendants, which he declined.[55] The highly publicised trial of two homosexual teenagers who had randomly kidnapped and murdered fourteen-year-old Bobby Franks exhibited the irresolvable tension between tradition and modernity, religion and science that characterised the decade. Clarence Darrow, celebrated defence lawyer who would later defend John Scopes for teaching evolution in Tennessee (see the case study below), argued against the death penalty for the boys on the basis that they were psychologically sick rather than morally diseased. This view of crime and human behaviour transformed subsequent advances in criminology but also indicated a new danger to society in the form of 'abnormal' psychology and mental disease. Yet it was also a highly publicised fact that Leopold was a self-confessed atheist who had been motivated to crime by his reading of the philosopher Nietzsche. Darrow's defence thereby also appeared an intellectual defence of modern atheism and philosophy and the trial illustrated that beneath the veneer of educated civilisation was a debased atavism, a belief that Freud's publications over the 1920s were only to confirm further. The importance of the psychoanalyst in detecting and curing psychoses and creating functioning citizens in a godless, amoral society seemed paramount but the trial also revealed the moral vacuum in which psychoanalysis now functioned.

The popularity of psychoanalysis as a cure for social and cultural problems led to the proliferation of books and magazines offering pop psychology as a solution to all ills. Although Freud was dismayed at the emergence of such eclectic psychoanalysis in America, his ideas did combine fruitfully with other disciplines to provide Americans with a new intellectual roadmap. Freud and Dewey's mutual admiration, for example, led to important developments in psychoanalytic education, and Freud was greatly influential in the development of social anthropology and criminology in the social sciences.[56] Rather than curtailing the tensions in American culture, however, the proliferation of psychoanalytic theories of the individual, society and culture intensified the paradoxical experience of modernity. To many, the new impact of psychoanalysis was associated with modern freedom and expressivity. To others, however, it became associated with enforcing and policing a new conformity and conservatism, one based on a consumerist or behavioural 'normalcy' rather than religious faith, politics or artistic expression.

Culture and Religion

Psychoanalytic theories enabled rebellious intellectuals to turn against traditional values, rejecting the heritage of Puritanism and the values associated with Victorian culture; at the same time these theories filled the gap left by the repudiation of traditional social and religious doctrines in the scientific age. To many, it seemed, psychoanalysis had replaced religion as Freud presented Americans with a 'sustained plea for a heroic and defiant atheism' through which the tension between the past and the future could be expressed and resolved.[57] Freud's publications over the 1920s only confirmed this view more fully. While *Group Psychology and the Analysis of the Ego* (1921) had shown that individual psychology was affected by a 'herd instinct' that was 'contagious' in a crowd, in *The Future of an Illusion* (1927) Freud asserted that religious belief was 'a store of ideas . . . born from man's need to make his helplessness tolerable and built up from the material of memories of the helplessness of his own childhood and the childhood of the human race'.[58] Sensationally reported in the *New York Times*, the headline read: 'Religion Doomed, Freud Asserts; Says It Is at Point Where It Must Give Way Before Science'.[59] Yet while Freud revealed the illusion, he also demonstrated how it had been essential in the development and survival of civilisation thus far – without religion, this implied, civilisation would struggle to function.

The growth and popularisation of scientific thought, instrumentalism, pragmatism and materialism all appeared on the surface to divide American society between Christians and those who believed in something else. Relativism and pluralism appeared to divest American culture of a moral framework on which social stability could be formed. Despite this, aspects of religious thinking were infused by new ideas. University of Chicago professor of divinity Shailer Matthews developed theories of a theological 'scientific modernism' using the socio-historical methods of the Chicago school; his *The Faith of Modernism* (1924) argued that '[Theological] Modernists endeavor to reach beliefs and their application in the same way that chemists or historians reach and apply their conclusions . . . [their] theological affirmations are the formulation of results of investigation both of human needs and the Christian religion'.[60]

To some, however, it was this theological liberalism that threatened American culture most of all.[61] In response to the growing secularisation of society and growing liberalism of religious belief, fundamentalism expanded in diverse and unprecedented ways. Theologians met and organised opposition to modernists and the demise of civilisation, coining the term 'fundamentalist' in 1920 for someone who went into battle for 'the fundamentals' of Protestant belief and interpreted the Bible literally.[62] Organising a growing network of associations and Bible institutes, fundamentalists emphasised the literal truth of the Bible and the Gospels and challenged scientific ideas that threatened this. The popular radio preacher Harry Emerson Fosdick called for reconciliation between modernisers and fundamentalists in his 1922 sermon 'Shall the Fundamentalists Win?'[63] However, the anti-evolutionary movement within fundamentalism had become a 'national fad' by 1925, epitomised in the trial of John Scopes for teaching evolution at a school in Dayton, Tennessee.

The Scopes Trial, 1925

The Scopes 'Monkey Trial' became the stage on which these key conflicts were played out in the public arena. The trial illustrated the irreconcilable tension that had emerged between science and religion, modernity and tradition, the urban and the rural, 'wets' and 'drys', and the intellectual liberal versus the conservative fundamentalist. At the time it gave a public platform to ideas and anxieties about modernity that were seething in the intellectual undercurrents of the 1920s.

During the war the American Civil Liberties Union had formed to defend the civil rights of those threatened by bigotry and conservatism, and continued after the war in the face of the rise of fundamentalism, nativism, racism and anti-communism. Their focus on legislation made them turn their attention in 1925 to a Tennessee statute, the Butler Act, a state law making it unlawful for a State-employed teacher to 'teach any theory that denies the divine creation of man as taught in the Bible, and to teach instead that man has descended from a lower order of animals'.[64] An apparently serious threat to intellectual and educational freedom, the ACLU approached a high-school science teacher in Dayton, Tennessee, asking him to act as a test-case for challenging the legitimacy of the statute. After teaching evolution from a biology textbook, John Scopes was arrested and charged according to the Butler Act.

The ensuing trial became a publicity feature of the decade, helped by the presence of 'two well-known verbal pugilists', William Jennings Bryan on the anti-evolutionist side, and Clarence Darrow for scientific modernism.[65] Over the 1920s, Bryan had become a leading campaigner for the funda-mentalist anti-evolution movement, arguing for the literal interpretation of the Bible. Despite this, he did not neatly fit into reactionary categories. As a familiar speaker on the Chautauqua circuit and a well-known popular and political figure, he had formerly led populist campaigns in the 1890s – notably the Free Silver campaign, anti-imperialism and pacifist campaigns – and had been a Democratic Presidential candidate three times, becom-ing Secretary of State in Woodrow Wilson's cabinet in 1913. In many ways, Bryan personified the disillusion with progressive reforms of the era. He saw the teaching of evolution as something that encouraged selfish, animalistic behaviour, equated Darwinism with unrestricted capitalism and saw the ravages of the war as a consequence of such scientific rationalism. In his career he had often renounced conservatism and capitalism, thus in Bryan 'reform and reaction lived happily, if somewhat incongruously, side by side'.[66]

Bryan's populist beliefs came into play to argue that in a state where a large percentage of the population were against the teaching of evolution, tax-payers should not be forced to pay the wages of teachers who taught contrary to the majority belief. Thus he became chief prosecutor, protect-ing 'the word of God against the greatest atheist or agnostic in the United States'.[67]

That atheist, Clarence Darrow, had a similar past of campaigning for liberal causes, fighting legal battles in the cause of labour against big business. He had even campaigned for Bryan's Presidential nomination, supporting Democratic campaigns against the exploitation of the common man. By 1925 Darrow had become the most famous criminal defence lawyer in the United States – fighting the death penalty for the Nietzschean 'thrill murderers' Loeb and Leopold – and offered his services to the ACLU for no charge. Despite his earlier connection with similar causes to Bryan, he had come to regard Christianity as a 'punitive slave-religion' and stated his aim in court as simply 'preventing bigots and ignoramuses from controlling the education of the United States'.[68]

Likened to the publicity given to sporting events, especially the famous boxing matches of the era, the preparations made for the world to descend on the small town of Dayton had a carnival atmosphere: the courtroom was repainted, 500 extra spectator seats were built and the room was filled with wires and microphones for the first ever live radio broadcast of such an event; a field was turned into an air strip to accommodate report-ers and journalists who would fly daily newsreels out to northern theatres, to be shown later that day; a loft in a downtown hardware store was turned into a press office for the hundreds of reporters who turned up from all over the world to report the bizarre American trial; extra trains were laid on and souvenir and hotdog stands appeared on the streets. More than 2,000 daily newspapers covered the trial, some with full stenographic transcriptions of the courtroom events, and when the trial moved onto the wooden stage outside the courthouse for fear that the floors would collapse, the performance could not have been more dramatic.[69]

That the trial was a 'set-up' in many ways did little to diminish interest in it. Darrow's dramatic speeches claimed world attention by illustrating that the trial represented nothing less than the future of culture: 'with flying banners and beating drums we are marching backward to the glorious ages of the sixteenth century when bigots lighted fagots to burn the men who dared to bring any intelligence and enlightenment and culture to the human mind'.[70] The works of Darwin, the Bible, anthropologists, archaeologists and biologists were all used as evidence in the attempt to determine the relationship between religion and evolution and whether John Scopes had denied creation by teaching from a standard biology textbook. It was Darrow's cross-examination of Bryan that electrified the trial, however, as he challenged Bryan on the literal interpretation of the Bible asking questions such as 'Do you believe that [Eve] was literally made out of Adam's rib?', and forcing Bryan to explain his fundamentalist belief in the Virgin birth, the creation of Earth, and whether Jonah was really swallowed by a whale or a huge fish. In the sparring between the two men Darrow showed fundamentalism to be essentially anti-intellectual, as shown in his cross-examination of Bryan about his belief in the age of the Earth and the beginnings of mankind:

> D: Do you know there are thousands of books in our libraries on all those subjects I have been asking you about?
> B: I couldn't say, but I will take your word for it . . .
> D: Did you ever read a book on primitive man? Like Tyler's *Primitive Culture*, or Boaz, or any of the great authorities?
> B: I don't think I have read the ones you mentioned.
> D: Have you read any?
> B: Well, I have read a little from time to time. But I didn't pursue it, because I didn't know I was to be called as a witness.
> D: You have never in your life made any attempt to find out about the other peoples of the earth – how old their civilisations are – how long they had existed on earth, have you?
> B: No sir, I have been so well satisfied with the Christian religion that I have spent no time trying to find arguments against it.[71]

The trial became a duel between old thought and new. That Bryan had so clearly refused to read the modern works of cultural anthropology and science appeared a rejection of modernity and the cultural knowledge upon which modern society depended. The contrast between the two worlds that these ideas inhabited could not have appeared greater to all of those following the trial, and it was this tension that made the case electrifying.

At the end of the eleven days, Scopes was found guilty and sentenced to pay $100. Despite this, the case was seen as Darrow's conquest; modernity had been brought to Dayton and the world had seen that scientific progress could not be stopped. At the same time fundamentalism was not crushed by defeat, and Darrow's antics in court merely highlighted rifts and tensions between moralists and atheists. Darrow's comparison of the trial with the witch-burning of the sixteenth century later resonated with other historical events in the 1950s, where the trial received popular treatment as a play and a film, *Inherit the Wind*, resonating with McCarthy's persecution of 'atheistic communism'.

The trial did nothing to reconcile or resolve the tensions of the 1920s. Instead, as the *Atlanta Constitution* stated, it was a 'stage-play between conflicting currents of thought'. The *Christian Century* claimed after the trial that few really cared about the legal issues involved but had turned up to be entertained by the self-publicising 'pugilists' in the 'Amateur Dramatics at Dayton'.[72] Satirist H. L. Mencken saw more danger than humour in the success of the prosecution: 'Let no one mistake it for comedy, farcical though it may be in all its details. It serves notice on the country that Neanderthal man is organizing in these forlorn backwaters of the land, led by a fanatic, rid of sense and devoid of conscience'.[73] While the trial had few intellectual or legal consequences for either side involved (the Butler Law was not repealed until 1967), the issues that it raised remain significant within American society today, in debates about freedom of speech, freedom of science, public education and the still-raging debates over evolution, creationism and 'intelligent design'.

The Scopes Trial profoundly illustrated that while America of the 1920s was fascinated with the rift between tradition and modernity, modern America was more a confused melting pot of the two. Commenting on Bryan's anti-evolution campaign in 1922, Dewey saw great danger in Bryan's mix of fundamentalism and populism, and perceived his mix of 'social and political liberalism combined with intellectual illiberality' as symptomatic of the confused and potentially dangerous climate of the 1920s. To Dewey, it raised 'fundamental questions about the quality of our democracy'.[74] Bryan's crusade reflected the illiberalism embedded within American democratic and liberal thought, where the desire for social and moral order in the midst of 'latent frontier disorderliness' operated to crush free inquiry and criticism where it didn't operate to enhance that moral order. To Dewey, this 'fixed limit to thought' closed down the potential use of art and science for liberating and elevating the human spirit; instead the function was limited: 'science and art as far as they refine and polish life, afford "culture," mark stations on an upward social road, and have direct useful applications, yes: but as emancipations, as radical guides to life, no'.[75]

Anti-science religious fundamentalism appeared to hamper both progress and freedom of thought and expression. The director of the Science Service, Edwin Slossen, equated the 'instinctive mass reaction against new ideas' to the 'common aversion to the foreigner', a bigotry that would have popular votes repeal Copernican, Newtonian and Einsteinian theories, he claimed.[76] The most obvious manifestation of the rise of a virulent religious bigotry was in the rapid growth of the Ku Klux Klan in the postwar period. As 'guardians' of white Protestantism and Victorian values, the Klan ascended to the height of its power in 1924, attracting up to five million supporters throughout the nation.[77] Decidedly anti-modern, the Klan voiced white working-class grievances against big business and economic exploitation as well as appealing to white supremacy with attacks on African Americans, immigrants, Jews, Catholics, feminists and radicals.[78] Despite this, even the Klan employed modern techniques of mass marketing and publicity gleaned from recent business culture.[79]

Modern mass culture came under regular assault in the sermons of traditionalists, who blamed immoral behaviour on developments in mass technology, especially cars, cinema and radio. However, like the KKK, fundamentalists also used and benefited from these new technologies with productions of their own. Pentecostal preacher Aimee Semple McPherson became the first female radio evangelist in 1922, acquiring her own radio station a year later to promote her unique brand of Christian fundamentalism. A conservative in faith and a moderniser in behaviour, McPherson neatly embodied the paradox of 1920s fundamentalism.

The modernisation of religion was no more visible than in the developing relationship between Church and business over the decade, symbolised in the appearance of the new journal *Church Management* in 1923.[80] Arguing for more business efficiency in church affairs and explaining how to run a church like a business, the role of the businessman became increasingly central to a successful religion. The rise of business culture did not necessarily trammel traditional moral ethics, for Shailer Matthews 'business does more than make money – it makes morals'.[81] Modernising Baptist minister Harry Fosdick called for *Adventurous Religion* in 1926, a title that evoked the excitement and risk-taking of business ventures rather than faith. Business and religion were not mutually exclusive, argued Bruce Barton in his bestselling *The Man Nobody Knows* (1925), which depicted Jesus as the most successful businessman the world had known. The writer Sinclair Lewis satirised this paradox of modern conservatism as moral confusion in both *Babbitt* (1922) and *Elmer Gantry* (1927).

Culture and Race

While the variety of religious experiments in the 1920s appeared to have shattered a unitary experience of faith, and business involvement in the Church further elided the secular with the religious, American society was less in the process of destroying God than diversifying a variety of faiths into an expanding number of areas. Religious revivals took on a variety of shapes and forms outside of the traditional perspective of Protestantism and at times provided a platform for new forms of liberation and expression. The 'modernisation' of spiritual faith worked in more radical ways for sections of believers and, indeed, served to revitalise spirituality for many African Americans during the period. The emergence of religious groups and cults preaching equality, self-improvement and economic independence contained both elements of a radical modernity and a rejection of past oppressions, alongside religious fundamentalism and patriarchal politics. The rising presence of African Americans in northern cities provided the impetus for a variety of new movements; among these were the Pentecostal cult leader 'Daddy Grace', who established the United House of Prayer for All People in 1919, 'Father Divine', founder of the International Peace Mission Movement, and F. S. Cherry, who founded the black Jewish 'Church of the Living God' in Philadelphia in 1915. The decade saw the rise of pan-Islamism with Nobel Drew Ali's Moorish Science Temple (later followed by the Nation of Islam movement in the 1930s). [82] These religious movements, which later became connected to the civil rights and freedom movements, provided African Americans with a faith-based rhetoric of empowerment as well as offering institutional support networks for activities that were not formally sponsored by the State such as relief, charity and cultural activities. [83] For many African Americans, embracing a new spiritual modernity became symbolic of the rejection of 'old' America, with its slavery and economic oppression that connected to the fundamentalist Christian South.

Marcus Garvey's United Negro Improvement Association was undoubtedly the most popular of all of these new movements. Jamaican-born Garvey had founded the movement in 1914, setting up a chapter in New York in 1916. By 1920 the UNIA had gained over four million members. [84] Garvey had tapped into a new black demographic; newly urbanised following the migration of over one million African Americans from the South since 1910, hopeful that the North would provide them with new economic and social freedom but victims nonetheless of race riots and prejudice in both the North and South. Garvey argued for a new pan-African solidarity to sustain black pride, economic self-sufficiency and self-governance. In contrast to earlier movements for African American civil rights, Garvey's philosophy was separatist and anti-assimilation.[85]

Garvey reversed the Darwinian-inspired notions of cultural evolution with which white supremacists justified their position, arguing that 'When the great white race of today had no civilization of its own, when white men lived in caves and were counted as savages, this race of ours boasted of a wonderful civilization on the Banks of the Nile'.[86] To Garvey, Africa was the fatherland of all people of African ancestry and a place that they should aim to return to, repossess and repopulate. Garvey argued for a social, economic and cultural separatism, setting up black-owned businesses and companies. Appearing ready for a fight in his paramilitary regalia, he argued that the postwar world offered the opportunity for those of African ancestry to fight for their rightful place in a world that had disinherited them.

To some white observers, this rise of Black nationalism and 'pan-Africanism' was part of a dangerous uprising of 'colored' people around the world. Behind the fears of 'cultural lag' and individual inability to keep up with the times were perceptions that the white race and Western civilisation were in decline – a theory promulgated by the popular reception of Oswald Spengler's *The Decline of the West*. In his organic conception of civilisation first published in Germany in 1918, Spengler wrote that Western civilisation was in its 'winter' phase and thereby racing towards its inexorable end. To many, the decline was specifically connected to modern patterns of culture and reproduction and Spengler's idea merely confirmed the well-established theories of 'race suicide' promoted by eugenicists over the previous two decades. It was in the aftermath of the Great War, however, that these ideas reached their zenith of popularity, epitomised by the 1920 publication of Lothrop Stoddard's *The Rising Tide of Color Against White World-Supremacy*.

The Rising Tide of Color (1920)

Lothrop Stoddard was a protégé of the naturalist and anthropologist Madison Grant, whose book *The Passing of the Great Race, or the Racial Basis of European History* was published to wide acclaim and effect in 1916. Grant's thesis epitomised 'scientific' racism of the era by arguing that the superior 'Nordic' culture was under threat in the US by the unprecedented immigration of other races and the massive migration of African Americans to the urban North. Grant's thesis was influenced by the combination of evolutionary thought with new scientific ideas about genetic inheritance, asserting that the races were in perpetual competition with each other for power, control and resources. Stoddard adopted many of Grant's ideas about the threat to 'Nordicism' from other races, but placed this threat in a world context and argued further that the Great War had highlighted and exacerbated the emergency now facing the white race.

Like *The Passing of the Great Race*, *The Rising Tide* argued that the 'conflict of color' was the 'fundamental problem of the twentieth century'. Stoddard's view of the centrality of race to the twentieth century had been pre-empted by the African American intellectual W. E. B. Du Bois, who had written in 1903 that 'The problem of the twentieth century is the problem of the color-line, – the relation of the darker to the lighter races of men'.[87] To white supremacists, however, any gain in power from 'inferior' races would result in the further collapse of civilisation. In his introduction to the book, Grant argued that 'If this great [Nordic] race, with its capacity for leadership and fighting, should ultimately pass, with it would pass that which we call civilization . . . succeeded by an unstable and bastardized population'. Grant argued that democracy was something that only applied to a homogenous population of 'Nordic blood' and that sharing blood and ideals with 'brown, yellow, black or red men' was 'suicide pure and simple'.[88] Stoddard expanded on the threat to white supremacy in his study of the rise of non-white races in all parts of the globe. Not only were whites outnumbered but white cultural advance had enabled the 'colored' world to increase, advance and thrive at alarming levels. White civilisation had thus sown the seeds of its own destruction by sharing its scientific and technological advances with 'inferior' races. While 'the white world was tearing itself to pieces' in war, and limiting its numbers with the increasing availability of birth control, the 'colored' world had been watching closely, increasing its numbers and waiting to 'shake off its fetters' and seize power and resources from the whites.[89] Stoddard charted, chapter by chapter, the rise of the 'colored' threat – the rise of Asian territories and 'Asiatic nationalism' (notably Japan's recent territorial aggression), the 'Mohammedan Revival' and the building of a coming 'Jehad' or 'Holy War' by Muslims, the rise of pan-Islamism and population growth in Africa, and the dangerous 'mongrelization', rebellion and radicalisation of Latin America – all of which added up to a 'cataclysmic' situation for 'Nordic' culture.

To Stoddard the war had added new factors to intensify the threat further; having destroyed the lives, youth, 'breeding' potential and economic infrastructure of 'white' Europe, the problematic peace settlement initiated further dangers and crises through the 'perpetuation of hatreds' among white Europeans. As well as the dysgenic 'slaughter of genius-bearing strains' in war, the recent revolution in Russia further illustrated the most 'gigantic triumph of dysgenics ever seen'. Bolshevism encouraged the underdog and the 'dysgenic' to rise up, to kill off the carriers of higher-quality genes – the aristocracy and educated elite – and created agitators in 'every quarter of the globe' to inspire further nationalist uprisings and agitate against every grievance. 'Bolshevism is "the arch-enemy of civilization" and must be "crushed out with iron heels, no matter what the cost"'.[90] Stoddard's interpretation depicted white America as the last post and refuge for civilisation, surrounded by seething hordes of 'coloreds' and Bolsheviks literally hammering at the door.

The impact of such ideas on politics and culture throughout the decade was huge. Both Grant's and Stoddard's ideas argued for the 'vital necessity of restriction and selection in immigration' and underpinned the enactment of new immigration laws in 1921 and 1924.[91] Stoddard's book came out at the height of postwar immigration to the United States and during the onset of economic depression, contributing to the scare that enabled the rapid enactment of the Emergency Immigration Act of 1921. This act limited immigration to 3 per cent of the foreign-born residing in America in 1910. The racial theories of those such as Grant and Stoddard continued to fuel fears over 'race suicide', so that even though America had entered a 'boom' period, in 1924 the National Origins Act was passed to further limit immigration, changing the quota to 2 per cent and adopting 1890 as the date on which to base the quotas (a time seen as more demographically favourable to 'Nordics'). Further restrictions effectively barred any Japanese immigration at all – the racial group that Stoddard had claimed to be the most immediately threatening to white America.[92] President Harding recommended Stoddard's book in a speech at Birmingham, Alabama, on 26 October 1921: 'Whoever will take the time to read and ponder Mr. Lothrop Stoddard's book on The Rising Tide of Color . . . must realise that our race problem here in the United States is only a phase of a race issue that the whole world confronts'.[93]

Following the success of his book, Stoddard penned many more. In The Revolt Against Civilization: The Menace of the Under-Man (1922), he argued that civilisations went into decline because of 'mongrelization' and the appearance of weaker 'germ plasms', causing the increasing appearance of degenerate types. Barely mentioning 'colored' races, The Revolt Against Civilization neatly summarises eugenic thinking of the 1920s, which blamed all social and political problems on genetic decline. The Saturday Evening Post complimented Stoddard on being the first to successfully 'present a scientific explanation of the worldwide epidemic of unrest that broke out during the Great War and still rages in both hemispheres'.[94] Stoddard complemented his theories with further books interpreting world history in racial terms: The New World of Islam and Racial Realities in Europe (1924). In Reforging America (1927) he highlighted how white America could rebuild its 'native' stocks and assimilate white immigrants into the fold. While Stoddard represented a trend rather than a founder of such ideas, his writings undoubtedly contributed to the widespread popularity and dissemination of racist ideology in the 1920s.

> Despite the overt racism of his books, with historical hindsight Stoddard appears to have predicted some key convulsions of the post-colonial world in the second part of the twentieth century. Not only does his book anticipate the downfall of European imperialism such as British rule in India and French rule in Africa and Asia, his dire warnings of forthcoming conflict appear to predict beyond World War II to the Cold War, the Vietnam War, The Gulf War, American military interventions in Latin America, War in Afghanistan and the 'War on Terror'.

However much the conflict over the 'color line' appeared as a black versus white issue – epitomised in 1929 when Stoddard and Du Bois stood together on a platform in Chicago to debate 'cultural equality' in front of a mainly black audience – neither the 'rising' nor the 'ebbing' tides were as homogenous in their racial identity or scientific beliefs as either side desired.[95] Eugenics not only inflected white modernism, black leaders such as Garvey, whose anti-miscegenation ideas mirrored white separatism, and Du Bois, whose claim that there was an elite 'talented tenth' among the black population, also subscribed to eugenic beliefs as a form of racial 'improvement'.[96]

Culture and the New Negro

Though inspiring fears of 'colored' races in the white populace, Stoddard's work indicated to racial minorities that their new world was indeed coming. To African American activists in the 1920s the promise of a new civilisation in which they would play a vital role presented both a challenge and an opportunity. While black rejection of white domination and demands for equal status and recognition had been growing over the past twenty years, the 1920s saw a fruition of black pride and activism in cultural and intellectual life, as well as in the social sphere. In contrast to both African nationalists and white supremacists, a cultural movement supported by Du Bois and a number of African American artists arose to proclaim that there was a 'New Negro' who would play a key role in the revitalisation of both black and white American culture. Black intellectuals and artists consciously ignited a new cultural movement that reflected this growing self-consciousness. Unlike white despair over the decline of civilisation, the movement exhibited a willing rejection of the past and a celebration of social and cultural change as progress. This celebratory modernism was reflected in the name given to the movement: the Harlem Renaissance.

The Harlem Renaissance was spurred forward by the support and patronage of Charles Spurgeon Johnson, a Chicago sociologist whose *The Negro In Chicago* (1922) reported the causes of the Chicago race riots of 1919 to the Chicago Commission on Race Relations. As publisher of *Opportunity: A Journal of Negro Life* he encouraged and published black writers and found white patrons for the artists. Johnson believed in cooperation rather than conflict between the races and worked to allow black artists self-expression.[97] At a literary dinner for the publication of Jessie Fauset's new novel *There is Confusion* (1925), the editor of *Survey Graphic*, a social science journal, proposed a whole issue devoted to black culture, which became *Harlem: The Mecca of the New Negro*.[98] This volume was expanded into an anthology in 1925, *The New Negro*, edited by Alain Locke.

The volume of essays, stories and poems printed in *The New Negro* anthology illustrated a new interconnectedness between the social sciences and the creative arts, with sections on black demographics, sociology, and history interspersed with poems and essays on the culture of jazz, spirituals, art and sculpture. Locke saw salvation for the African American in the realm of such intellectual and cultural production, and his seminal essay 'Enter the New Negro' argued that a new psychology was emerging which shook off the 'old chrysalis of the Negro problem', showing a new self-respect and self-dependence. This new psychology would release 'our talented group from the arid fields of controversy and debate to the productive fields of creative expression'. Thus the 'New Negro' was the epitome of modernity, of cultural pluralism, self-making and the conscious rejection of the past. 'The American mind,' he argued, 'must reckon with a fundamentally changed negro'.[99]

Although Locke barely mentioned Garvey, the volume was certainly linked to a rising nationalist politics throughout the world following the war. Locke, however, argued for a cultural pluralism reliant on white cooperation and acceptance rather than separatism. 'This wider race consciousness,' he argued, was a 'different thing from the much asserted rising tide of color'; rather than threatening civilisation it was essential to its rejuvenation and progress.[100] While the new centrality of African American artistry would provide uplift through cultural pursuit and refinement, all of American culture would be advanced. An example of this is shown in his essay 'The Legacy of Ancestral Arts', where Locke claimed that African cultural heritage had saved the European avant-garde culture from 'decadence and sterility'.[101] To Locke, then, pluralist culture was in itself a form of progress, politics and racial advancement.

Despite the claims for a new group psychology based on these ideas, rifts in the movement were always present. Locke's promotion of intellectuals and artists struck some as elitist and highly selective.[102] The young journalist George Schulyer called the Harvard-educated scholar 'the high priest of the intellectual snobbocracy'.[103] Others felt that Locke – educated in traditions of European thought – had papered over the everyday experiences of ordinary African Americans in order to promote a hygienic vision of the 'New Negro' with which white reformers and patrons would feel comfortable. At the same time the tension between past and future is clear in much of the anthology: in trying to establish a tradition for African American culture, while at the same time make claims for an entirely new modern age, the message was at times contradictory or paradoxical. Despite this, the Harlem Renaissance and the conditions that gave rise to it were both 'molding a new Negro [and] molding a new American attitude'.[104]

Women and Culture

Like the New Negro, the New Woman was not an innovation of the 1920s, yet rapid social change made women's role in society a topic of heightened prominence and cultural concern. In the years preceding, women had played key parts in progressive and reform movements by using a moral authority garnered from their domestic roles as mothers, carers and homemakers. At the same time the transformation from an agrarian economy to an industrial one had created new opportunities for women, particularly single, working-class women. The image of the modern woman was further transformed by women's participation in industrial work during the war, leading to an emergence of new expectations and social norms. Enjoying the freedom that came from having an independent source of income, many working-class women created a new culture for themselves that centred on consumption and mass entertainment. The postwar boom enabled these women to further explore their new autonomy and individuality and reject their mothers' ways for more modern choices.

In 1920 two key successes of the women's movement appeared to herald a new feminine future: temperance and suffrage. For decades reformers had argued that these two gains would fundamentally transform society, as women would vote more ethically than men (whose involvement in the world of business and politics corrupted them) and prohibition would stop the abuse and disintegration of the family that was a key feature of modern urban life. On the eve of the decade it seemed that a new female-improved culture was dawning. Despite this success, the feminist ideal of the reform-minded club-woman, the settlement worker or the liberated, free-loving, bohemian intellectual of the 1910s was being replaced with a more individualistic image of female liberation: one that was based on freedom of expression, sexuality (notably heterosexuality) and consumption.

In many ways the problem for American women in the 1920s lay in the tension between tradition and progress that had been embedded in their success: reformers had relied on traditional feminine stereotypes in order to push through their radical goals for social change. In arguing for equality the women's movement had been forced to defend women's traditional roles and moral superiority against the tide of modern social change. As social change led to new roles for women, where they did not use their newly gained freedoms to further reform and improve society, the attempt to sustain the paradox collapsed, leading to a decade of contradiction and critique. The disappointments of the morning after were bitter: women's votes did not radicalise society; instead there emerged a decade of political conservatism, individualism and apparent indifference.

Contradictory images of new women thus emerged on the social scene as racism, fundamentalism, conservatism, crime, corruption and cultural anxiety over modernity reached a zenith. At the same time women entered into the workplace in unprecedented numbers, attained a new cultural voice in literature, film and radio, expressed new sexual freedoms with support from Freudian analysis and freer access to birth control, and helped fuel the consumer boom that has characterised the decade. Some blamed the women's movement for the rising tide of reactionary politics, others blamed it for the changing gender roles which appeared to lead to increased divorce and family breakdown, others equated femininity with mass consumer culture; in all cases the backlash to feminist ideology was strong enough to last until the 1960s.[105]

Behind many of the concerns and anxieties over the transformation to modernity lay a deeply embedded gender critique that expressed a concern over the apparent dominance of American woman in cultural life. According to Harold Stearns 'the extraordinary feminization of American social life' had caused the spiritual impoverishment of culture.[106] Even the 'remarkable growth of pragmatism' and 'its sturdy offspring instrumentalism' was only possible due to an intellectual atmosphere 'surcharged with this feminized utilitarianism', for 'what women usually understand by the intellectual life is the application of modern scientific methods to a sort of enlarged and subtler course in domestic science'.[107] As intellectuals rejected the repressions of Puritanism, Puritanism became associated with domineering, evangelical womanhood. The shallowness, materialism and functionalism that Stearns saw as a feature of American culture could be blamed on women, to whom 'intellectual life is an instrument of moral reform . . . a sociological activity' compounded by the 'satisfied marital felicity of the bacteria-less suburbanite in his concrete villa'.[108] Rather than cultural improvement, he argued, the culture of the new woman and female reform had contributed to cultural and spiritual decline.

According to Van Wyck Brooks, artists and writers were similarly affected by this cultural emasculation, sterility and impotency; like Samson, the writer had 'lost his virility before the philistines bound him'.[109] Likewise, cultural infantilism could be blamed on the overvaluation of the mother figure according to Alfred Kutter, where Americans' 'exaggerated mother-love' had reached 'cultic proportions', leading to the 'sexual infantilism' of the American male.[110]

These ideas were connected as much to the changing nature of American society as to the changing roles of women within it. Mass production soared in the 1920s, creating a huge consumer boom in which women appeared to play a key role. By the end of the 1920s consumer culture appeared as a new type of matriarchy, in which women controlled the nation's pocketbook. Stearns used the example of the popular cartoon strip 'Bringing up Father' as an example of women's relationship to modern cultural life. In the strip a nouveau riche wife aspired to a bourgeois lifestyle while her husband remained stuck to his gauche working-class habits. 'Bringing up' father meant forcing him to adopt materialistic and superficial habits that had rapidly become associated with middle-brow, anti-intellectual, feminine bourgeoisification. Using 'rolling-pin' humour, the strip highlighted the new power of women in a world of showy artificiality and consumption – inevitably 'mother' was twice the size of 'father', although her reform project continuously fails.

Women's smoking, drinking and jazz dancing represented a further rejection of prohibitive Victorianism and feminism as 'the flapper' emerged as the most overt rejection of the 'old'. Connected to a new sexual freedom and the mass production of ready-to-wear items, the flapper style entailed a minimum of undergarments, short skirts, filmy fabrics and sheer hosiery. Her bobbed hair (a release from the weight of tradition) represented female daring and eroticism. Smoking, drinking and cosmetics – traditionally associated with prostitutes – further underscored women's right to sexuality and personal expression.

Movies also projected visions of women who had physical freedom, energy and independence.

To some feminists and radicals, however, the flapper did not represent choice but consumer conformity. Former suffragists were dismayed to see women using their new-found freedoms to display themselves to men in competition for a husband in the restrictive environment of 1920s heterosexuality – the first Miss America contest held in 1921 at Atlantic City was an apotheosis of this new superficiality. Blamed for a new amorality and seen as a threat to the family, women reformers saw the nihilism of the flapper as a contradiction to the values of the earlier women's movement.

In this climate some women exercised their new political voices to defend older patriarchal gender roles and racial hierarchies. From 1923 The Women's Ku Klux Klan (WKKK) became flooded by those who continued to link the preservation of the family to women's political activism, whose goals were 'to cleanse and purify the civil, political and ecclesiastical atmosphere of our country; to provide a common meeting ground for American Protestant women who are willing to co-operate in bringing about better conditions in the home, church and social circles; to assist all Protestant women in the study of practical politics; to encourage a study by Protestant wives, mothers and daughters of questions concerning the happiness of the home and the welfare of the state'.[111] As Kathleen Blee has argued, 'anti-immigrant and racist sentiments within the women's suffrage, moral reform, and temperance movements created the historical possibility for a post-suffrage women's Klan that espoused women's rights while denying the rights of nonwhites, non-Protestants, and the foreign-born'.[112]

Many women reformers continued to see the educated woman as central to the progress of a new civilisation yet based their ideas of progress on 'scientific breeding' and reversing 'race suicide' rather than political or economic reform. Activist Margaret Sanger, central to making birth control more accessible in America during this period and thereby enabling the new sexual freedom for women, departed from feminist and socialist arguments to adopt a eugenic panacea for the problem of civilisation. Tapping into the wide body of intellectual perceptions about the genetic decline of American civilisation, she argued that birth control would enable a new civilisation by preventing the propagation of the 'unfit'.[113] Published in the same year as Stoddard's *The Revolt Against Civilization*, Sanger's *The Pivot of Civilization* (1922) argued '[t]he lack of balance between the birth-rate of the "unfit" and the "fit" was the greatest present menace to

Figure I.1 Women in Ku Klux Klan demonstration, Washington DC, 1928 (© The Art Archive/ National Archives Washington DC).

the civilization'. In his introduction, H. G. Wells highlighted how Sanger's book presented 'the case of the new order against the old':

> The New Civilization is saying to the Old now: 'We cannot go on making power for you to spend upon international conflict . . . we cannot go on giving you health, freedom, enlargement, limitless wealth, if all our gifts to you are to be swamped by an indiscriminate torrent of progeny. We want fewer and better children who can be reared up to their full possibilities in unencumbered homes, and we cannot make the social life and the world-peace we are determined to make, with the ill-bred, ill-trained swarms of inferior citizens that you inflict upon us'.[114]

The new civilisation evoked by Wells and Sanger tapped into modern scientific thought: 'Recent developments in the realm of science, – in psychology, in physiology, in chemistry and physics – all tend to emphasized the immediate necessity for human control over the great forces of nature', she argued. Birth control was 'pivotal' to progress, and educated women's choices were vital to this new civilisation: 'The new civilization can become a glorious reality only with the awakening of woman's now dormant qualities of strength, courage, and vigor ... The physical and psychic power of woman is more indispensable to the well-being and power of the human race than that even of man'. Women thus remained central to the progress of civilisation but their emancipation was only of benefit if they used it for scientific efficiency and racial uplift. Despite the class and race bias in the birth control movement, however, many black, immigrant and working-class women subscribed to these ideas as a necessity (and boon) to modern womanhood, sexual freedom and the progress of civilisation.

The shift toward negative eugenics (the prevention of breeding among the 'unfit') in this decade was closely tied to beliefs about modern civilisation and decline promulgated in the arts. As schemes to increase the breeding of 'the fit' remained unfocused, the prevention of an unwanted rising tide of misfits became a focus of social and cultural improvement. America had enacted the world's first compulsory sterilisation law in 1907 – providing for involuntary sterilisation of 'confirmed criminals, idiots, imbeciles and rapists'. By 1927 the law was revised to include those deemed 'feeble-minded, epileptic and the potential parents of socially inadequate offspring'.[115] In the same year the Supreme Court upheld the 1924 forced sterilisation of Carrie Buck (in the now infamous *Buck* v. *Bell* case) making compulsory sterilisation constitutional.

The celebratory modernism of the new woman was thus more complex than a simple rejection of traditional roles and the adoption of new 'flapper' lifestyles. African American women had to negotiate a new terrain that celebrated her sexuality without reverting to primitive stereotypes associated with the sexual exploitation of slavery. Similarly, overt sexual expression in young working-class women could lead to a stint in the reformatory and even to sterilisation if she were deemed 'unfit' to become a mother, while homosexuality in both men and women was increasingly classified by psychoanalysts as a sign of 'abnormal' sexual development that needed correction.

Conclusion

Just as Einstein's discoveries dismantled the old Newtonian order of reality, the character of modernity was an apparently chaotic battle to re-establish stability. As John Dewey noted:

The chief intellectual characteristic of the present age is its despair
of any constructive philosophy . . . the formation of a new, coherent
view of nature and man based upon facts consonant with science and
actual social conditions is still to be had. What we call the Victorian
Age seemed to have such a philosophy. It was a philosophy of hope, of
progress, of all that is called liberalism. The growing sense of unsolved
social problems, accentuated by the war, has shaken that faith. It is
impossible to recover its mood.[116]

Baker Brownall claimed in his book *The New Universe* (1926) that
'[t]oday is a crevice between two worlds': 'In music, and poetry, in
geometry, physics, in space, time, chemistry, in painting and dancing,
in religion, in politics, in trade and sculpture, the old forms shift and
deliquesce and new formulations of the world appear'.[117] In his 1929
essay 'The Modern Temper', literary critic Joseph Wood Krutch
argued that a crevice had indeed opened up in which 'man seems
caught in a dilemma which his intellect has devised. Any deliberately
managed return to a state of relative ignorance . . . is obviously out
of the question', for '[t]he values which he thought established have
been swept along with the rules by which he thought they might be
attained'. While there was no going back, ('[n]o one can tell how
many of the old values must go or how new the new will be') what
was certain was that the gulf left behind by the loss of stability meant
'either extinction [of the human spirit] or a readjustment more stupendous than any made before'.[118] Culture, in all its varieties, was the
sphere in which this stupendous readjustment took place.

Chapter 1

Fiction, Poetry and Drama

Although America had attained a new cultural dominance in the 1920s and its writers an exuberance, confidence and readership to accompany it, literary productions did not reflect the boosterism of the business elite; instead, writers cast a critical eye over the myths and claims of the founding dream of abundance and democracy, finding their new position a source of discomfort and tension. In *The Professor's House* (1925) Willa Cather used the metaphor of the intellectual trapped between the old and new to illustrate the tension of the era:

> [H]is new house, his old house, everything around him, seemed insupportable, as the boat on which he is imprisoned seems to a sea-sick man. Yes, it was possible that the little world, on its voyage among all the stars, might become like that; a boat on which one could travel no longer, from which one could no longer look up and confront those bright rings or revolution.[1]

This tension between the past and the present, life and death, and the experience of lacking destination were themes explored by young writers who became known as 'the lost generation'. The term first appeared in the epigraph to Ernest Hemingway's novel *The Sun Also Rises* (1926), which quoted modernist writer Gertrude Stein declaring 'you are all a lost generation'.[2] Although referring specifically to a group of young writers who chose to spend some, or all, of the decade in Europe, the notion of a 'lost generation' also expressed a wider abandonment of traditional beliefs among American intellectuals in the postwar period. As Malcolm Cowley wrote in his memoir of the decade *Exile's Return*, 'they were not a lost generation in the sense of being unfortunate or thwarted', instead the generation was 'lost, first of all, because uprooted . . . lost because its training had prepared it for

another world than existed after the war . . . lost because it tried to live
in exile . . . lost because it accepted no older guides to conduct'.[3] Yet,
as Joseph Krutch noted, these exiles were 'seceding from the old and
yet could adhere to nothing new'.[4]

Stuck between two irreconcilable worlds, this inability to be at
home in either appeared an inexorable path towards self-destruction,
violence or death. To philosopher George Santayana, the patterns of
restlessness that he witnessed around him in 1920 summarised the
national character:

> Consider now the great emptiness of America: not merely the primi-
> tive physical emptiness, surviving in some regions, and the continental
> spacing of the chief natural features, but also the moral emptiness of
> a settlement where men and even houses are easily moved about, and
> no one, almost, lives where he was born or believes what he has been
> taught.[5]

In their personal lives the writers of the lost generation famously
pursued destructive lifestyles, drinking excessively, driving care-
lessly or obsessed with the primal scenes of violence. So many of the
writers in the decade were alcoholics, Ann Douglas has noted, that
'this was the generation that made the terms "alcoholic" and "writer"
synonyms'.[6] Writers such as F. Scott Fitzgerald, Ernest Hemingway,
Dorothy Parker, Djuna Barnes, Hart Crane, Harry Crosby, Sinclair
Lewis, Jean Toomer, Wallace Thurman, Eugene O'Neill and William
Faulkner all battled with alcohol problems during the thirteen-year
period of national prohibition.

Fitzgerald wrote that by 1927 'contemporaries of mine had begun to
disappear into the dark maw of violence. A classmate killed his wife and
himself on Long Island, another tumbled "accidentally" from a skyscraper in Philadelphia, another purposely from a skyscraper in New
York. One was killed in a speak-easy in Chicago; another was beaten to
death in a speak-easy in New York and crawled home to the Princeton
Club to die; still another had his skull crushed by a maniac's axe in
an insane asylum where he was confined. These are not catastrophes
that I went out of my way to look for—these were my friends'.[7] The
tension between violence and the pursuit of pleasure exhibited by the
Lost Generation was central to Freud's work in the postwar period. In
his search for the psychological causes of violent obsessions, which he
termed the 'death-instinct', he turned to the traumatised soldier. Freud
claimed that humans had an inherent urge 'to restore an earlier state of

things which the living entity has been obliged to abandon under the pressure of external disturbing forces'.[8] This idea, published in *Beyond the Pleasure Principle* (1920), explained the self-destructiveness of nostalgic longing as a desire to enter an idealised state that created a longing for death. Freud's theory revealed that behind destructiveness and violence was a compulsion to repeat or re-enact the moment of trauma or loss in order to gain mastery or control over that which was feared. The death-instinct was thereby a compulsion to revisit the trauma (something that had happened in the past) in order to find what had been lost (in the present), and restore it (in the future). Freud expanded his ideas over the decade to show how this idea applied to the modern subject within civilisation more generally.

Writers of the period certainly explored this modern sense of loss and trauma in their work but unlike Freud they offered few cures and little comfort. A prevalent image underpinning such spiritual desertion and geographic or historical confusion was that of the wasteland. As a symbol for modernity the wasteland was not a cultural desert but a place of chaotic and fragmented cultural detritus, where past and present merged in nauseating profusion, chaos and overabundance. The most celebrated depiction of this warped cultural fecundity appeared in T. S. Eliot's landmark poem 'The Waste Land' (1922). '[W]ithered stumps of time' depicted the spiritual and cultural chaos of a world broken by war and dehumanised by mass production, making him question what future could grow from such corruption: 'April is the cruellest month, breeding/ Lilacs out of the dead land' . . . 'What are the roots that clutch, what branches grow/ Out of this stony rubbish?'[9] The fractured civilisation of 'The Waste Land' showed the individual searching for order and meaning in the rubble of burnt-out ideas and beliefs. In it, the modern subject was literally 'lost' in time.

Fiction written about the recent war compounded and underwrote this sense of loss. The young writer John Dos Passos fictionalised his war experiences in his first novel, *One Man's Initiation: 1917* (1920).[10] The initially idealistic young hero, Martin Howe, sees the destruction of civilisation and culture first-hand, causing him to describe war-devastated France as a wasteland: '[i]t's all so like an ash-heap, a huge garbage dump of men and equipment'.[11] Later in the novel, the relationship of American culture with this European wasteland is discussed among the soldiers:

In exchange for all the quiet and the civilization and the beauty of ordered lives that Europeans gave up in going to the new world we

gave them opportunity to earn luxury, and, infinitely more important, freedom from the past, that gangrened ghost of the past that is
killing Europe to-day with its infection of hate and greed of murder.
'America has turned traitor to all that, you see; that's the way we look
at it. Now we're a military nation, an organized pirate like France and
England and Germany.'[12]

The devastation of the ancient structures represented a collapse of
time, a collapse of faith and the belief in lineal progress, where civilisation, the past, has become a 'gangrened ghost' that has infected the
founding ideals of the nation.

The destruction of civilisation and the dehumanisation of war
shaped Dos Passos' novel *Three Soldiers* (1921). The novel is divided
into sections reflecting an industrial production line as the army
processes the soldiers through war: 'Making the Mould'; 'The Metal
Cools'; 'Machines'; 'Rust'; 'The World Outside'; 'Under the Wheels'.
As in T. S. Eliot's 'The Waste Land' the lost past emerges in the pal-
impsest of the present: as the wounded soldier John Andrews finds
himself returning to consciousness in a Renaissance Palace that has
been converted into a field hospital, he observes the figures on the
decorated ceiling seeming 'to wink and wriggle in shadowy mockery
of the rows of prostrate bodies in the room beneath them . . . in which
all the little routine of the army seemed unreal, and the wounded men
discarded automatons, broken toys laid away in rows'.[13]

The wounded and broken man featured prominently in Ernest
Hemingway's series of interlinked short stories, *In Our Time* (1925),
which explored the death-instinct beneath everyday social relationships. Between each short story he interspersed abstract violent scenes
from war or bullfighting, making death a subtext that highlights the violence of 'normalcy' within everyday life. In 'Soldier's Home' society's
demand for a mythical heroism annihilates the individual, hollowing
out his existence and leaving him a meaningless cipher. The impossibility of translating the immediacy of his experience in war makes Krebs,
the returning hero, fabricate the past: by telling lies about his wartime
experience, Hemingway wrote, 'he lost everything'.[14]

Idealist myths were further debunked in his celebrated war novel, *A
Farewell to Arms* (1929), with the depiction of random atrocities, mass
death and retreating soldiers shot by their own side and where future
promise ends with a mother's death in childbirth and a stillborn baby.
This bleak refutation of idealism and romanticism emerged in the style
of writing as well as in the narrative. Under the tutelage of Gertrude

Stein and Ezra Pound, Hemingway utilised the continuous present and the results presented a new type of psychological realism that was indebted to pragmatic philosopher William James's idea that modern experience was a 'stream of consciousness'. Hemingway's style aimed to overthrow past literary conventions that readers had grown too familiar with and his writing attempted to reveal only the essential truth of the experienced situation and to abandon any distracting embellishments. To Hemingway, all abstractions in literature were 'romance'; decorative, fake and ultimately meaningless. As Frederick Henry states in *A Farewell to Arms*, 'Abstract words such as glory, honor, courage, or hallow were obscene beside the concrete names of villages, the numbers of roads, the names of rivers, the numbers of regiments and the dates'.[15]

In *The Sun Also Rises* (1926), Hemingway further exposed the fantasy of a romantic past as something sinister and destructive. When Jake Barnes discovers that his friend Robert Cohn had been reading and rereading a book called *The Purple Land* that recounts the 'splendid imaginary amorous adventures of a perfect English gentleman in an intensely romantic land, the scenery of which is very well described', Barnes calls it an 'innocent occupation' becoming sinister 'if read too late in life': 'For a man to take it at thirty-four as a guidebook to what life holds is about as safe as it would be for a man of the same age to enter Wall Street direct from a French convent, equipped with a complete set of the more practical Alger books'.[16] Hemingway and the Lost Generation thereby explored more than just death, but the possibility of escape from the corruption of the old dreams – of being able to 'resume again unknowing' – without returning to the past.

For African Americans the experience of exile and return was less a choice than an imposition caused by social, economic and legal exclusion. In the opening line of his poem 'The White House' (1922) Claude McKay stressed that for the black soldier homecoming was also exile, as 'Your door is shut against my tightened face'.[17] The experience, however, led many writers to explore new models of liberation and black subjectivity that had a direct influence on the emergence of the Harlem Renaissance, signified by the radical potential of violence as self-definition in McKay's poem 'If We Must Die' (1919). The migration, persecution and exile that characterised the African American experience made the definition of 'home' problematic to non-white writers. Caribbean expatriate McKay contentiously portrayed this in *Home to Harlem* (1928), where Jake, a black working-class southern war deserter, befriends Ray,

an exile of American-occupied Haiti, who experiences his alienation as a sensation of being 'in the middle of the world, suspended
in space'.[18] To such exiles Harlem became the ironically fleeting and
subaltern home for fleeing or seeking migrants, be it from the South,
Haiti, the Caribbean or Africa. For Alain Locke, however, Harlem
was a 'Mecca' for the New Negro and the 'home for the Negro's
"Zionism"'.[19] In *The New Negro* Locke wrote that Harlem was the
place where the modern American was made, a 'laboratory of a great
race-welding' in which the modern human was forged.[20] To Locke,
black exodus from the South was less exile – the African American in
the South had been in exile since slavery anyway – than a 'deliberate
flight not only from countryside to city, but from medieval America
to modern' and a grand project of self-making.[21]

   Despite this, as Jessie Fauset pointed out in her essay 'Nostalgia',
for the migrant the feeling of homesickness was always a longing to
be somewhere else, a permanent sense of 'spiritual nostalgia' caused
by alienation and exile from equal citizenship.[22] As lamentations of
loss and longing, blues and folk songs gave voice to the experience
of those in the margins and interstices of culture. Langston Hughes'
poem 'The Weary Blues' (1923) expressed this nostalgia as a state of
permanent longing that underpinned black folk expression: 'I got
the Weary Blues/ And I can't be satisfied'.[23] To Harlem Renaissance
writers, exiles and migrants occupied the interstices of race and gender
as well as of time and space, a liminal position of 'inbetweenness'
examined in the many novels of racial passing such as Nella Larsen's
Quicksand (1928) and *Passing* (1929); Walter White's *Flight* (1926) and
Jessie Fauset's *Plum Bun: A Novel Without a Moral* (1928). Novels of
passing explored the migrancy of existing within and outside of two
mutually exclusive worlds, at home and an outcast in both. Langston
Hughes summarised the liminal world of the racial outcast in 'Cross'
(1925): 'My old man died in a big fine house./ My ma died in a shack./
I wonder where I'm gonna die,/ Being neither white nor black'.

   While African American writers were acutely aware that 'old'
dwelled within 'new', the theme was prevalent throughout the literature of the decade. In *The Modern Temper* (1929) Krutch called the
1920s a time 'haunted by ghosts from a dead world and not yet at
home in its own', a theme explored by Willa Cather in *The Professor's
House* (1925). While not a war novel, the effects of the war haunt
the text in the character of Tom Outland, a young inventor killed in
action. Attempting to write up Tom's diaries, historian Godfrey St.
Peter undergoes a psychical crisis closely resembling Freud's death-

instinct: under 'pressures of external change' St. Peter resists a move into his new house, but spends his time in the attic of his old house reading Outland's diaries and conjuring memories from his earlier life. His retreat into memory makes him wish for death, a wish only just averted through a chance visit from the family seamstress. In all parts of the fragmented narrative the past and youth is being, or has been, destroyed; at the same time the story fights to put the narrative back together and 'reconstruct' the unknowable past. To St. Peter there is no longer any satisfactory model or vision of the future on which new structures can be based. The new houses imitate the 'old' but they are hollowed of meaning and history – especially disturbing to St. Peter is his daughter's new house, called 'Outland', built in Norwegian manor house style out of the profits of Outland's invention, 'the Outland Vacuum'. Outland thus becomes a place and a non-place, a symbol of what is missing (hence 'a vacuum') among the modern debris of material culture.

Longing, nostalgia and self-destruction highlighted an experience of modernity that went beyond the soldier's experience. The war and increasing pace of change had triggered a widespread feeling that modern living was an accident waiting to happen, and it was the expectancy of such a collision that propelled the tension in what has become the most celebrated novel of the period, F. Scott Fitzgerald's *The Great Gatsby* (1925).

F. Scott Fitzgerald, *The Great Gatsby* (1925)

F. Scott Fitzgerald's *The Great Gatsby* is the story of Jay Gatsby's attempt to win back his former girlfriend, Daisy, who has married the wealthy Tom Buchanan. Like all of Fitzgerald's stories the characters are superficial, sometimes vapid, and usually wealthy enough to try and disconnect themselves from the harsh realities of contemporary life. Despite being celebrated for his depiction of a privileged elite and carefree flappers, Fitzgerald managed to tap the plethora of intellectual and social anxieties in *The Great Gatsby* to make it far more than just a novel of manners or high society. The key to this lies not in Jay Gatsby's relationship with Daisy but in his relationship with the American past, which ultimately propels the novel: Gatsby's acquisition and display of huge wealth is motivated not just by love but by the desire to remake the past, so that when the novel's narrator Nick Carraway tells Gatsby '"You can't repeat the past"', Gatsby responds incredulously, '"Can't repeat the past?" . . . "Why of course you can!"'[24]

Gatsby's house and possessions illustrate his impossible desire to create a new history for himself. His books in the library are unread, and his house a bricolage of failed dreams and ambitions: a Georgian colonial mansion containing a patchwork of historical styles from Marie Antoinette music-rooms, Restoration salons, a 'Merton college library' and numerous undefined period bedrooms. The faked realism only highlights Gatsby's isolation, emphasising that he has no true home. Gatsby's identity is one-dimensional, created out of the objects that surround him – 'you resemble the advertisement of the man,' Daisy comments, drawing unintentional attention to his semiotic display and emptiness.[25] Gatsby's imperial quest to gain Daisy means that he must display his possessions like a 'World's Fair', but this makes him a cheap peddler of outdated ideas and attractive to the wrong type of guests who behave more like patrons of an amusement park than the elite he wishes to join.[26]

Yet to Nick, Gatsby represented 'something gorgeous', showing 'a gift for hope, a romantic readiness such as I have never found in any other person'. Despite this, Gatsby's romanticism is also a futile desire to return to a former state that resembles Freud's death-instinct: '[Gatsby] talked a lot about the past, and I gathered that he wanted to recover something, some idea of himself perhaps, that had gone into loving Daisy. His life had been confused and disordered . . . but if he could once return to a certain starting place and go over it all slowly, he could find out what that thing was . . .'[27]

The past that Gatsby conceals and erases in his self-formulation is working-class immigrant. As Nick pieces together the fragments of Gatsby's past – much of which he has fabricated to conceal his former class status and remake himself – he learns of Gatsby's earlier relationship with Daisy (his military uniform acted as an 'invisible cloak' that covered his true class identity) which ended while he was fighting in Europe, during which she married Tom. With a vast fortune accumulated within three years following the war (an implied result of profiteering or black-market activities) Gatsby has bought a huge mansion across the bay from Daisy where he holds lavish parties in the hope of winning her back. When Nick first encounters Gatsby he is staring at the bay that separates him from Daisy, stretching out his arms to the green light at the end of Daisy's dock in a gesture of desire and hope. Nick becomes central to their reunion as Gatsby uses Nick's acquaintance with the Buchanans to solicit a meeting between himself and Daisy. Despite this, his dream of returning to the past is shown as futile and outdated: Gatsby in fact exists between the world he creates and the world he tried to escape, between the faked happiness and hollow luxury of the sumptuous parties, filled with jazz music and actresses, and the dust-covered reality of the vast wasteland between New York and Long Island called the valley of ashes. Ultimately, Gatsby remains a class outcast (Tom calls him 'Mr Nobody from Nowhere') and his dream results in cataclysmic violence and death.

The novel implicitly examines the anomie resulting from social change following the war. Nick's decision to go East at the start of the story is based in his own sense of restlessness after the war – an event that he calls an enjoyable 'counter-raid' to 'Teutonic migration' after which his home feels 'like the ragged end of the universe'.[28] Like Gatsby, his move East becomes another counter-migration, one almost as violent as the war, and a negative mirror-image of the American Dream that propelled Western migration in search of freedom and material gain. The drunken marauding that punctuates the novel shows the nihilism beneath this reversal, an alienation that is summarised by Nick as a casual careless-ness: 'It was all very careless and confused. They were careless people, Tom and Daisy – they smashed up things and creatures and then retreated back into their money or their vast carelessness, or whatever it was that kept them together, and let other people clean up the mess they had made . . .'[29]

This mess is rudely exposed in Fitzgerald's portrait of the valley of ashes – 'a fantastic farm where ashes grow like wheat into ridges and hills and grotesque gardens; where ashes take the forms of houses and chimneys and rising smoke'.[30] A huge waste tip, the 'ash-grey' workers in the valley of ashes are screened by an 'impenetrable cloud' over which appeared the faded 'blue and gigantic' eyes of Doctor T. J. Eckleburg, a massive billboard advertisement for an oculist who has long since disappeared. The obscuration of vision, meaning and truth, a central theme of the novel, is represented by these unseeing eyes that overlook the garage in which Tom's working-class mistress, Myrtle Wilson, lives with her mechanic husband. It is here where the collision finally happens and the vital body of Myrtle Wilson is extinguished by Daisy who is driving Gatsby's car – a hit-and-run accident that leaves her 'violently extinguished', her left-breast 'swinging loose like a flap' . . . 'the mouth wide open and ripped a little at the corners'.[31]

Like his real-life contemporaries Henry Ford and William Randolph Hearst, the millionaire's fantasy of perfection in the imagined past is fuelled by his own destruction of it.[32] Through Gatsby and his material acquisi-tions, Fitzgerald shows that the dream of progress and upward mobility is connected to a deep sense of loss and destruction that is particular to Americans: cutting themselves adrift from history and smashing up idols and links with an old world has left them bereft of meaning; living, like the title of Eliot's poem, as 'The Hollow Men' (1925). Rather than its story of wealth, money or love, what makes *The Great Gatsby* supremely emblem-atic of 'jazz age' psychology is the way it reveals the sublimation of social unease and anxiety necessary to enjoy the glib and fleeting pleasures associated with the pursuit of happiness and material gain. Fitzgerald's writing hints at the class and race violence that lies beneath the American Dream of success and self-invention but remains ambivalent, torn between the dream and its destruction, just as Nick attempts to sustain the romantic ideal of a Gatsby being 'Great' despite his failure. Fitzgerald posits this ambivalence as the representative condition of modern America caught between progress and the past, and ends the novel with Nick's ambivalent reflection:

> Gatsby believed in the green light, the orgiastic future that year by year
> recedes before us. It eluded us then, but that's no matter – tomorrow we will
> run faster, stretch out our arms further . . . And one fine morning –
> So we beat on, boats against the current, borne back ceaselessly into the
> past.[33]

The New Poetry

The desire to 'make it new' while being 'borne ceaselessly back into the
past' produced a characteristic tension in avant-garde poetry expressed
by Gertrude Stein's 'Beginning again and again and again'.[34] Ezra
Pound, foremost in the promotion of the artist as a cultural renova-
tor, encouraged numerous poets and writers to adopt a minimalist
directness and economy of expression that became highly visible in
the literature of the 1920s. Pound believed that 'making it new' in
poetry, art and music could lead to the restoration and rejuvenation
of civilisation, yet while he demanded that new poetry should jettison
abstractions and old habits, he also held up the best examples from the
cultural past to guide the modern reader and writer, something he later
called 'pragmatic aesthetics'.[35]

Pragmatic aesthetics signified an experimentalism in art that
employed methods and ideas coming out of experimental psychology,
sociology, philosophy, maths, science and technology. New ideas
about the composition of organic structures and their relationship with
the perceiving subject stimulated writers to new forms of expression
that broke with tradition.[36] Like Pound, Gertrude Stein encouraged
writers to take up the challenge of the 'new realism' that had emerged
from the scientist's observations. Stein's work challenged lineal narratives of historical progress by positing that human experience was a
series of perceptions in the continuous present that were relative and
transitional. Her *Making of Americans* (1925) showed, however, that
within the continuous present there was always a past: 'The old people
in a new world, the new people made out of the old, that is the story
that I mean to tell, for that is what really is and what I really know'.[37]
This was confirmed in her essay 'Composition as Explanation' (1926)
where repeating the past ('Beginning again and again and again') creates
something new. To Stein, this aesthetic was particularly appropriate to
America because migration and exile had meant that Americans had
to continually reinvent themselves: 'The nature in every one is always
coming out of them from their beginning to their ending by the repeating always in them, by the repeating always coming out of them'.[38]

Eliot also explained this dynamic between past and present as a new temporal order, where the past was 'altered by the present as much as the present is directed by the past'.[39] The poet, he claimed, 'is not likely to know what is to be done unless he lives in what is not merely the present, but the present moment of the past, unless he is conscious, not of what is dead, but of what is already living'.[40] Such ideas show that Gatsby's frustratingly impossible dream of repeating or altering the past made him less a symbol of romantic loss than of supreme American modernity.

The modification of the past in the present offered an exciting promise to young writers who were fascinated with the new knowledge of objects offered them by science and psychology. Marianne Moore's *Observations* (1924) explored the natural world with the precision of a naturalist, botanist or archaeologist – 'Contractility,' she said of the snail 'is a virtue'.[41] To these poets, objects needed no embellishment, ornamentation or Godlike creator to make them wondrous. Similarly, William Carlos Williams and Archibald MacLeish saw Einstein's theory of relativity as liberation from the past and inspiration for new poetic expression. In Williams' poem 'St. Francis Einstein of the Daffodils' (1921), Einstein was the bringer of spring, the liberator from 'oldfashioned knowledge'.[42] Like Pound, Williams eschewed literary abstraction for concrete expression; using mechanisation as a model for his literary efficiency he argued in 1921 that writers should have the 'inventive intelligence of our engineers' and later explained the poem as a 'machine made of words'.[43] His joy in the scientific understanding of the unadorned object is famously expressed in 'The Red Wheelbarrow' from *Spring and All* (1923), a collection that jettisoned archaism and literary convention. 'The rose is obsolete,' he stated at the start of 'The Rose', (echoing Gertrude Stein's 'Rose is a rose is a rose') yet it could be revivified through geometric rather than romantic appreciation. MacLeish's long poem 'Einstein' (1926) also illustrated the vast potential of a world seen anew, yet hinted at the vertiginous psychological shift that the scientist's work entailed: 'Still he stands/ Watching the vortex widen and involve/ In swirling dissolution the whole earth/ And circle through the skies till swaying time/ Collapses, crumpling into dark the stars,/ And motion ceases and the sifting world/ Opens beneath'.[44] Williams also saw the knowledge of relativity as painful moments of epiphany 'that somehow seems to destroy us' and leaves 'no one to drive the car' ('To Elsie').[45]

While science left in its wake a moral relativism and spiritual disorder that threatened civilisation, Wallace Stevens showed that the

new structural understanding offered its own fragile order that could
be harmonious. His first collection, *Harmonium* (1923), was particularly concerned with ways of portraying the impact of this shifting
order on the structure and perception of reality. Each of the five sections of 'Sea Surface Full of Clouds' begins with 'In that November
off Tehuantepac' and offers a repetition with variation of the section
before it – each a description as 'real' as the other while remaining different, showing how the perceiving subject structures external reality.
This kaleidoscopic and shifting heterogeneity was further underscored
in 'Thirteen Ways of Looking at a Blackbird' that illustrated the
impossibility of a single way of knowing.

These new aesthetics enabled the defamiliarisation of common
objects and thoughts in order to revivify the everyday experience
of modern machine culture and mass production. The aesthetics of
the machine age, Pound insisted, should at least meet the profound
transformations that the sciences had revealed. To Pound, observing the machine allowed the artist to study form with a detachment
that enabled a radical departure from outmoded forms of expression
associated with pre-formulated emotional responses. Henry Ford's
workshop, he thereby argued, had produced a new musical rhythm
and pace to life that had been incorporated in the work of his friend
and composer Antheil.[46]

Few poets could detach themselves from an emotional response
to the machine in the way that Pound wished, however.[47] The most
ambitious attempt to construct poetry by surrendering to urban
experience or the 'jazz rhythm' of the city was visible in Hart Crane's
The Bridge (1930). In the metaphor of the bridge Crane celebrated
the contemporary experience as a connection between old and new,
celebrating American modernity as a union, rather than disjuncture,
of machine culture and the pioneer past. Williams also attempted to
depict this particularly American experience in his iconoclastic prose
works *The Great American Novel* (1923) and *In the American Grain*
(1925).

These poets found new rhythms not in the machine but in the mix
of folk or working-class culture and the urban or everyday experience. Harlem provided the best example of this productive synthesis
between old and new, man and machine. The rhythm of Harlem
nightlife and music inspired Langston Hughes, who drew on blues
songs and jazz music in an innovative mix of modern music, vernacular sounds and machine culture in *The Weary Blues* (1926) and *Fine
Clothes to the Jew* (1927). To Hughes this was the beat of the new

America: 'jazz to me is one of the inherent expressions of Negro life in America: the eternal tom-tom beating in the Negro soul – the tom-tom of revolt against weariness in a white world, a world of subway trains, and work, work, work; the tom-tom of joy and laughter, and pain swallowed in a smile'.[48]

Drama: The Mind and the Machine

The psychological effects of the man-made world on the individual were key themes explored in new and experimental drama. As one observer noted, new ideas about the relationship between the individual and the world being developed in the sciences emerged in drama: 'Just as in all of the other arts, the material of the theatre has been affected thoroughly by modern scientific thinking. It has been influenced by all the "ologies and isms" – neurology, psychology, pathology – by free, independent, daring thinking'.[49] While it was correct to note a vibrant experimentalism that engaged with ideas coming out of the sciences, the influence of European experiments in drama, most notably German expressionism, was sometimes unacknowledged. John Dos Passos, however, whose expressionist play *The Garbage Man* (1925) was being produced in the same year his experimental novel *Manhattan Transfer* was published, wrote about the impact of European modernism on the Americans in postwar Paris.[50] One result of this ferment between native and foreign influences alongside contemporary artistic and scientific theories was that modern American theatre started to develop a unique identity that would make American drama internationally ascendant.

The growth of independent theatre groups and 'little theatre' in the previous decade provided the impetus for experiments that were shocking to conventional audiences in the 1920s. Alternative theatre provided outlets for young, female and immigrant writers more easily than the mainstream commercial theatre. In these alternative and independent theatre groups (which included the Provincetown Players, the Washington Square Players, the Neighborhood Playhouse, various African American community theatres and university Laboratory Theatres) the impact of the war, the Russian Revolution, Freud and feminism were expressed in experiments with theatrical space, time, dialogue, character, subject and setting that changed the landscape of American drama.[51] Out of these groups emerged the foremost writers of the decade, among whom Eugene O'Neill became the most celebrated.

Eugene O'Neill

Eugene O'Neill's work over the 1920s was continually experimental and expressed the alienation of modern culture and the anxieties over gender, race and class that dominated American social thought. O'Neill first came to popular notice with *The Emperor Jones* (1920), an expressionist play about the rise of a working-class African American murderer to totalitarian leadership on a West Indian island and his subsequent psychological collapse and self-annihilation.[52] The play opened in November 1920, just three months after Marcus Garvey's First International Convention of the Negro Peoples of the World in New York, and can thus be seen as a reflection on the 'rising tide' of black self-determination and declining European empires, as well as the rising imperialism of the United States in the Caribbean (having invaded Haiti in 1915). Despite this, O'Neill saw Brutus Jones as a universal or paradigmatic figure, who illustrated that a material rise became also an atavistic descent, showing the rapidity with which the 'civilised' man returned to savagery – something that Jung and Freud's theories of mankind's compulsion towards racial primitivism and violence confirmed at the time. Unusual though this plot was for conventional theatre, the style was even more revolutionary – the setting of expressionist silhouettes and silent shadowy figures reflects Jones' emotional hysteria as he is haunted by the past, accompanied by incessant drumbeats that increase in tempo and intensity until the protagonist dies.

Expressionism intended to depict the nightmare of human existence through sparse and distorted scenery, automaton 'everyman' characters and themes of the senseless mechanised horror of industrial society. Most central to the expressionist play, however, was the exploration and dramatisation of inner states of being that recent psychoanalytic studies had revealed. *The Emperor Jones* thus explored Jung's idea of a collective racial unconscious in the individual mind of a man haunted by his origins.[53] O'Neill's second expressionist play, *The Hairy Ape* (1922), explored this further through the inability of 'Yank', a seaman, to connect with the world around him. Yank is only happy when he is part of the machine – literally feeding coal into the engine of a cruise steamer that carries the wealthy leisured classes above his head. Once his alienation is made apparent to him, his search for a place in society propels him towards death. The play ends when Yank, entering into the gorilla cage in Central Park Zoo to return to his 'family', is crushed by a gorilla, his alienation compounded as he asks 'Where do I fit in?'

O'Neill continued to explore these ideas of alienation and estrangement using controversial themes and expressionist stage techniques to explore every religious and social taboo: in *Desire Under the Elms* (1924) it was greed, sex, incest and infanticide; in *All God's Chillun' Got Wings* (1924) interracial marriage, miscegenation and sexual slavery; in *The Great God Brown* (1926) business materialism and the death of art and spirituality; in the Pulitzer prize-winning *Strange Interlude* (1928), a six-hour play, he explored promiscuity and eugenic abortion. Although he downplayed the importance of Freud to his work O'Neill, along with many of his contemporaries, was certainly familiar with Freud's *Totem and Taboo* and *The Pleasure Principle* as well as Jung's *Psychology of the Unconscious*.[54]

O'Neill's plays captured the nation's engagement and fascination with Freudian ideas to an unprecedented extent. In his expressionistic and psychoanalytic explorations of religion, sex, materialism and race, he dramatised key issues of the 1920s. His use of masks gave dramatic illustration of personality complexes and types that had entered into current discourse and illustrated the battle between the surface image and the hidden subconscious. His characters often spoke an inner monologue alongside their 'public' dialogue, illustrating the 'inner reality' of the battle between the individual and society alongside the conscious and subconscious drives that motivated their actions. By 1927 O'Neill was himself undergoing psychoanalytic therapy for his alcoholism, and his plays continued to express his search for dramatic devices 'to penetrate the conscious surface of the personality'.[55]

Psychoanalysis was a particularly apt device for the dramatist as it illustrated not just the tensions experienced by the individual in society, but those between the past and the future in which the present was a chaotic 'jungle' of collective memory. Like the psychoanalyst who attempted to get to the bottom of present psychopathic behaviours by examining the patient's past, O'Neill's play *Strange Interlude* exposed the way that past inheritances shaped subsequent events. As the central protagonist, Nina, states in the play: 'The only living life is in the past and future – the present is an interlude – strange interlude in which we call on past and future to bear witness we are living!'[56]

The nihilism of commercial modern culture also appeared in O'Neill's plays. The far less successful *Marco Millions* (1928) presented a satire of Marco Polo as a thirteenth-century commercial traveller, a mercenary, self-centred historical 'Babbitt' who reflected the soullessness of modern business America. By 1929 O'Neill embarked further on a theme that would 'dig at the roots of the sickness of today as I feel it – the death of an old God and the failure of science and materialism to give any satisfactory new one for the surviving religious instinct to find a meaning for life in, and to comfort its fear of death with'.[57] The subsequent play *Dynamo* (1929) follows the downward trajectory of Reuben, a fundamentalist preacher's son, who renounces his father's faith, rapes and kills his girlfriend, and replaces her with a womb-shaped humming dynamo, by which he is electrocuted as he grasps the machine he calls 'mother'. As Reuben renounces his faith he takes to studying science: 'books on astronomy, biology and physics and chemistry and evolution. What the fool preachers call God is in electricity somewhere'.[58] Although the play was not successful it dramatised the tension between faith and the worship of science that had been epitomised in the Scopes trial and Henry Adams' discussion of 'The Dynamo and the Virgin': 'the dynamo became a symbol of infinity.

As he grew accustomed to the great gallery of machines, he began to feel the forty-foot dynamos as a moral force, much as the early Christians felt the Cross . . . Before the end, one began to pray to it'.[59] O'Neill's play illustrated the calamitous outcome of this loss of faith in the modern world.

Figure 1.1 Paul Robeson in the film of Eugene O'Neill's *The Emperor Jones*, 1933 (© United Artists/The Kobal Collection).

Numerous other dramatists rebelled from the realistic dramaturgy of the day in their attempts to express modern alienation as a psychotic withdrawal from 'civilised' values in a dehumanising machine-made culture.[60] Elmer Rice's *The Adding Machine* (1923) opened twelve months after O'Neill's *The Hairy Ape* and incorporated similar expressionist-inspired techniques to illustrate the individual as a cipher or cog in the modern industrial machine. In the strikingly absurd play the central character, Mr. Zero, kills his boss when he replaces him with an adding machine. The play follows his trial, execution, and his after-life, where he fails to take up the emancipation he is offered, choosing instead to operate another adding machine. After twenty-five years operating the machine Zero is eventually 'sent back' to become a baby again, only to become another unwitting cog in the machine. Zero's self-subordination turns him into a waste product of the machine-age; the lieutenant who is sending him back to his 'sunless groove' declares: 'You're a failure, Zero, a failure. A waste product. A slave to a contraption of steel and iron ... Back you go – back to your sunless groove – the ready prey of the first jingo or demagogue or political adventurer who takes the trouble to play upon your ignorance and credulity and provincialism'.[61]

Rice further explored the individual trapped in the mechanistic world in his next play, *The Subway* (1929), which dramatised the downward trajectory of a filing clerk, Sophie Smith, who is seduced by the businessman Eugene Landray. Eugene describes his feelings for the city as a new form of sexual passion: 'It fills me ... obsesses me ... The city ... the city ... steel and concrete ... industrialism, rearing its towers arrogantly to the skies ... Higher and higher ... deeper and deeper ... Up and up'.[62] Finding herself with an illegitimate pregnancy, Sophie commits suicide by jumping in front of the subway train that has become symbolic of her trapped existence.

The theme of the woman trapped by her biological role in a mechanistic environment to which she is unable to adapt was pursued in Sophie Treadwell's *Machinal* (1928) – based on the infamous Judd Gray/Ruth Snyder murder case that Treadwell had covered as a journalist. (The same murder plot was later to provide the story for James M. Cain's serialised novel *Double Indemnity*.) Treadwell sympathetically depicted the killer as an 'everywoman' trapped within patriarchal capitalism, highlighted by cage-like stage settings and the continual presence of offstage noises such as adding machines, telegraph bells, airplanes, radios, buzzers and other mechanical instruments. In the final scene the machinery has finally triumphed and she is executed in an electric chair, a scene gruesomely paralleling the real-life execution of Snyder that was secretly photographed and splashed across the daily news the following day.

The mechanisation of the individual within the contemporary urban scene again appeared in Edward Faragoh's *Pinwheel* (1927), which he called 'a rapid patterned dance of multitudes to the music of a gigantic hurdy-gurdy of steel and concrete'.[63] The play explored the mechanised work and leisure of the female office worker, 'The Jane', whose office is dominated by an enormous typewriter like the oversized adding machine in Rice's play. The play sees 'the Jane' pursued by men and going on dates to the dance hall and the movies, and features an 'orgiastic' shopping spree and a Coney Island debauch – similarities that it shared with the expressionistic movies *Sunrise* (1927) and *The Crowd* (1928).[64]

As expressionist cinema reached its height with the American release of Fritz Lang's *Metropolis* in 1927, politicised expressionist dramas continued to appear on the stage. The e. e. cummings play *Him* (1927) began with an anaesthetised pregnant woman on a table whose unconscious thoughts become objectified in the surreal performance that unfolds. Michael Gold's *Hoboken Blues* (1928) demanded an all-black cast (with white characters played using white masks) with reality depicted through the mind of the unemployed Negro Sam Pickens, suggesting a 'battle of jungle and modern industrialism'.[65] Similar political attacks on capitalism were *The Belt* (1927) by Paul Sifton and John Dos Passos and Upton Sinclair's *Singing Jailbirds* (1928). In *The Belt* the workers of an automobile plant revolt and destroy the assembly line when Old Man, a Henry Ford figure, tries to shut down the factory. The play depicted the Ford factory process with a procession of automobile frames moving slowly across the stage as men worked 'monotonously' around it.[66] By the end of the 1920s, experimental drama had had a huge impact on theatre and performance, influencing Broadway productions, trends in crime fiction and film noir, works produced in the 1930s by Group Theatre and the Federal Theater Project and drama of the forties and fifties by those such as Arthur Miller and Edward Albee.[67] Although the height of the expressionist trend only lasted until the end of the decade (and the majority of plays were more traditional in theme and setting) the themes of the expressionist play tapped the anxieties of the lost generation concerning estrangement and alienation in capitalist mass culture.

The Novel and Mass Culture

Consumer capitalism's effect on human behaviour was central to Theodore Dreiser's *An American Tragedy* (1925). Dreiser depicted the pathological impact of the new materialism through the moral descent of Clyde Griffiths, who, having rejected his parents' evangelical and repressive lifestyles, has no moral map to follow. His pursuit of pleasure and lust for social status turns him sociopathic and his attempt to improve his lot leads only to the execution chamber. The pursuit of 'normalcy' and success, Dreiser thus implied, encouraged a greedy individualism that led to modern neuroses and compulsions.

The dehumanising impact of mass production, standardisation and psychological repressions in small-town America came under satiric critique in Sinclair Lewis's *Main Street* (1920). Central protagonist Carol Kennicott observes 'an unimaginatively standardised background, a sluggishness of speech and manners, a rigid ruling of the spirit by the desire to appear respectable'.[68] To Carol, the townsfolk are: 'A savorless people, gulping tasteless food, and sitting afterward, coatless and thoughtless, in rocking-chairs prickly with inane decorations, listening to mechanical music, saying mechanical things about the excellence of Ford automobiles, and viewing themselves as the greatest race in the world'.[69]

American 'normalcy' also came under attack in Sinclair Lewis's story of passive consumerism in *Babbitt* (1922), a book that displayed a deep disdain for the commodity fetishism and materialism of the era that had turned culture into an adornment and advertisement for capitalist values. In the opening chapter the city of Zenith is described as a streamlined machine: the skyscrapers are towers of steel, as sturdy as silver rods, a car moves over the concrete bridge noiselessly and as the train runs past 'twenty lines of polished steel leaped into the glare'.[70]

In contrast to this smoothly running productive machine, the sleeping Babbitt is described as babyish and flabby, an archetypal consumer. Not a loner or alienated outsider, however, Babbitt is Mr Average. A fictional parallel to the sociological description of life in *Middletown* (1929), Lewis charts Babbitt's mundane daily activities to highlight how much of his life is structured by the material objects he has purchased. The alarm clock that wakes him is 'the best of nationally advertised and quantitatively produced alarm-clocks' and just seeing it in the morning makes him feel proud and socially 'creditable'. The objects surrounding him perform a semiotic function, symbolising dreams and aspirations that are never fulfilled: his camping blanket 'suggests' freedom and heroism to him, although he bought it for a camping trip that never happened. Babbitt's 'wasteland' is created by the abundance of consumer goods surrounding him out of which he constructs meaning – the objects take on a life and meaning of their own and formulate a narrative of display (just as Jay Gatsby's house and possessions 'narrate' him). In the bathroom, for example, 'above the set bowl was a sensational exhibit of tooth-brush holder, shaving brush holder, soap-dish, sponge dish and medicine cabinet, so glittering, so ingenious that they resembled an electrical instrument board'.[71]

The objects satisfy Babbitt not to use but to see, as displays of his success, modernity and efficiency. Despite this, Babbitt isn't content. By making modern appliances his 'God', Babbitt experiences a constant feeling of undefined dissatisfaction. Lewis showed that because Babbitt allowed objects to replace authentic feelings he also experienced displacement and homelessness: 'there was but one thing wrong with the Babbitt house: It was not a home'.[72] Through *Babbitt* Lewis criticised consumer democracy as proto-fascist, alienating and dehumanising – showing that it was not just workers on the production line who experienced anomie. As one critic noted in 1928,

> Babbitt, as a representative man, is possible only in America. His gestures, his foibles, his words and phrases, are explained by the country where millions of human beings are cut on the same pattern, made in series like automobiles or harvesters, because it cannot be done otherwise. Quantity versus quality, the masses against the individual, – this is the great American problem and George Babbitt is the half-sarcastic, half-tragic example of it. He is conformism incarnate.[73]

Average Americans enjoyed Lewis's portrait and the huge popularity of the book among the middle classes at the time led 'Babbitt' to become a dictionary definition of shallow consumerism and pompous middle-class narrow-mindedness.

Southern Renaissance

Two major literary phenomena of the decade also grew out of the changes experienced as a result of the rapid industrialisation that had been accelerated by wartime production: the Southern Renaissance and the Harlem Renaissance.

A cultural renaissance in the South did not appear possible to H. L. Mencken in 1917, who likened the South to a cultural wasteland or desert. In his famous essay 'The Sahara of the Bozart' (1917), Mencken depicted the South as culturally retarded, a place far more sterile and degenerate than anything T. S. Eliot had yet to imagine: 'It is, indeed, amazing to contemplate so vast a vacuity . . . It would be impossible in all history to match so complete a drying-up of a civilization'.[74] To Mencken the South was not just un-modern but anti-modern, a place where religious fundamentalism and ignorance reigned, of which the Ku Klux Klan was a prime example. The imposition of crass material-ism from the North had only exacerbated things: 'the liberated lower orders of whites have borrowed the worst commercial bounderism of the Yankee and superimposed it upon a culture that, at bottom, is but little removed from savagery'.[75] As the Scopes trial was to confirm, the South appeared a place that time and progress had forgotten.

That this barren, infertile wasteland would sustain some of the best writers of the decade had not been apparent to Mencken, yet after the war a flowering of southern literary magazines provided the stimulus for new cultural production. Magazines such as the *Double Dealer*, *The Reviewer* and *The Fugitive* became publishing outlets for young, innovative writers.[76] *The Fugitive* (1922–5), founded by John Crowe Ransom at Vanderbilt University, became the most famous of these, publishing verse and critical pieces by young southern writers who were later to become known as 'the Southern Agrarians'; Ransom, Allen Tate, Robert Penn Warren and Donald Davidson. These writers also saw themselves as exiles; the Fugitive, claimed Allen Tate, was 'a Poet: the Wanderer, . . . the Outcast'.[77] To these writers, industrialism and 'progress' imposed an alien and abstracted consumerist culture that was spiritually sterile and fragmenting; their criticism dismissed modern capitalist progress as a chimera that offered the South no remedies or security, no culture and no faith.[78]

As in 'The Waste Land', Allen Tate's poetry mourned the loss of God in this mechanically produced civilisation, where the machine was a figureless 'mathematical shroud' that prevented a genuine capac-ity for faith and belief. Like Eliot, Tate also employed ancient culture to show the decline into modernity, using Homer and Virgil as critics of twentieth-century culture in comparisons with the cheapening of mass-produced culture, where 'the Parthenon/ In Tennessee stucco, [was] art for the sake of death'.[79] Although the agrarians looked backwards to the pre-industrial South, as Tate's poetry showed, their aesthetic links were to modernist or European traditions.[80] Tate wrote that rather than resurrecting the past, 'my attempt is to see the present from the past, yet remain immersed in the present and committed to it'.[81] Rather than a return to the past, the poets and writers of the Southern Renaissance set about to consciously forge a 'new' southern tradition that would represent more accurately the condition of the South as the 'lost' country within a country.

Rediscovering that lost country led to a resurgence of poetry, prose and non-fiction that resurrected southern figures or considered matters central to the agrarian mission: as well as collections of poems these included Allen Tate's biographies of Stonewall Jackson (1928) and Jefferson Davis (1929), Warren's iconoclastic *John Brown* (1929) and Ransom's dismissal of science and defence of fundamentalism in *God without Thunder: An Unorthodox Defence of Orthodoxy* (1930).[82] Their 'radical conservatism' reached its apotheosis in the 1930 publication of *I'll Take My Stand*, a collection of essays from twelve contributors from different disciplines – 'which vigorously stated their preference for the social models of the white aristocratic planter of the Old South or the self-sufficient white yeoman farmer over the city-bound, clock-watching George Babbitts of the 1920s'.[83] *I'll Take My Stand* was the battle-cry of revisionist writers in search of a harmonious system, a white male vision of an organic South whose shared tradition depended on the exclusion of African American and female.

By re-commanding history the agrarians hoped to heal past wounds and restore masculinity to the Southern landowner, eviscerated by the dominance of northern financial and economic systems. The impact of World War I caused southern writers to revisit the losses of the Civil War, where the problem of modernity, the fracturing of culture and the imposition of a northern version of national history had begun. Loss of innocence, traditions and heroic causes inflected the fugitive's poems. Yet, in trying to capture the heroic past at the moment of its loss, the southern writer revisited the painful events only to find he was unable to restore or change the past. The poet was thus forced into a frustrating repetition of loss and impotency. Tate's 'Ode to the Confederate Dead' (first version written in 1926) illustrated such stasis, charting less a return to the past than a frustrating loss whereby the past cannot be re-experienced in the present.[84] The writing of the agrarians was nearly always retrospective, exploring the decomposition or deconstruction of the past as it emerged in the present,[85] an experience that Tate referred to as the 'cut-off-ness of the "modern intellectual man" from the world'.[86]

Other southern writers also experienced this 'cut-off-ness' from the past as a loss or absence that fuelled their search for 'home' and connected them, despite their regional focus, to the modernism of the lost generation. Thomas Wolfe's epigraph in *Look Homeward Angel* (1929) described birth itself as an exile and the earth as an 'unspeakable and incommunicable' prison, lamenting 'O Waste of loss, in the hot mazes, lost, among bright stars on this most unweary unbright cinder, lost! Remembering speechlessly we seek the great forgotten language, the lost lane-end into heaven, a stone, a leaf, an unfound door'. Wolfe's autobiographical essay 'God's Lonely Man' confirmed his belief that such isolation and atomisation was the universal human condition.

Both southern and modernist, William Faulkner wrote in his journal about this sense of dislocation on returning to the South at the end of the war: 'When the war was over – the other war – William Faulkner went back to Oxford, Mississippi . . . Now he was home again and not at home, or at least not able to accept the postwar world . . .'[87] To Faulkner the South was haunted by the ever present but inaccessible and fragmented past that can only be expressed (and then inadequately so) through fragmented and elliptical narratives. His first novel, *Soldiers' Pay* (1926), narrated the homecoming of a disfigured aviator who has returned home to die. Donald Mahon returns changed to a changed world, where his scar marks him as an outsider. As Richard Gray has noted, the theme of 'the absent centre or central figure who is both there and not there' was to become a trademark of Faulkner's later work.[88]

In *Sartoris* (1929) Faulkner depicted the destructiveness of the past in the present as he juxtaposed the Sartoris family's experience of the Civil War with the recent World War. The effect of this past's presence is always destruction and decline. As the young aviator Bayard Sartoris returns to the family at the end of World War I, bereaved and guilty at the death of his twin brother in an air battle, legendary stories about Bayard's Confederate grandfather, Colonel John Sartoris, continue to circulate around him. These are filled with chivalry, bravery and heroism, yet Bayard cannot connect these stories to his present or to the memories of the war that destroyed his brother. Bayard manifests Freud's death-instinct in his persistent reckless driving and self-destructiveness, eventually dying, like his twin, in a plane crash. Like Krebs in Hemingway's 'Soldiers Home', Bayard cannot adapt to the changes following the war and Faulkner connects his self-destructiveness and family decay to the violent fracture of the southern past that re-emerges within industrial modernity.

The experience of time and memory as loss or confusion was central to Faulkner's other novel of 1929, *The Sound and the Fury*, in which he collapsed time around a non-lineal narrative of Candace Compson's

absence in the lives of four different narrators. The impossibility
of achieving or even aiming for a single ideal or vision is illustrated
through the multiple perspectives of the narrators, who all experience
individual versions of the loss of Caddy. Just as the autistic Benjy
'could not remember his sister but only the loss of her', Faulkner did
not aim to represent a stable past, only the loss of it – the results of
such a loss.[89]

Rather than resort to nostalgia, however, the 'stable past' itself is
shown as an unsustainable illusion. On the day of his suicide Caddy's
elder brother Quentin (the second narrator) begins by destroying his
watch while he remembers his father's words as he hands him the
heirloom:

> I give it to you not that you may remember time, but that you might
> forget it now and then for a moment and not spend all your breath trying
> to conquer it. Because no battle is ever won he said. They are not even
> fought. The field only reveals to man his own folly and despair, and
> victory is an illusion of philosophers and fools.[90]

In this sentence Quentin's father summarises the nihilism that propels
his son towards death: the loss of the battle, the Old South, lineal time
and Caddy's virginity are not even losses but illusions of something
whole that never was. Like Henry Adams, whose encounter with
modernity convinced him that 'the sequence of men led to nothing and
that the sequence of their society could lead no further, while the mere
sequence of time was artificial, and the sequence of thought was chaos',
Quentin Compson's fragmented watch, like the fragmented narrative
that depicted it, symbolised the destruction of the old order replaced
with an arrangement of events ultimately 'signifying nothing'.[91]

'Other' Renaissances

While the agrarians and Caddy Compson's brothers propelled a vision
of the lost South as a fantasy of masculine order and white control,
women and non-white writers found Mencken's desert to be a fruit-
ful terrain, one that was also gaining a nationwide audience. Southern
women writers achieved unprecedented popularity in this period with
their portraits of overlooked or 'lost' Americans who existed on the
margins of progressive urban society, examining rural existence with
sociological realism. These stories gave a relenting image of the grind-
ing nature of poverty in the South that contrasted with 'local color'

fiction or idealistic notions of the rural past promulgated by some
agrarian visions. Edith Summers Kelley's *Weeds* (1922) focused on the
grim life of a sharecropper's daughter as she became resigned to the
monotony and hopelessness of rural poverty, while Elizabeth Madox
Roberts' *The Time of Man* (1926) depicted with sociological realism
a woman's struggle for self-definition while trapped in a cycle of
poverty and childbearing within a Kentucky farming community.

Although these mostly upper- or middle-class southern writers
found a feminist subtext in poor white female lives, white writers
also found a literary harvest in writing about poor black existence. At
times this fascination barely differed from the slumming of northern
white Harlemites, or writers who used experimentalism to explore
the edges of their subconscious revulsion and salacious fascination
with 'savagery' and primitivism.[92] Elizabeth Madox Roberts' *My
Heart and Flesh* (1927), for example, showed the 'hell' of a young
white woman's encounter with savagery when she discovers that, as
a result of her father's miscegenation, she has two sexually inconti-
nent mulatto half-sisters and a half-witted brother; her subsequent
identity crisis leads to a breakdown and final retreat into the purity
of the mountains.

One southern plantation owner, however, received unusual
approval from the black intelligentsia with her ethnographical portraits
and stories that were written using southern speech forms or Gullah,
a Creole dialect that combined English with a variety of West African
dialects. Julia Peterkin wrote from observation in the fields and cabins
of Lang Syne, the cotton plantation she owned with her husband
in South Carolina and her books *Green Thursday* (1924) and *Black
April* (1927) were highly praised by champions of the New Negro
movement Alain Locke, W. E. B. Du Bois, James Weldon Johnson,
Paul Robeson, Langston Hughes and Walter White. Although modernists H. L. Mencken and Carl Sandburg promoted her, genteel
white southerners were outraged by her work and she lived in fear
of Klan reprisals. Her novel *Scarlet Sister Mary* (a comedic take on
the Puritan morality that was the subject of Nathaniel Hawthorne's
The Scarlet Letter) depicted a plantation harlot who has nine children
by nine different fathers. Although banned for obscenity in parts of
the South it won a Pulitzer Prize in 1929. While Peterkin upset the
southern gentry, her work achieved widespread popularity because
of its unusual sensitivity to black speech patterns and observation of
plantation life, goals that were in keeping with black intellectual goals
to dignify the oral traditions of the black past.

Like Peterkin, white male writers also found rejuvenation for their aesthetic by writing 'blackface': DuBose Heyward depicted life in Charleston's black slums in his *Porgy* (1925), the story of a crippled beggar who falls in love with the drug addict Bess (later adapted into George Gershwin's opera *Porgy and Bess* in 1935); Roark Bradford wrote *Ol Man Adam an His Chillun* (1928), a collection of stories in black folklore style. Waldo Frank's experimental *Holiday* (1923), depicting the events of one day that lead to a lynching, was written from an African American perspective (and, indeed, Frank himself 'passed' for black when he travelled South with Jean Toomer to research the novel). Thomas S. Stribling explored the social and political issues of the South in his iconoclastic socio-journalistic works that were castigated by the Southern Agrarians; his *Birthright* (1922) – later adapted into a silent film by black film director Oscar Micheaux in 1924 – provided a damning critique of segregation and racial hierarchies as encountered by a Harvard-educated mulatto returning 'home' to the South.[93] Howard W. Odum, founder of the Department of Sociology at the University of North Carolina at Chapel Hill in 1920, also employed the voice of a black migrant worker in his fictionalised narrative *Rainbow Round My Shoulder: The Blue Trail of Black Ulysses* (1928).[94]

More than just minstrelsy or entertainment, however, white writers' fascination with black life in the South offered them an alternative vision to the cultural degeneracy associated with Western civilisation that the war had revealed. In *Civilization and Its Discontents* (1929), Freud noted a common perception that 'what we call our civilization is largely responsible for our misery, and that we should be much happier if we gave it up and returned to primitive conditions'.[95] In folk culture, writers saw a way to reject the false values of alienated industrial capitalism as well as the Puritan past and used 'pre-civilised' lifestyles to denote the restoration of spirituality that had been lost in modern culture. As a celebratory alternative to the decline or corruption of Western culture, 'primitivism' seemed a way to transform culture into something better and restore the authenticity that mass production had taken away.[96]

The desire to protect and document an 'authentic' folk culture existing outside of mass-produced culture led to increasing numbers of fictional productions that used fieldwork and sociological observations in an attempt to portray an authentic southern culture. A rage for collecting and collating the southern past resulted in numerous folk and sociological studies that examined the forgotten, ephemeral, oral or overlooked aspects of southern culture, many of which are now seen as products not of the Southern Renaissance but of the New Negro or Harlem Renaissance. While on the surface it seemed that the Harlem Renaissance was the mirror opposite of the Southern Renaissance – based in the North and associated with the urban, the modern and the future rather than the past – the interest in southern folk culture and the re-evaluation of black contributions to American cultural life were central to the development of the literature of the Harlem Renaissance. Indeed, many of the writers, artists and musicians who fuelled the New Negro movement were part of the huge migration of black Americans from the South who fused folk knowledge and traditional artistic practices with their experience of industrial culture in the North. To Houston A. Baker it is this very fusion that created and defined American literary modernism.[97] Jean Toomer's *Cane* (1923) provided a pivotal representation of this complex hybrid aesthetic with its fusion of multiple genres, northern and southern intersections, transgressive racial politics and incorporation of blues and folksong within the fragmentary narratives.

Jean Toomer, *Cane* (1923)

To Waldo Frank, *Cane* translated the essence of the South into poetic form, capturing a primitive beauty and the dying folk-spirit of rural life at threat from industrial encroachment and northern progress.[98] At the same time Toomer became the flagship writer of Harlem's New Negro Movement, 'a bright morning star of a new day' in literature.[99] Toomer, however, defied any singular categorisation – not only had he grown up comfortably in the North, he later refuted racial classifications, and *Cane* was to be his only recognised literary achievement.

Born in Washington DC in 1894, Toomer was raised by his grandfather, P. B. S. Pinchback, a fair-skinned reconstruction-era politician who became the first US state governor of African American heritage. Toomer studied peripatetically in Wisconsin, Massachusetts, Chicago and New York before settling in Greenwich Village in 1919. In 1921 he accepted a position as a substitute teacher at a black school in rural Georgia. His experience of northern city life at the height of the race riots along with his encounter – as an educated, light-skinned African American – with rural poverty, folk song, segregation and lynching in the South, provided the material and impetus for what would become one of the Harlem Renaissance's most experimental texts: *Cane*.

Cane gathered together a set of connected writings that Toomer had been composing for several years since his experience in rural Georgia; his immersion in the South unleashed a sense of spiritual and artistic awakening that he had not found in his academic studies or intellectual circles. To Toomer, 'The folk-spirit was walking in to die on the modern desert. That spirit was so beautiful. Its death was tragic'.[100] Despite this, his South is not a simple place of natural harmony. Although Toomer saw a spiritual identity in Georgia that he connected to natural rhythms and expression, he also explored a painful repression and biological determinism behind the structures of an exploitative racial and gender economy. In 'Karintha' a beautiful girl's soul is attenuated by premature sexuality, which has 'ripened too soon' under the lustful attentions of townsfolk.[101] The forced ripening mirrors the economic exploitation of the South in the poem 'November Cotton Flower' where the unnatural blossom becomes a harbinger of drought and hardship.[102] This is not a South of natural harmony but one ruled by violence and sexual passion ('Carma'), one inhabited by a race of slaves who are 'dark purple ripened plums,/ Squeezed and bursting in the pine-wood air'.[103]

Divided into three sections, the book is a tapestry of poetry, prose and drama (sometimes all three genres appear in a single narrative such as in 'Kabnis') that incorporated folklore, folk songs, spirituals and the shifting sensibilities of rural and urbanised characters to create a kaleidoscope of places and situations that refuted categorization. The shifting text was intentionally non-lineal, hybrid and ambiguous: Toomer wrote in a letter to his mentor Waldo Frank in 1922 that 'From three angles, Cane's design is a circle. Aesthetically, from simple forms to complex ones, and back to simple forms. Regionally, from the South up to the North, and back into the South again. Or, from the North down into the South, and then a return North'.[104] The endless circular motion that this implied makes migration, exile and place (or home) central themes in each section, themes mimicked in the fragmentary roaming style of the text. To the literary critic Gorham B. Munson the 'period of shifting and drifting without settled harborage' finds resolution in the South: 'Weary of homeless waters, he turns back to the ancestral soil, opens himself to its folk art and its folk ways, tries to find his roots, his origins'.[105] Despite this, Cane depicts violence rather than safety in origins: the story 'Becky' shows the social exclusion and alienation of sexual and racial transgression in the story of a white woman who gives birth to two Negro sons. An outcast who lives 'on the narrow strip of land between the railroad and the road', Becky becomes an ethereal presence, a ghost reminding the townsfolk of submerged transgressions and alienation.[106] The level of violence resulting from such repression varies from self-annihilation, as in Esther's internalised racism ('Esther') and sexual frustration, to violent lynching ('Blood-burning Moon'). The 'narrow strip of land' occupied by the sexual and racial outcast in Cane is thereby a place of both poetic beauty and extreme violence.

In the second section, mostly set in Washington DC, Toomer continued to explore the themes of repression and racial transgression. Prohibition and the war have created a 'bastard' culture of jazz songs and love in the 'whitewashed' wood of Washington where white standards of civilisation are shown as spiritually repressive and suffocating, like Rhobert's house, which he wears 'like a monstrous diver's helmet' ('Rhobert').[107] Trapped between the two worlds, white and black, intellectual and physical, the story of Ralph Kabnis who goes South to teach and write completes the circle. Contrary to Toomer's literary awakening in the South, however, Kabnis finds himself petrified with fear of racial violence, surrounded by stories of lynchings (stories based on real lynchings that had happened during Toomer's southern sojourn) and an outcast among the southern black community.[108] Kabnis, however, cannot disconnect himself from the past. northern civil rights activist Lewis reminds Kabnis of his connection:

Kabnis: . . . my ancestors were Southern blue-bloods –
Lewis: And black.
Kabnis: Aint much difference between blue an black.
Lewis: Enough to draw a denial from you. Can't hold them, can you? Master; slave. Soil; and the overarching heavens. Dusk; dawn. They fight and bastardize you.[109]

Toomer's elliptic and 'bastardised' text was feted by the intellectuals of the Harlem Renaissance – although *Cane*'s complexity and hybridity led to its neglect in subsequent years. *Cane* was reprinted in limited quantity in 1927, after which it remained out of print until interest from the black arts movement revived it in the 1960s and 1970s. After publication Toomer found the label of 'Negro' increasingly problematic and restricting, writing to James Weldon Johnson that 'My poems are not Negro poems, nor are they Anglo-Saxon or white or English poems. My prose, likewise . . .'[110] Toomer's quest for spirituality led him to follow the Armenian mystic Georges Gurdjieff, whose theories of self-creation contained no racial classification and fitted in with Toomer's belief in self-development. In 1922 he had written to Waldo Frank of this ambiguous racial identity: 'My own life has been equally divided between the two racial groups. My grandfather, owing to his emphasis upon a fraction of Negro blood in his veins, attained prominence in Reconstruction politics. And the family, for the most part, ever since has lived between the two worlds, now dipping into the Negro, now into the white. Some few are definitely white; others definitely colored. I alone have stood for a synthesis in the matters of the mind and spirit analogous, perhaps, to the actual fact of at least six blood minglings'.[111] *Cane* displays the writer's exploration of such racial synthesis and ambiguity through an experimental literary modernism that illustrated such complex modern subjectivity. As both a violent death and a rebirth, the condition he described was one of unavoidable modernity.

In his construction of a hybrid racial subjectivity, Toomer showed that the past was deeply intertwined with visions of the new. African American collector and archivist Arthur Schomburg wrote that the Negro needed to 'remake his past in order to make his future'.[112] To Schomburg, remaking the past would restore the human values and rights that slavery had taken away. Other African American writers of the Harlem Renaissance, such as James Weldon Johnson, were pivotal in highlighting the creativity and originality of black cultural productions originating from the South; over the 1920s his work included *The Book of American Negro Poetry* (1922), *The Book of American Negro Spirituals* (1925), *Second Book of American Negro Spirituals* (1926), *God's Trombones: Seven Negro Sermons in Verse* (1927) and *Black Manhattan* (1930).[113]

The social sciences were therefore at the forefront of the new literary vision. In 1926 anthropologist Franz Boas encouraged his student, Harlem Renaissance writer Zora Neale Hurston, to undertake folk-life research in the South that resulted in her subsequent collection *Mules and Men* (1935) as well as many plays, stories and musical revues. The previously overlooked African American became the focus of numerous studies: *Negro Workaday Songs* by Howard Odum (1926), *Folk Beliefs of the Southern Negro* (1926) by Newbell Niles Puckett, *Congaree Sketches* (1927) by E. C. L. Adams, *Singing Soldiers* (1927) by John J. Niles and Margaret Thorniley Williamson, *Plays of Negro Life* (1927) edited by Alain Locke, Montgomery Gregory and Aaron Douglas, *Caroling Dusk* (1927) by Countee Cullen and Aaron Douglas, *Ebony and Topaz: A Collectanea* (1927) by Charles Johnson and *Religious Folk-Songs of the Negro* (1927) by R. Nathaniel Dett.[114] Such publications further propelled the writing of white dramatists Heywood Broun and Paul Green, indicating that the new folk aesthetic had become a publishing phenomenon of the decade.[115]

Despite this interest in folk life, the New Negro and pan-African movements worked to dispel any sense that African Americans were historic or primitive throwbacks. They persistently rejected white stereotypes of the 'old' Negro, insisting that through a 'new aesthetic and a new philosophy of life' they had become modern players on a contemporary, international and intercultural stage.[116] Often combining urban with rural, the fusion and tension of multiple geographical, chronological and racial spaces underpinned the hybrid aesthetics of the Harlem Renaissance. Linking the African American with a disappearing folk past while also laying claim to representative modernity inevitably led to dissension. The publication of Sherwood Anderson's

Dark Laughter (1925) and Carl Van Vechten's *Nigger Heaven* (1926) brought this debate out into the open as intellectuals supported or rejected white characterisations of African American low-life. Locke, Du Bois and Weldon Johnson denigrated white 'Negrophilia' and saw degenerate portrayals of black life as capitulation to 'old' stereotypes of black life as primitive or regressive. In his essay 'Criteria of Negro Art' (1926), Du Bois claimed that all art was propaganda and that it was the duty of the black artist to represent the beauty of his people rather than their degradation.[117] Younger writers like Hughes, Toomer, Hurston, McKay and Wallace Thurman rejected what they saw as an attempt to police racial representation in art by the 'Niggerati'.

In the same year George Schuyler's 'Negro Art Hokum' argued that 'blackness' was no more a useful category of judgement in art than 'whiteness' and that 'the Africamerican is subject to the same economic and social forces that mold the actions and thoughts of the white Americans'.[118] Langston Hughes saw this as a denial of African American uniqueness, stating that 'Nordicised' black intellectuals were sustaining the 'urge within the race toward whiteness, the desire to pour racial individuality into the mold of American standardization, and to be as little Negro and as much American as possible'. While the 'present vogue in things Negro' may do some harm, he added, it had 'brought him forcibly to the attention of his own people' who for so long had valued him only through white eyes. Hughes declared that 'We younger Negro artists who create now intend to express our individual dark-skinned selves without fear or shame'.[119]

Insisting on artistic freedom, the self-consciously transgressive Harlem libertarians refused to conform to the boundaries of the 'talented tenth'. These arguments over internalised racism and representational politics spilled into Wallace Thurman's satire *The Blacker the Berry* (1929), Rudolph Fisher's *Walls of Jericho* (1928) and Schulyer's satire *Black No More* (1931). Rather than portraying Harlem as a mecca, Thurman's and William Rapp's play *Harlem: A Melodrama of Negro Life in Harlem* showed the hardships of migration there, with scenes of deprivation and illicit rent parties that upset both black and white critics.

A further liminal space was explored by gay Harlemites such as Countee Cullen, Langston Hughes, Claude McKay, Wallace Thurman and Richard Nugent. Although the margins could be hostile and only Nugent was open about his sexuality (in his 1926 'Smoke, Lilies, Jade' he expressed frank joy in his sexuality in an unpunctuated dream-like stream-of-consciousness narrative) Harlem's diversity enabled previously unmapped representations that the rebels were keen to turn into literary art.[120] Similarly, Hurston's explorations of folk practices showed that forms such as spirituals and stories were not museum pieces but fluid, performative, interactive and constantly changing. Neither denying her past nor letting it prevail over her self-construction, she described herself as a 'brown bag of miscellany . . . a jumble of small things priceless and worthless'.[121] Instead of a waste-land, however, the detritus formed a spectacular quilt in which the past was recast into something new and unique.

Yet Hurston's gaze Southwards among the 'lost generation' of black southerners was also a repudiation of a masculinised northern progressivism.[122] Hurston understood the double-oppression and double-standard that structured black female identity and explored this theme in many of her works. Her play *Color Struck* (1926), for example, exposed the destructiveness of black female self-loathing due to the social fetishisation of whiteness.[123] Like Hurston, Marita Bonner exposed the disempowerment and alienation that resulted from race and gender oppression in 'On Being Young – A Woman – and Colored' (1925).[124] Bonner showed that the experience of northern migration and entry into modernity was particularly difficult for the young black female. Bonner further explored this alienation and destructive marginalisation of black women in her unconventional expressionist plays *Exit, An Illusion* (1923), *The Pot Maker* (1927) and *The Purple Flower* (1928).[125] *Exit: An Illusion* illustrated the fatal destructiveness of internalised racism in a female protagonist who passes for white but who dies as a result of her self-loathing. Expressionist techniques enabled Bonner to disconnect her characters from time and place in order to expose and deconstruct oppressive hierarchies of race. The abstract setting of *The Purple Flower* was therefore a no-man's-land in which time was the 'Middle-of-Things-as-They-Are. (Which means the End-of-Things for some of the characters and the Beginning-of-Things for others)', and the place 'Might be here, there or anywhere – or even nowhere'.[126] As Hurston and Bonner showed, there was nothing uniquely white or uniquely male about self-destruction, violence, exile and alienation.

Women of the Lost Generation

To many modern writers the rejection of the past was a rejection of oppressive gender relations as well as racial stereotypes. In their novels, motherhood, marriage and domesticity were depicted as sites of patriarchal control or monstrous biological femininity. Experimental southern writer Evelyn Scott explored the problems and possibilities of female empowerment within patriarchal culture in her portraits of repressed female desire and sexuality within the narrow restrictions of traditional (white) southern womanhood. Her novels, *The Narrow House* (1921), *Narcissus* (1922), *The Golden Door* (1925), *Ideals* (1927) and *Migrations* (1927), and her autobiography *Escapade* (1923) showed the family and tradition as dysfunctional and repressive. Similarly, Frances Newman focused on female sexuality in her bestselling novels *The Hard-Boiled Virgin* (1926) and *Dead Lovers Are Faithful Lovers* (1928), which satirised the traditional role of the southern belle, the sexual double-standard and repressions of patriarchal domesticity. Although their work antagonised the agrarians, these women were central to the broader Southern Renaissance; yet they displayed no nostalgia for a lost past – the rejection of traditional southern womanhood was a strike for female sexual and social independence.

Women writers in the 1920s also included unprecedented portrayals of pre-marital sex, birth control, lesbianism and abortion in their novels: exploring modern sexuality in literature became a way that women could challenge the boundaries of their traditional social exclusion and domestic confinement. While Dorinda Oakley in Ellen Glasgow's *Barren Ground* (1925) eventually finds independence through miscarriage and land ownership, Agnes Smedley's feminist novel *Daughter of Earth* (1929) portrayed Marie Rogers' liberation from biological determinism through her abortion, use of birth control and divorce. Although often reluctant to see themselves as part of any women's movement, unconventional women writers did not submit to marginalisation quietly or politely.

Women's writing of the decade was particularly notable for the emergence of the bawdy or outspoken woman writer who openly discussed sex and sexuality and lived as intemperately as her male contemporaries. On Broadway, Mae West became the most iconic of the rebellious new women writers; her plays, *Sex* (1926), *The Drag* (1927), *The Pleasure Man* (1928) and *Diamond Lil* (1928) challenged the boundaries of puritanical America with topics ranging from sex addiction, prostitution, homosexuality and interracial relationships. Famous for her dialogue and dirty street-talk taken from the speakeasies and familiar vaudeville routines, West's prostitutes and fallen women were no victims or failures. Even though her characters sinned without punishment, by daring to challenge the boundaries of decency, West endured periods of imprisonment and censorship (as well as increasing fame and renown).

Bawdiness, blasphemy, and sexual and literary experimentation also characterised the work of writer-journalist Djuna Barnes. Barnes experimented with literary form as well as openly exploring lesbian sexuality and desire in her anarchistic and surreal writings; her mock-medieval text of lesbian instruction *The Ladies Almanack* (1928) was banned for obscenity, and her satire of promiscuous domesticity and fecund patriarchy, *Ryder* (1928), was censored before publication in New York (though she rebelliously insisted on showing the censor's hand by putting asterisks to expose the 'havoc of this nicety'). Barnes' carnivalesque fiction drew attention to the constructed nature of the text in order to playfully expose male authority and biological deter-minism and her anti-puritan parable of the politics of sexual repro-duction 'upturned literary, religious and sexual orthodoxy through linguistic and thematic misrule'.[127]

While stylistically very different from Barnes' overwrought parody-narratives, another Paris-based lesbian writer of the era, Gertrude Stein, also used playful linguistic misrule to overthrow sexual and literary orthodoxy. Stein's long poem 'Patriarchal Poetry' (1927) is seen by critics as a 'mock epic' counterpart to *The Waste Land*, in which she rejects 'the Western literary past and . . . attempt[s] to erect a new literature on the ruins of that demolished culture'.[128] For modern-ist women writers the non-lineal anti-narrative radically exposed the patriarchal structures that were buried within language and enabled them to experiment with alternative forms of expression that went beyond feminist 'protest' literature of the progressive period.

The new assertive presence of the female writer did not automati-cally lead to the feminist heroine. In popular stories and novels the new woman was flawed, assertively independent and selfishly indi-vidualistic in her attempts to subvert patriarchal conventions. In her acerbic and witty stories, the outspoken Dorothy Parker criticised superficial modern relationships, domesticity and materialism through her various depictions of wisecracking broads, weedy girlfriends and wives, snobbish party hosts or female alcoholics. Parker's own suicide attempts, failed marriages, alcoholism and abortions became well known, and her short stories drew on this unhappiness to portray the hypocrisy of modern culture and the dilemmas of the new female inde-pendence. In her story 'Big Blonde' (1929), a blonde ex-model falls into self-destructive domesticity and alcoholism that finally leads to a failed suicide attempt that displayed all the characteristics of Freud's death-instinct: 'The thought of death came and stayed with her and lent her a sort of drowsy cheer. It would be nice, nice and restful, to be dead'.[129]

Not all women found their new-found sexual freedom problematic: Anita Loos offered a satirical reflection on the working-girl in her novel *Gentlemen Prefer Blondes: The Illuminating Diary of a Professional Lady* (1926), in which the semi-literate showgirl Lorelei Lee recorded her gold-digging quest for riches and status around Europe. A satire on upward mobility, popular self-help and success literature, Lorelei Lee goes to Freud for analysis and later writes in her diary that 'Dr. Froyd said that all I needed was to cultivate a few inhibitions and get some sleep'. While more comedic than tragic, Lorelei is a female Gatsby: her sexually charged performance of gender enables her to gain upward mobility in a world that continued to create and silence the 'dumb' blonde.[130]

Conclusion

The dumbing-down of culture and the threat to civilisation remained an intellectual concern throughout the 1920s. Popular novels like *Gentlemen Prefer Blondes* lampooned cultural degeneration but also seemed to fuel it: Loos' novel became a bestseller, making the author extremely rich, while other 'high-brow', experimental and serious works struggled to gain a readership. The appearance of tabloid newspapers, book-of-the-month clubs and the *Reader's Digest* all added to a host of concerns about the quality of mass culture. The relationship between high and low, however, was becoming less distinct as writers buoyed up their careers by contributing to popular magazines and the film and radio industries: both Fitzgerald and Faulkner wrote scripts for Hollywood, while Mencken and George Nathan began the pulp crime magazine *Black Mask* in 1920, in order to financially prop up their high-brow literary magazine *The Smart Set*.

It was this hybridity of high and low, black and white, old and new that made the literary wasteland so richly innovative over the decade. Although the war and cultural change left writers anxious about the future, the literature of the 1920s did not turn its back on the present and retreat into the past. The 'Lost Generation' were deeply committed to representing the emotional trauma caused by social and political change even if they were unable to provide any clear solutions to it. While faith in democracy, progress and founding Puritan principles were at an all time low, postwar abundance appeared excessive and frivolous, and freedom remained a highly valued but contested terrain. Fitzgerald called the 1920s 'The Jazz Age' not because his wealthy elite expressed their desultory freedom by dancing to jazz, but because jazz was the experimental and improvisational score that set the pace for this new America. Jazz was the beat and rhythm of unavoidable cultural change, a hybrid sound of the southern past and the industrial North, the 'primitive' keeping time with Ford's production line. As we shall see in the next chapter, hybridity, spontaneity and boundary-stretching transgression were central to the anxious pleasures of the age.

Chapter 2

Music and Performance

No other music has defined a decade so definitively as jazz in the 1920s. With hybrid origins in both African and European musical traditions it was quintessentially representative of America in the post-war world: modern, mongrelised, energetic and vernacular. To white bandleader Paul Whiteman, jazz reflected 'the spirit of a new country', the confusions, paradoxes and 'cheerfulness of despair' that was 'deep in America':

> Behind the rush of achievement is a restlessness of dissatisfaction, a vague nostalgia and yearning for something indefinable, beyond our grasp . . . That is the thing expressed by that wail, that longing, that pain, behind all the surface clamor and rhythm and energy of jazz.[1]

As the ultimate symbol of American modernity, jazz and the dances it generated embodied social and cultural changes surrounding class, race and gender that made it a site of both innovation and anxiety.[2]

Seen as 'a distortion of the conventional, a revolt against tradition, a deliberate twisting of established formulas', jazz seemed to diminish social hierarchy and mock the cultural distinctions of the past, changing the cultural lexicon as it challenged traditional boundaries and conventions.[3] While the function of culture had always been the creation of harmony and beauty, jazz seemed to upset this balance: one observer wrote that it 'disorganizes all regular laws and order; it stimulates to extreme deeds, to a breaking away from all rules and conventions; it is harmful and dangerous, and its influence is wholly bad'.[4] Yet, by the end of the decade jazz was widely considered as 'an expression of the soul of America' and had become the prime arena of the battle between dominant and emergent, or old and new, cultural values.[5]

While jazz expressed a communal exuberance and energy, its musical cousin, the blues, expressed the sorrow and alienation of the outcast. The lyrics of Bessie Smith's 'Lonesome Desert Blues' (1925) expressed a loss and disorientation that was contiguous with Lost Generation sentiments. The antithesis of 'normalcy', conformity and Babbittry, the blues portrayed the isolation of the migrant experience. The spread of blues through the recording industry from 1920, however, turned this art of the margins into a mass-produced aesthetic that reflected the contradictions of 1920s America: 'Wanna be happy? then buy our BLUES!' asserted Okeh Records' advertisement for Victoria Spivey's 'T.B. Blues' (1927).[6]

While neither jazz nor blues began in the decade, their remarkable spread and rapid development brought them to the unprecedented attention of mass audiences in a way that seemed to signal a musical revolution. This revolution was interlinked with the rise of a 'dance mania' that propelled the music in new directions. At the same time, jazz and blues also provided a bridge between the past and present, rural and industrial, by blending the old with new. As folklore collectors went South into the folk past to preserve the voice of the rural sharecropper, southern musical culture had been migrating North to form exciting new hybrids in urban areas, giving expression and cultural leadership to a host of artists from minority groups whose voices had previously been ignored, denigrated or repressed within high-art cultural traditions.

The booming economy alongside developments in recording, radio and sound technology sustained the jazz craze – but what was most revolutionary was that this music of multiracial origins came to be considered representatively American at a time when the majority of Americans still lived racially segregated lives. Few were more aware of prevailing racism than the performers and musicians who created the sound of the era, yet nothing worked harder to challenge that racial divide and penetrate those boundaries than the music they created. To Harlem Renaissance writer J. A. Rogers, jazz was an energetic, improvisatory, multiracial music that illustrated progress towards a national identity that knew neither colour lines nor class boundaries. He celebrated it as the rise of a 'nobody's child of the levee and the city slum' to the status of a national 'common property' symbolic of 'that tremendous spirit of go, the nervousness, lack of conventionality and boisterous good-nature characteristic of the American, white or black'.[7] To Leopold Stokowski, conductor of the Philadelphia Symphony Orchestra, jazz added an unprecedented dynamism to American culture:

> Jazz has come to stay because it is an expression of the times, of the breathless, energetic, superactive times in which we are living, it is useless to fight against it. Already its new vigor, its new vitality is beginning to manifest itself . . . America's contribution to the music of the past will have the same revivifying effect as the injection of new, and in the larger sense, vulgar blood into dying aristocracy.[8]

Jazz music didn't just overturn accepted norms of European musical styles, it appeared to presage a multicultural American future where universality was no longer coloured white and democracy was truly enacted. Rogers noted that this made jazz 'a marvel of paradox': 'too fundamentally human . . . to be typically racial, too international to be characteristically national, too much abroad in the world to have a special home. And yet jazz in spite of it all is one part American and three parts American Negro'.[9] By referring to the 'one-drop' definition of race in his essay, Rogers upturned the prevalent fear of racial mixing that had underpinned segregation since the Civil War, turning blackness into a proudly visible percentage that was now cause for celebration. This 'marvel of paradox' was visible every day, as millions of Americans imitated, bought, stole and shared what had previously been considered the 'low-life' music and dance styles that had developed in the barrel-houses, jook-joints, honky-tonks and brothels of the South.

Although jazz represented a new celebratory modernism, careful repressions and controls lay beneath the anarchy of such mass-cultural democracy. F. Scott Fitzgerald subtly highlighted these in *The Great Gatsby*, showing how his class-crossing protagonist attempted to distance himself from his past by using music and dance to illustrate his personal evolution out of the gutter: Gatsby's controlled 'graceful' and 'conservative' foxtrot as he dances with Daisy revealed a strenuous politeness that distanced him from the low racial origins of jazz dancing, while his instructions to his orchestra to perform 'Vladimir Tostoff's "Jazz History of the World"' illustrated his cultured – thereby 'civilised' – standing.[10] His paradoxical attempts to disassociate from the 'improper' implications of jazz, while appropriating it for his seduction of Daisy, is indeed paradigmatic of the wider social and cultural response to the rising popularity of jazz in the 1920s.

Being positioned precariously on an intersection of racial and social divisions, jazz formed a conscious and subconscious cultural front that exposed and reformulated prevailing cultural and social hypocrisy. Vachel Lindsay, for example, expressed a virulent dislike of the music even though he had become famous as America's premier jazz-poet who wrote in jazz style: '[J]azz is hectic, has the leer of the bad-lands in it, and first, last and always is hysteric. It is full of the dust of the dirty dance,' he stated, further adding that 'The Saxophone . . . is the most diseased instrument in all modern music'.[11] Lindsay's open disgust for jazz did not prevent him from becoming a mentor and patron of the jazz-loving blues poet Langston Hughes, while in that same year admitting that 'I have always hated jazz'; it is 'our most Babylonian disease'.[12]

The Growth of Jazz

While Fitzgerald dated the beginning of the jazz age with the civil unrest of 1919, most music histories of the era chart its beginning from the phonograph recordings 'Livery Stable Blues' and 'Dixie Jass Band One Step' by the Original Dixieland Jass Band in 1917. Although they were a white band recording in New York, all five members of the band were southerners who had picked up tunes and instrumental styles from the black jazz musicians of Storyville, a New Orleans district famed for its legal prostitution and bordellos that employed musicians to draw in brothel patrons. The closure of Storyville by the Secretary of the Navy in 1917, due to concerns over the demoralising effect on troops now engaged in the World War, led jazz musicians to seek work elsewhere. Many of these, including Louis Armstrong, Kid Ory and Joe 'King' Oliver, found work on the Mississippi river boats that travelled to port cities such as Memphis, Kansas City and St. Louis, finally settling in northern cities where they joined a burgeoning population of migrants from the South. Patterns of migration connected to wartime production and industrialisation meant that these musicians found an eager audience for southern jazz music as they moved northwards: while almost one million blacks migrated from the South between 1916 and 1930, between 1917 and 1923 over 50,000 migrants from the South settled in Chicago alone, making commercial jazz recordings, dance-halls and cabarets a profitable venture on Chicago's South Side, so that by 1920 the centre of jazz had shifted from New Orleans to Chicago in just a few years.

Although jazz had been played in the South for many years prior to the recording of 'Livery Stable Blues', because it was unwritten, improvisatory or performance-based, the commercial sheet music and phonograph record producers of Tin Pan Alley in New York had not seen it as commercially viable. Indeed, transcribing jazz music onto sheet music was not even possible until new musical notations were devised to express the unusual 'rips, slurs, swoops, [and] slides' that it incorporated.[13] 'Livery Stable Blues', however, showed that jazz recordings could be commercially lucrative and companies began to target their consumers with novelty syncopated numbers recorded by white bands.

It was the first recording of a blues song sung by a black performer in 1920 that indicated the huge market for jazz recordings among African Americans as well.[14] The success of Perry Bradford's 'Crazy Blues' (1920) – sung by the first black recording artist, Mamie Smith – ushered in a new era of commercial success for other black musicians. The record sold 10,000 in the first week, over 75,000 within a month, and one million in seven months.[15] By the end of the year Smith had recorded another twenty-three songs and the success of these saved the Okeh record company from financial disaster. Other record companies, such as Victor, Paramount and Columbia, followed suit, all starting up a line in 'race records' that were marketed to black consumers.[16]

Race records may have reflected market segregation but the rise in the artistic and economic viability of black art fuelled businesses such as Harry Pace's Black Swan records, whose slogan ironically reversed racial hierarchy: 'The Only Genuine Colored Record. Others Are Only Passing For Colored'.[17] Black Swan was owned and run by African Americans in keeping with the goal of racial uplift promoted by Harlem Renaissance intellectuals. Pace appointed W. E. B. Du Bois as a company director and the black composer with William Grant Still and Fletcher Henderson (see below) as musical directors, although the company ran into financial difficulty and was bought out by Columbia in 1923. By the end of the decade, however, vast numbers of such recordings were available: one Victor Records 'race record' catalogue contained over forty-four pages listing hundreds of records by black artists that were now available, a market that had not existed in 1920 and one that virtually disappeared with the onset of the Great Depression.[18]

The popularity of these records signified a shift in American cultural taste. Central to the aesthetic of the new sound was an exuberant, seemingly crude or untutored, anti-intellectual appearance that contrasted with the traditional image of the classically trained musician and purveyor of culture. Discarding their music sheets and learning songs by rote and repetition, the Original Dixieland Jass Band attempted to appear as improvisatory and spontaneous as the black musicians they emulated and admired such as Ferdinand 'Jelly Roll' Morton and his Orchestra, Kid Ory's Original Creole Jazz Band and Joe 'King' Oliver.[19]

Figure 2.1 Kid Ory on the trombone, with his Original Creole Jazz Band, c.1922 (© The Art Archive/Culver Pictures).

Although Dixieland jazz remained racially segregated and appealed more to white audiences, the white band The New Orleans Rhythm Kings recorded the first interracial Chicago jazz record with Jelly Roll Morton in 1923, and white musicians jammed with their black counterparts even if their bands were segregated for performances.[20] Mentor to the young Louis Armstrong, Joe 'King' Oliver moved from New Orleans to Chicago with Kid Ory in 1918, later inviting Armstrong to join him there in 1922. Although he didn't make his first recording, 'Chimes Blues', until 1923, Oliver's Creole Jazz Band had a huge influence on the development of Chicago-style 'hot' jazz music at the time. These musicians formed a network of influence for new musical expression and gained the admiration of the talented young musicians who watched them perform; after seeing Oliver and Armstrong play, the cornetist Leon Bismarck 'Bix' Beiderbecke was inspired to form his band the Wolverines in 1923 and his friend the singer-songwriter Hoagy Carmichael similarly formed Carmichael's Collegians in 1924.

While Beiderbecke never achieved the seemingly effortless style of his idol Armstrong, the tension and drive that fuelled these musicians set a new 'white hot' standard for jazz in the era that contrasted with the commercialised 'sweet jazz' and the frenetic Dixieland jazz appearing in mainstream culture. By adopting and emulating the music of Chicago's Black Belt, young white musicians found a way to escape the bourgeois restriction and multi-ethnic tensions of middle-class suburbia, rebelling against the traditional and dominant cultural values of the day. Through jazz, white 'Chicagoans' such as Bud Freeman, Mezz Mezzrow, Jimmy McPartland and Eddie Condon found a multicultural home in urban America that contrasted with the dizzying fragmentation experienced by their 'Lost Generation' counterparts.[21]

Urbanisation, migration and a postwar boom in nightlife that led to the proliferation of hotel and restaurant ballrooms, made Chicago the centre of jazz in the early 1920s, a position boosted by prohibition, which created an urban subculture that funded and proliferated jazz music. Gangsters bankrolled speakeasies as music and dance became a way of attracting customers as well as covering illegal activities. By sending alcohol drinking underground, prohibition in effect sent New Orleans-style jazz into a separate cultural space where it became further connected to bootlegging, gambling, drugs and prostitution. Celebrated nightclubs were run by the mob: Chicago's Sunset Café, where Louis Armstrong and others played, was controlled by Al Capone's gang, and New York's Cotton Club was operated by gangster Owney Madden during Duke Ellington's reign there.

Jazz developed in other urban areas in the North, West, Midwest and Southwest, where it absorbed local regional styles as well as those of touring musicians from the urban North. This spread was further enabled by the first radio broadcast in 1920, making it a familiar sound from coast to coast. Within two years there were over five hundred radio stations throughout the United States and where three-quarters of the broadcasting over the decade consisted of music, 75 per cent of this was jazz.[22] Technical developments in the recording industry also aided the music boom: the introduction of the electrical condenser microphone in 1925 allowed for higher-quality recordings as well as increased portability, making records sound better but also making it possible to record away from the big studios, leading to a boom in country music and southern folk recordings.

While the economic boom fuelled nightlife, record and radio sales, economic hardship within migrant culture caused by high rents and low wages also created an environment in which jazz musicians received a regular supply of work. 'Rent Parties' and underground activities had become commonplace in urban African American life by the early 1920s and provided a musical proving ground and valuable source of income for many emerging jazz artists. Of these, Louis Armstrong emerged as the leading exponent of the 'hot' jazz style.

An illegitimate child born in a New Orleans ghetto, Armstrong's tuition was in the reform schools and brothels of Storyville. After his mentor Joe Oliver left for Chicago in 1918, Armstrong replaced him in Kid Ory's band, later working on the Mississippi river boat ballrooms, joining Oliver in Chicago in 1922. Wanting fewer musical restrictions (he was playing as second cornetist to Oliver), he left the band in 1924 to join Fletcher Henderson's band at the whites-only Roseland Ballroom in New York, where he developed his unique solo playing and 'scat' singing style – epitomised by his celebrated 'Heebie Jeebies' (1926) and 'West End Blues' (1928). Armstrong's innovations in singing, along with his exaggerated use of vibrato, high notes and trumpet shakes to 'bend' the notes, set a new standard in American music.[23] Even though Armstrong returned to Chicago in 1925 the move to New York represented a wider drift as the centre of jazz moved from Chicago to New York, notably Broadway and Harlem, and the fashion in jazz shifted from Dixie to the 'swinging' dance styles that dominated the late 1920s.

Between 1925 and 1928 Armstrong made a series of recordings with his Hot Five and Hot Seven bands that became massive hits. The replacement of acoustic with electronic recording made the quality of all records higher, but Armstrong's unique sound and musical ability made him famous among African American audiences, to whom his records were chiefly marketed. Armstrong's solos linked jazz more fully to the blues boom, where his wailing trumpet called a counterpart to the individualistic, soulful expression of the blues singer. He recorded with all of the top blues singers of the day but the epitome of this union between jazz and blues was perhaps the recordings he made with Bessie Smith in 1925, most notably W. C. Handy's 1912 song 'St. Louis Blues'.

Female Blues and Bessie Smith

The demarcation of the colour line in jazz was traversed by a similar segregation in musical culture along a gender line. Beginning with Mamie Smith's success with 'Crazy Blues', however, the 1920s witnessed the unprecedented success of black female singers such as Ma Rainey, Bessie Smith, Ethel Waters, Clara Smith, Trixie Smith, Rosa Henderson, Alberta Hunter, Lucille Hegamin, Edith Wilson, Victoria Spivey, Sippie Wallace and Ida Cox. The majority of their songs were sung from the personal female perspective, expressing ideas and responses to life that reached millions of listeners. To Ann Douglas, this ascent illustrated a key moment in feminist history as 'the only major exception in the patriarchal story of jazz'.[24] Not all classic blues singers were women – blues musicians W. C. Handy and Perry Bradford had also worked in black minstrel troupes as entertainers – but performing as part of a travelling show was one of the very few employment options available to black women that could offer significant financial reward. Female or 'classic' blues music thereby developed differently from the country blues, which was associated with itinerant male workers and solitary singers or guitar pickers such as Lonnie Johnson, Huddie Ledbetter, or Leadbelly, and Blind Lemon Jefferson, who wrote and recorded songs that became popular later in the decade with the rise in interest in black folk culture and music.

The majority of classic blues singers, however, learned their craft as professional entertainers on the vaudeville, musical-hall or minstrel circuit where they performed blues along with folk songs, spirituals, ballads, comedy and ragtime music. Female performers developed their repertoire on a touring circuit where lines were borrowed and songs patched together from cabaret, vaudeville, Tin Pan Alley tunes, folk songs and ballads.[25] Not only did these women achieve financial success, which they typically flaunted on stage with showy costumes, diamonds and gold teeth, they often asserted musical directorship over their songs, created new songs and performed songs that expressed an assertive sexuality and independence previously unheard outside the ghetto, brothel or vaudeville show. The blues and jazz that they performed was thus closely associated with the rise of freer sexual expression and the assertion of a rebellious unconventionality.

Bessie Smith

Bessie Smith's career is paradigmatic of the story of classic blues in the era. Born into poverty in Chattanooga, Tennessee in the 1890s, Smith was orphaned at a young age and started out as a street performer to raise money. In 1912 she joined Ma Rainey's 'Rabbit Foot Minstrels'; the self-billed 'mother of the blues' was a leading blues singer whose impressive career was eventually outshone by Smith despite cutting nearly one hundred records with Paramount between 1924 and 1928. Smith's earthy 'down-home' sonorous style came from Rainey, who helped her develop her voice into an expressive instrument that was powerful enough to be heard acoustically above the accompanying jazz band.

After leaving Rainey's troupe she performed in a variety of cabarets and dance halls throughout the South on the Theater Owners Booking Agency circuit. By 1919 she was successful enough to earn up to $75 a week plus tips.[26] In 1920 she began performing in northern circuits for the first time where she came into contact with the emerging jazz musicians with whom she would later work and record. Her sonorous and instrumental voice had a huge impact on the jazz musicians who saw her; the use of small jazz combos for accompanying the blues singer ultimately led to the merger of the individual art of the blues with the collective aesthetic of jazz from the mid-1920s, noted in the rise of jazz solo instrumentalists leading in blues style.

Smith incorporated groans, moans and unusual phrasing in an idiosyncratic style that gained her huge popularity at sell-out concerts but which shocked recording agents at first. Her voice and her personality were seen as too crude and raw by the race record companies who denied her recording contracts; even Black Swan turned her down in 1922. Eventually she was signed to Columbia Records in 1923 and her first recordings, 'Down Hearted Blues' and 'Gulf Coast Blues' were instant hits, saving the record company from financial ruin. Bessie's subsequent recording success was phenomenal and she sold over ten million records between 1923 and 1933.[27] She relied on live performance for her income, however, as she only received a lump sum for her recordings and gained little in royalties.[28] Like all classic blues singers, Smith borrowed from the repertoire of songs that she learned during her early touring years and employed them for her later recordings and performances, something that makes the search for the origins and ownership of particular songs almost impossible. However, she did write many of her own songs and claimed credit for 'Jailhouse Blues' (1923), 'Dixie-Flyer Blues' (1925), 'Lonesome Desert Blues' (1925), 'Hard Time Blues' (1926), 'Young Woman's Blues' (1926), 'Foolish Man Blues' (1927), 'Backwater Blues' (1927), 'Thinking Blues' (1928) and 'Wasted Life Blues' (1929), among others.

Like Ma Rainey and Mamie Smith, Bessie Smith enjoyed dressing in elaborately luxurious style. On tour she commanded her own railroad car, dressed in jewels and fur, and lived up to the regal title of 'Empress of Blues'. Between 1926 and 1927 she had her own touring show called 'Harlem Follies' or 'Bessie Smith and Her All-Star Revue', consisting of a troupe of about forty entertainers travelling throughout the country. At her peak of popularity she worked with leading jazz musicians of the day, such as Fletcher Henderson, James P. Johnson and Louis Armstrong, becoming the most popular and highest-paid blues performer of the decade.

While her success may have represented personal uplift, her performances and recordings were not seen as uplifting for her race at the time. Angela Davis has noted that although the era of classic blues coincided with the Harlem Renaissance, black intellectuals ignored performers like Bessie Smith because she represented the 'low' culture of working-class southern blacks that they wished to disassociate from.[29] Smith was certainly physically and verbally tough, a heavy drinker, openly bisexual and lascivious. Her sexually assertive and uncompromising identity was reflected in her lyrics: 'I'm as good as any woman in your town/ I ain't no high yeller, I'm a deep killer of brown/ I ain't gonna marry, ain't gonna settle down'.[30] Smith firmly rejected the 'high-brow' in favour of the 'low down'. This gave her strong appeal to working-class blacks and upper-class whites like Carl Van Vechten, author of the notorious *Nigger Heaven* (1926). Van Vechten wrote of her that she was 'an elemental conjure woman', a 'rich ripe beauty of Southern darkness', whose 'volcanic' and 'sensuous' voice sent audiences into hysterical and semi-religious frenzies.[31] When Van Vechten adoringly invited her to sing at his party she demanded whiskey and became extremely drunk, though managing to sing an ironic 'Work House Blues' to the wealthy audience before pushing over Van Vechten's wife with a 'get the fuck away from me' as she tried to kiss her goodbye. Not appreciating the 'ofays' treating her like some kind of 'singin monkey', she showed no aspiration to fit in with the intellectual crowd of Harlem.[32]

Smith's heavy drinking didn't help but by the late 1920s a number of factors contributed to her gradual career decline. The introduction of electronic sound recording created a new fashion in gentler, melodic singing rather than the powerful acoustic sound that she was familiar with. The success of female blues recordings also led to a recording boom for male country blues from the mid-1920s, which became more fashionable as 'authentic' folk documents than the commercial blues of the classic style. Vaudeville and live acts became increasingly threatened by the introduction of talking films in 1927 and in 1929 the economic crash hit phonograph record sales and the income of the black communities who worshipped her. Although Smith starred in the all-black sound film *St. Louis Blues* (1929), which told the story of a young woman named Bessie driven to drink by her unfaithful boyfriend, it was her only appearance in the talkies as the Hollywood musical in the thirties provided little opening for even the most celebrated black entertainers.

Smith made her last recording in 1933 with a session that included the up-and-coming jazz musician Benny Goodman.[33] Although she was working intermittently, her career had gone into decline and she died in a car accident in 1938 just as she was making a comeback. Although she was rumoured to have bled to death when a segregated hospital refused her admission, the story has been disproven on several occasions. Despite this, the tale was immortalised by playwright Edward Albee in his play *The Death of Bessie Smith* (1959) and has become an apocryphal tale that summarises the racism faced by African American artists within segregated America.

Sweet Jazz

In the process of the transmission to mass audiences jazz was continually reinvented and reinterpreted. In popular culture revised versions of the blues and 'hot jazz' sound dominated white culture. In fact the word 'jazz' usually referred to popular music in general, which included syncopated band music played up-tempo, songs from

Figure 2.2 Film still from *The King of Jazz* (1930) (© Universal/The Kobal Collection).

Broadway shows by Irving Berlin and George Gershwin, or concert music that used jazz idioms. Most of the recording hits of the decade were actually 'danceable' popular songs or show tunes recorded by white bandleaders that are not considered 'real' or 'authentic' jazz by critics and musicologists today.[34] 'Sweet jazz' was the term for this popular jazz dance music and 'symphonic jazz' referred to longer jazz-inflected academic arrangements (discussed below). Sweet jazz dominated the radio airwaves; behind its widespread popularity was Paul Whiteman, the classically trained conductor who by the end of the decade became widely known as the 'King of Jazz'.[35]

Whiteman had grown up in Denver and had begun his career in the San Francisco Symphony Orchestra, but found more rewards in popular dance music. Following the huge success of his first recordings, 'Whispering' and 'Japanese Sandman', which sold over a million copies in November 1920, Whiteman expanded his popular jazz repertoire so that by 1922 he controlled twenty-eight bands on the East Coast and commanded a salary of over a million dollars per annum.[36] Whiteman's success led to numerous imitators who were interested in the big band jazz sound, including the black bandleader Fletcher Henderson at the start of his career. The Whiteman sound was a 'jazzed-up' orchestrated waltz, foxtrot or tango music that was carefully arranged and rehearsed and his orchestra became the most popular dance band of the decade. The inspiration for the movie *King of Jazz* (1930), Whiteman starred in the spectacular Technicolor musical revue that showcased him as the musical star of the 1920s.

The fluidity of jazz as a style and cultural metaphor made it a malleable term for both artists and writers. In one of the first serious assessments of popular culture, *The Seven Lively Arts* (1924), Gilbert Seldes wrote that: '[The] word jazz is already so complicated that it ought not to be subjected to any new definitions, . . . it is the symbol, or the byword, for a great many elements in the spirit of the time – as far as America is concerned it is actually our characteristic expression'.[37] At the end of the decade the popular composer George Gershwin also noted that jazz was not definable by a single word, but had become a term used 'for at least five or six different types of music. It is really a conglomeration of many things. It has a little bit of ragtime, the blues, classicism and spirituals'.[38] The musical, cultural and racial miscegenation that this implied was exactly what made jazz the pre-eminent symbol of what was both good and bad about American culture. While jazz-loving Americans paradoxically created new hybrids in their attempt to 'clean up' and 'civilise' jazz for the commercial market, those who hated jazz attempted to introduce alternative dance music in its place, or suppress it altogether.

Opposition to Jazz

Despite attempts to create refined jazz, the music was frequently dismissed as 'low-brow', 'degenerate', 'savage' and 'uncivilised', and its spread caused national concern. The words 'jazz' and 'culture' were seen as oppositional terms; the former was modern, discordant, improvisatory and accessible, while the latter was traditional, harmonious, rehearsed and intellectual.[39] Jazz quickly became associated with youthful rebellion and the rejection of tradition, causing fears to erupt over the effect that the sexually charged lyrics and illegal milieu would have over the morals of impressionable youths. One observer noted that the postwar environment was ripe for such 'Bolshevik' rebellion: 'There is always a revolutionary period of the breaking down of old conventions and customs which follows after every great war; and this rebellion against existing conditions is to be noticed in all life to-day'.[40]

On top of a fear of rebellion was added the racist judgement that jazz was a 'primitive' art that encouraged savage instincts to emerge, for 'Jazz originally was the accompaniment of the voodoo dancer, stimulating the half-crazed barbarian to the vilest deeds'.[41] Widespread evolutionary beliefs promoted by eugenicists regarding the superiority of white civilisation and culture led to a flurry of similar articles, many of which received credence from the scientific and medical community. In Anne Shaw Faulkner's view, scientists had clinically proven that 'the effect of jazz on the normal brain produces an atrophied condition on the brain cells of conception' where 'those under the demoralizing influence of the persistent use of syncopation, combined with inharmonic partial tones, are actually incapable of distinguishing between good and evil, right and wrong'.[42] Similar stories ran in numerous newspapers and magazines.

Of central concern to reformers was the relationship between jazz and the new sexual openness of modern America. Critics of jazz often blurred the lines between the music and the sociology and demography surrounding it. With its roots in the bordellos and brothels of the South and further associations with the underworld prohibition culture of illegal gambling, alcohol consumption, drugs and vice, many reformers believed the music encouraged an immoral and sexually charged atmosphere in which traditional controls were loosened. Before censorship and self-censorship by the music and broadcasting agencies in the late 1920s, jazz lyrics were replete with sexual innuendo, or contained references to hardship, death or violent retribution, which, reformers feared, would demoralise America's youth.[43]

As a 'sexual symbol of an inferior race', jazz was linked to the rejection of white cultural authority by youth, as blacks were considered 'an adolescent race' whose musical immaturity rejected 'the adult repression of the whites'.[44] What bothered these observers was the way that such youth rebellion breached traditional class and race barriers and threatened to 'pollute' the gene pool of the white elite. Jazz was ruining girls, declared the headline of a 1922 article in the *New York American*: 'Moral disaster is coming to hundreds of young American girls through the pathological, nerve-irritating, sex-exciting music of jazz orchestras . . . Girls in small towns, as well as the big cities, in poor homes and rich homes, are victims of the weird, insidious, neurotic music that accompanies modern dancing'.[45]

Even though Paul Whiteman was central to the refinement and acceptance of 'society' jazz music and his performances were almost exclusively white, he clearly recognised the racist motivations behind the anti-jazz movement. Associating the censorship and repression of the critics to the witch-hunt activities of the Ku Klux Klan, he stated in his book *Jazz* (1926) that 'I wish the preachers and club lady uplifters who put on sheets and pillowcases to go jazzclanning wouldn't concentrate on me'.[46]

The Harlem Renaissance Jazz of Henderson and Ellington

African Americans also expressed objections to jazz, though often for different reasons from those stated by the white reformers. In their attempt to place black Americans on an equal cultural footing with whites, some leaders of the Harlem Renaissance distanced themselves from 'vulgar' popular performances that did not fit in with the image of a highly cultured educated black elite.[47] Although they promoted traditional musical forms like spirituals or folk songs as evidence of foundational musical skill among blacks, jazz was too closely connected with the image of a sexually degenerate, violent low-life that the black middle classes associated with the negative stereotypes that they had fought hard to escape. Alain Locke, for example, claimed that the racier music and dance of the Harlem cabarets represented an 'exotic fringe' enjoyed by 'the connoisseur in diversion as well as the undiscriminating sightseer'.[48]

Younger and more rebellious writers such as Langston Hughes called for the 'talented tenth' to recognise jazz as a unique and creative art form of which they should be proud: 'Let the blare of Negro jazz bands and the bellowing voice of Bessie Smith singing Blues penetrate the closed ears of the colored near-intellectuals until they listen and perhaps understand'.[49] Despite this, class divisions clearly emerged in the reception of jazz as the black elite attempted to impose classical standards of formal musical training and genteel musical performance as a way of illustrating a cultured refinement that counteracted images of primitivism.[50] Black singers of spirituals were particularly in demand among upper-class blacks and whites in concert halls, with those such as Roland Hayes, Marian Anderson, Jules Bledsoe, Harry T. Burleigh and Paul Robeson becoming highly regarded as cultured performers who counteracted the secular, erotic, vulgar and primitive image of the jazz and blues performers.

Two African American bandleaders became central to the fusion of 'hot' with 'sweet' and 'symphonic' jazz and created an original sound in commercial dance music that operated in a spirit of cultural and racial uplift promoted by intellectuals of the Harlem Renaissance.[51] Fletcher Henderson and Duke Ellington were educated middle-class pianists with classical training who cultivated an aristocratic bearing that garnered widespread respect for jazz. Although both led house bands at white-only establishments – Henderson at the Roseland Ballroom from 1921 and Ellington at the Cotton Club from 1927 – both fought the cultural stereotype of the 'primitive Negro' that plagued black jazz musicians and used their musical versatility to challenge race, class and cultural divisions.[52] Henderson arrived in New York in 1920 to study for a master's degree in Chemistry at Columbia University but became a musical director for the Black Swan record company instead. Henderson emulated Whiteman's smooth jazz style to become the most popular and commercially successful African American bandleader of the 1920s. When Edward 'Duke' Ellington arrived in Harlem a few years later, it was Henderson's band that he encouraged his own musicians to emulate.

Ellington's upbringing and education in black middle-class Washington DC fostered a strong sense of race pride and ambition that led him to view black musical traditions as an art form that could foster pride and racial uplift, as well as pleasure. He was already a professional musician when he moved with his band 'The Washingtonians' to New York in 1922 and entered into the vibrant culture of Harlem nightlife.[53] By 1927 the band was featured as the house band at the mob-run Cotton Club, which showcased Ellington's 'jungle music' sound between the years 1927 and 1931. Weekly radio broadcasts from the Cotton Club spread Ellington's sound throughout the country and the band became a top attraction in over thirty cities, commandeering their own separate Pullman car while on tour.[54] Although the Cotton Club shows and revues were notorious for exploiting the white taste for primitivist fantasy, Ellington's emphasis on high-quality performance and respectability led him to become 'Harlem's Aristocrat of Jazz' and the representative 'New Negro' of the music world.[55]

Ellington fulfilled the ideals of the Harlem Renaissance for economic, social and cultural equality with whites by giving high-class respectability to black musical styles. Like others in the 'New Negro' movement, he worked to portray an authentic portrait of black life in art, composing over fifty songs in the decade, many of which reflected on Harlem culture and the African American experience in a style he called 'tonal portraits', which included numbers such as 'Black and Tan Fantasy' (1927), 'Rent Party Blues' (1929), 'Saturday Night Function' (1929) and 'Harlem Flat Blues' (1929).[56] As 'a bridge between two continental traditions', he linked avant-garde music with idiom of jazz as well as keeping up traditions of group composition and improvisation within an orchestrated environment.[57] Alain Locke called him 'the pioneer of super-jazz' who had huge potential as a great composer to carry symphonic jazz to a 'higher level'.[58]

By the early thirties Ellington would write that 'I am proud of that part my race is playing in the artistic life of the world. Paul Robeson, Roland Hayes . . . are names already high in the lists of serious music; that from the welter of negro dance musicians now before the public will come something noble I am convinced'.[59] His desire to record the African American experience in music culminated in *Black, Brown and Beige*, performed at Carnegie Hall in 1943, a musical suite that reflected on the history of slavery, racial segregation, mass migration, urbanisation, war and the battle for democracy. Ellington's desire for respect and his race pride propelled him to create unique musical forms that synthesised tradition with the new. Although his regal style alienated some, both he and Henderson mocked 'dicty' or stuck-up intellectuals – Henderson in 'Dicty Blues' (1923) and Ellington in 'Dicty Glide' (1929) – and their desire to reduce the division between high and low culture as well as the class divide among African Americans was pivotal to the development of the big-band 'swing' style that dominated the 1930s and 1940s popular music scene.

Experiments in Modern Music: Symphonic Jazz and Jazz Symphonies

Whiteman, Henderson and Ellington's music highlighted the cultural possibilities of the call-and-response between classical and popular music.[60] This intertextual exchange also breached traditional class and race boundaries as modern American composers of classical symphonic music began to adopt jazz elements in their compositions. The incorporation of the popular was not just a way of making jazz respectable or classical more popular, but formed a dialogue between musicians that creatively explored the construction of modern American identity.

In the 1910s, European composers had been exposed to the widespread popularity of ragtime, a style that influenced the works of Debussy, Milhaud, Honegger, Ravel, Satie and Stravinsky. The war further exposed European classicists to the 'jazz germ' by bringing black soldiers and bandsmen such as James Reese Europe to France.[61] European classical modernists were in turn highly influential over young American composers in the 1920s, many of whom spent periods of study in Paris alongside the lost generation of modernist writers and artists. George Gershwin, the leading exponent of this merger between popular and classical music, saw the classical use of jazz as a new pattern of intercultural musical exchange that positioned America at the forefront of the musical avant-garde:

Unquestionably modern musical America has been influenced by
modern musical Europe. But it seems to me that modern European composers, in turn, have very largely received their stimulus, their rhythms
and impulses from Machine Age America . . . The Machine Age has
influenced practically everything. I do not mean only music but everything from the arts to finance. The machine has not affected our age in
form as much as in tempo, speed and sound.[62]

Not only did this acknowledge America's importance on the world
stage, it signified a reversal of the accepted hierarchy that art and
culture originated in Europe and that high art flowed into low.

Over the 1920s, American composers such as George Antheil, John
Alden Carpenter, Aaron Copland and Louis Gruenberg incorporated
vernacular folk and jazz idioms into their modernist classical works
as a way of expressing this new cultural identity. In their works jazz
was freely interpreted as a 'musical symbol of the melting-pot' and
was represented as both folk idiom and machine-age urbanism.[63]
The pianist and composer Antheil was most famous for his mechanical, abstract style, becoming closely associated with the modernist
avant-garde in Paris where he lived from 1922 to 1927.[64] His music
incorporated sirens, typewriters, buzzers, bells, telephones, aeroplane
propellers and automatic player-pianos in a radical rejection of classical romantic traditions. While Ezra Pound saw this as the music of
a Ford workshop, Antheil also tied his anarchic experiments closely
to the innovations of jazz, calling the 1920s 'a Negroid epoch'.[65] His
Symphony no. 1 (1920) was one of the earliest examples of jazz-inspired
dissonance, a non-conformity to musical tradition that he quickly followed in Jazz Sonata (1922) and Jazz Symphony (1925), which was
originally written to be played by Whiteman's orchestra.[66] Antheil's
famous collaboration with the artist Fernand Léger and cinematogra-
pher Dudley Murphy produced his most celebrated and iconoclastic
work of this era, Ballet Mécanique (1926), composed as the score to a
short film of Dadaist animated montages. Ballet Mécanique was first
performed in Carnegie Hall in 1927 along with his Jazz Symphony,
played by the W. C. Handy orchestra and conducted by the African
American Allie Ross.[67]

John Alden Carpenter also acknowledged the multiculturalism
of the urban American sound in his classical works by incorporating
an eclectic mix of classical, folk and popular Tin Pan Alley songs. In
the 1920s he expressed a particular fascination for African American
culture in his experimentation with popular mass culture genres,

producing a ballet, or 'jazz-pantomime', called *Krazy Kat* (1921) based on the popular comic strip by George Herriman. Following this success the Russian Serge Diaghilev commissioned *Skyscrapers*, which premiered at the Metropolitan Opera House in 1926.[68] *Skyscrapers* presented a musical interpretation of modern urban America, a ballet of the urban workers' day followed through work and leisure and then returning back to work, all with the construction of a 'huge and sinister skyscraper' looming over the action, with sounds mimicked by the orchestra.[69] While the performance of *Skyscrapers* presented one of the first racially mixed ballets to appear on stage in New York, and included performers from popular theatrical shows in the large black chorus, as well as classical musicians, the show still resorted to white performers in blackface for lead African American parts.[70] That same year, however, Carpenter also wrote *Four Negro Songs* (1926), which incorporated text by Langston Hughes.

These composers expressed the ideals of American democracy and identity by juxtaposing high and low culture, as well as black and white, in their music. Aaron Copland, who was central to the development of an American idiom in the interwar period, explored nativism and national identity in an experimental fusion of jazz with classical modernism. His works over the 1920s, including *The Cat and the Mouse: Scherzo Piano Piece* (1920), *Symphony for Organ and Orchestra* (1924), *Music for the Theater* (1925), *Concerto for Piano and Orchestra* (1926), *Symphonic Ode* (1927–9) and *Dance Symphony* (1925), all explored the potential of jazz to add a new dimension to American musical expression. In a 1927 article titled 'Jazz Structure and Influence', Copland called jazz an indigenous music that could reinvigorate symphonies and concertos. If 'freed of its present connotations,' he added cautiously, the synthesis of jazz with classical provided a startling instrument of musical expression.[71] However, as jazz became increasingly associated with the commercial and mass produced, the left-wing Copland turned to less commercial folk traditions, although he did write a clarinet concerto for jazz clarinetist Benny Goodman in the 1940s.

To many musicians jazz rejuvenated classical music by injecting it with dynamic new sounds that communicated a revolutionary modernity. This revolution did not reject the past but employed indigenous traditions in new ways. Classical symphonist Louis Gruenberg claimed that America needed to turn away from Europe and look at its own cultural traditions for new expression, stating '[a] new technic should be invented which will combine a knowledge of tradition and the modern experiment, if for no other reason than to avoid the pitfall of imitation'.[72] This modernity was tied closely to the racial hybridity of jazz expressions. Gruenberg's works utilised spirituals, folk songs, blues and popular jazz in symphonic style, notably in his *Jazzberries* (1925), *Jazz-Suite* (1925) and *Jazzettes* (1926). His work was also linked with other cultural producers: *The Daniel Jazz* (1925) set music to Vachel Lindsay's poem of the same name and *The Creation: A Negro Sermon* (1926) was accompanied with text by James Weldon Johnson, whose 'The Creation' was published the next year as part of *God's Trombones – Seven Negro Sermons in Verse*.[73] Still fascinated with African American themed work, Gruenberg later composed an operatic version of Eugene O'Neill's *The Emperor Jones* that was performed in 1933.

African American composers also blurred class, race and genre boundaries in their work. James Price Johnson and William Grant Still worked in both symphonic and popular styles. A key figure in the development of jazz for his innovation of 'stride' piano style that bridged ragtime with jazz, Johnson worked in musical theatre (composing the music for 'The Charleston' in the hit all-black revue *Runnin Wild*, discussed below), taught Fats Waller, performed with Bessie Smith and Fletcher Henderson, and was influential on the music of George Gershwin and Duke Ellington. At the same time, he also wrote several symphonic concerts. His *Yamekraw* (1927), orchestrated by William Grant Still and conducted by blues composer W. C. Handy, with a piano solo by Fats Waller, premiered at Carnegie Hall, presented a definitive statement of the centrality of African American artists to American 'high' culture.[74]

William Grant Still also bridged the divide between high and low culture, even though his later work was almost entirely in the classical sphere. Moving to New York in 1920, Still was quickly caught up in the ideals of the Harlem Renaissance. Yet while he aimed 'to elevate Negro musical idioms to a position of dignity and effectiveness in the field of symphonic and operatic music', he also worked in musical theatre and recording over the decade.[75] He became a musical director for Black Swan soon after he arrived in Harlem, and arranged music for many jazz bands while composing orchestral music such as *Levee Land* (1926), written for the jazz singer Florence Mills to perform, *From the Black Belt* (1926) and *Darker America* (1926).[76] Jazz provided a communal and interactive model for composers such as Still, whose *Symphony no. 1: Afro-American Symphony* (1930) incorporated jazz and blues with citations from Gershwin, who, in return, cited Still's

Symphony in his 'I Got Rhythm' (1930).[77] Still also wrote works based on texts by Harlem Renaissance writers Langston Hughes, Zora Neale Hurston, Arna Bontemps and Countee Cullen.[78]

The promotion of symphonic jazz by Paul Whiteman early in the decade gave added impetus to the movement of jazz into the concert hall. Although Whiteman had begun as a classical musician and George Gershwin had started out recording popular songs for the player-piano in Tin Pan Alley, the two men met while working together on George White's musical revue *Scandals of 1922* (1922), for which Gershwin wrote his first serious piece, a one-act opera called *Blue Monday*. Gershwin then began work on his celebrated piano concerto *Rhapsody in Blue* (1924), performed for the first time at Whiteman's 'Experiment in Modern Music' concert held at Aeolian Hall in New York in February 1924.

Whiteman organised the concert to illustrate the progress that jazz had made, showing that it was now 'a great deal more than savage rhythm from the jungle'.[79] The concert charted this chronological progression with twenty-four works starting with 'Livery Stable Blues' to illustrate how jazz had developed from 'the discordant early jazz to the melodious form of the present'.[80] Among the composers and performers were John Alden Carpenter, Aaron Copland, Louis Gruenberg, James P. Johnson and William Grant Still, with Sergei Rachmaninoff as one of the judges.[81] The concert was a sell-out and was attended by all of New York's leading figures. Of all of the performances, however, it was George Gershwin playing 'Rhapsody in Blue' that was the biggest sensation. To the music critic Henry Osgood, Gershwin raised jazz to a higher level and was 'the only one to take the elements of jazz and employ them with a distinct degree of success in forms of composition higher and larger than popular songs and musical comedy; he is, in sporting parlance, the "White Hope" of Jazz'.[82]

In response others began organising concerts. Nine days later, Vincent Lopez and his orchestra appeared at the Metropolitan Opera House in a 'Symphonic Jazz Concert', featuring white and black musicians together – including Fletcher Henderson with 'Meanest Blues' and W. C. Handy's 'The Evolution of the Blues'. Lopez also commissioned Gershwin to write *Concerto in F* for a concert at Carnegie Hall – written not for a big band but for a full symphony orchestra.[83] In December 1925, Whiteman responded with a 'Second Experiment in Modern Music', featuring the opera *135th Street* (earlier titled *Blue Monday*) by Gershwin, and *A Little Bit of Jazz* by Carpenter.[84]

Serge Koussevitzky, conductor of the Boston Symphony Orchestra, saw jazz as 'an important contribution to modern musical literature. It has an epochal significance – it is not superficial, it is fundamental. Jazz comes from the soil, where all music has its beginning'.[85] Even though the emphasis in concert music remained on the educated, controlled, written and arranged, rather than the improvised, jazz was still seen as a way of accessing the primitive and emotional in the mechanical age. To Rogers, 'jazz is rejuvenation, a recharging of the batteries of civilization with primitive new vigor', a belief echoed by Gilbert Seldes who argued that Negro art 'has kept alive things without which our lives would be perceptibly meaner, paler, and nearer to atrophy and decay'.[86] Whiteman also claimed that 'jazz is at once a revolt and a release. Through it we get back to a savage . . . joy in being alive'.[87]

Not everyone felt that this was an advance. The critic Lawrence Gilman complained of Whiteman's 1924 concert that 'this music is only half alive . . . How trite and feeble and conventional the tunes are, how sentimental and vapid the harmonic treatment . . . Old stuff it is . . . Recall the most ambitious piece . . . the 'Rhapsody in Blue' . . . and weep over the lifelessness of its melody and harmony, so derivative, so stale, so inexpressive'.[88] The conductor of the Boston Symphony Orchestra also received letters of complaint during the season of 1925–6 that blamed a crime wave on 'his introduction of so much modernistic music'.[89] Musical critic Paul Rosenfeld dismissed jazz altogether as a superficial entertainment: 'AMERICAN music is not jazz. Jazz is not music . . . [f]or jazz heartily and consistently violates the identity of its medium,' he wrote.[90] However, by 1926 Otto Kahn of the Metropolitan Opera Company stated that '[a]ll the classics have been jazzed by now, and it has resulted in getting the people interested in them in their original form'.[91] Whether symphonic jazz actually created new fans for 'real' jazz or not, it certainly paid serious attention to an art form that had long been denigrated or dismissed.

Jazz and Dance

While symphonic jazz offered recognition of the significance of jazz as an art form, the appearance of jazz in the concert hall disregarded the central role that dancing played in the music's development.[92] Dancers often set the tempo for the musicians and used their bodies to accompany the music through syncopated hand clapping, foot stomping, tap dancing and shouting. The increasing pace of industrial society had caused a psychological and social shift that was reflected in movements on the dance floor.[93] The call-and-response relationship between the performer and the audience further dismantled accepted hierarchical behaviour in cultural appreciation that was traditionally based on the passive reception of the cultural artefact.[94]

Black vernacular dance rhythms had become a fad in popular dancing with the ragtime craze of the 1910s. Such dances threw away the controlled steps and prescriptions of etiquette manuals in favour of the improvisatory and self-expressive steps of the 'turkey trot', 'bunny hug', 'grizzly bear' and 'monkey glide'. Many saw these animalistic dances as scandalously liberated, where partners were free to choose who they danced with and would swap around or improvise steps. Such dances became more widespread when such moves were made popular and respectable by the dance partners Irene and Vernon Castle, who taught Americans how to dance the new styles in a more traditional, upright and controlled ballroom style, notably introducing the Foxtrot, which became the most popular dance step of the era.[95] However, the popular introduction of jazz in the form of 'Livery Stable Blues' and the death of Vernon Castle, both in 1917, started a new era for jazz dancing that took increasing inspiration from African American dance styles despite attempts to refine, control or even ban the steps.

The rejection of white cultural values was represented by a musical event that, Langston Hughes claimed, ushered in the Harlem Renaissance. To Hughes it was the all-black musical revue 'Shuffle Along' (1921) that chimed the new era for African American art and the ascendancy of black vernacular culture.[96] The musical revue written by Eubie Blake and Noble Sissle featured some of the newest and most talented black artists of the 1920s, such as Josephine Baker, Ethel Waters, Paul Robeson and William Grant Still.[97] The success of 'Shuffle Along' led to a flurry of all-black or mixed-race revues. Like 'Shuffle Along' the musicals incorporated conventions from minstrel theatre and many were owned and produced by whites and continued to segregate mixed performances. Not only were white dance instructors frequently employed to give the shows some Broadway 'finesse', many of the themes and sets contained stereotypical 'old Negro', exotic or primitive images that contained the black performances within stereotypical cultural discourses.[98]

Despite this, the revues offered increased employment opportunities and national prominence to black performers and musicians, as well as a national showcase for their dance styles: 'Chocolate Dandies' featured the rising star Josephine Baker, who eventually found herself feted in Paris; 'Blackbirds of 1928' led to the national discovery of the tap-dance star Bill 'Bojangles' Robinson; 'Blackbirds' made Florence Mills an international star; 'Africana' (1927) starred the blues singer Ethel Waters; and 'Hot Chocolates', written by Fats Waller and Andy Razaf, had Louis Armstrong in the orchestra and made Waller's 'Ain't Misbehavin'' a hit song.[99]

The popularity of African American revues in Harlem and Broadway generated a wave of new dances that were copied and imitated around the country, most notably the national dance sensation that defined the era: 'The Charleston'.

The Charleston

Although the Charleston became the quintessential dance of the flapper, when the film *The Flapper* (1920) was released white audiences would have not connected the city in South Carolina with the dance that, in 1923, became the emblem of the decade. Influenced by the sensational success of the all-black revue 'Shuffle Along', producers Flournoy Miller and Aubrey Lyles approached the white producer George White to put on another revue called 'Runnin Wild' (1923), this time with music by James P. Johnson and lyrics by Cecil Mack. The show featured a song by Johnson that he had originally composed in 1913 to play at African American dance halls in Harlem, responding to the familiarity of African Americans with the dance moves.[100] Like other cultural trends the dance had been popular long before it came to mass attention and had a complex cultural heritage. Certain elements of the dance, such as the body slapping and hand crossing on the knees, were inherited from the 'Patting Juba', a slave dance derived from early African dance moves that were devised to circumvent bans on drumming by using slapping and foot tapping instead, which later became popular in minstrel performances where it absorbed aspects of Irish folk dancing.[101] Like all dance crazes of the 1920s, it had been a popular dance widely performed among African Americans in honky-tonks throughout the South in the two decades prior to its appearance in the urban North.[102] Black performers and dancers like Noble Sissle and the Whitman Sisters had seen or even performed the Charleston as early as 1905, and it had already appeared in the black musical revues 'Liza' (1922), 'How Come' (1923) and Ziegfield's 'Follies of 1923'.[103]

The dance was performed in 4/4 time with fast-paced syncopated kick-steps, with the arms swinging alternately to the leg kicks. During the show the Charleston was danced to hand clapping and foot stamping by the rest of the chorus. James Weldon Johnson said of this that, 'The effect was electrical . . . '[s]uch a demonstration of beating out complex rhythms had never been seen on a stage in New York'.[104] The pace, speed and precision of the dance made it appear modern and machine-age while allowing innovation, individuality and creative expression to flourish through stylistic variations. To most Broadway audiences the dance was new and revolutionary, appearing to liberate American dance from upright European styles with its focus on the lower body that used unconventional or humorous styles such as 'rubber-legging'.[105] Gilbert Seldes in the *New Republic* commented that 'the first impression made by the Charleston was extraordinary. You felt a new rhythm, you saw new postures, you heard a new frenzy . . . gay and orgiastic and wild'.[106] Another critic announced that the Charleston number in 'Runnin Wild' 'pronounced the beat for the lost generation, and liberated the world of jazz movement'.[107]

The Charleston soon became the signature dance of rebellious youth and the 'flapper', and a fad that performed rebellion and the rejection of traditional social norms. A writer for the *New York Times* commented in 1926 that 'the Charleston has now been received with such enthusiasm as only America can express. Dancers young and not so young enjoy the barbarous rhythm of its syncopation; they like the tricky steps and the recklessness that is somehow injected into them'.[108] It led to new fashions of shorter and less restrictive clothing that enabled the energetic and athletic moves and signified the liberation of the new sexuality with free movement of the hips, thighs and buttocks and high kick-steps that revealed the dancer's underwear to the audience or her partner. Its popularity was enhanced by its versatility, as it could be danced solo by either sex, or with a partner (unlike other dance fads of the decade such as 'the Shimmy' and the 'Black Bottom'). The Charleston also broke down the hierarchy between dancing as performance and social dancing that anyone could do, merging the two into a more culturally democratic style.

By 1925 it seemed that everyone wanted to learn how to Charleston: 'schools are teaching it, the movie houses hold Charleston contests, little children imitate its steps on the sidewalks,' claimed Gilbert Seldes.[109] Films were shown to movie audiences with titles such as 'How To Dance Charleston' (1925) and movie houses were assured a return attendance with the six-reel 'The Charleston in Six Lessons' (1926). Magazine and newspaper sales also increased by promising 'how to' instructions on the Charleston, and *How to Charleston Correctly* (1926) appeared on bookshelves. Hotel ballrooms and dance halls held Charleston competitions throughout the nation. To actresses Joan Crawford and Ginger Rogers career success was intimately linked to the Charleston as both began in show business by winning Charleston competitions. Rogers was billed as 'Queen of the Charleston' and Crawford later showed off her skills in the lead role of *Our Dancing Daughters* (1928).[110] Ability in the Charleston, this implied, enabled young women to fulfil the dream of upward mobility, fame and money.

The extent of the dance fad inevitably led to an outbreak of public concern over the possible health and moral impact of the craze. Sociologists undertook studies of dance halls in order to establish their function in urban life. A 1924 investigation of San Francisco dance halls concluded that 'all of the social problems of modern life are met within the dance hall: sickness, marital difficulties, unmarried motherhood, unemployment, vocational maladjustment, desertion, feeble-mindedness, poverty, ignorance of social hygiene, of American manners and customs, lack of sex education'.[111] When a ballroom at the Pickwick Club in Boston collapsed in July 1925, killing forty-four dancers, the explosive energy of the Charleston was claimed to be the cause. The tumultuous energy and danger that this event symbolised led the dance to be banned in many dance halls as authorities reacted to an apparently uncontrollable dance mania.

In newspaper articles headlines such as: 'Charleston? Heart Shimmy? Health Director Blames Strenuous Dance for Prevalence of Organic Troubles Among Young People', doctors and medical experts confirmed the risks and dangers associated with the dance and prevailed on flappers to avoid knee and heart injury.[112] In an attempt to curb the craze, dance experts met to invent alternative dances to try and replace it, or set about to encourage more traditional and sedate dance styles. These efforts met with no success at all.

According to newspapers and headlines at the peak of the craze, the dance represented a manifestation of the 'Lost Generation' death-instinct. In 1926 several national newspapers carried the story of the death of a teenager who had died, according to her doctor, from 'dancing the Charleston'.[113] In June this was followed by the death of a sixteen year old who, doctors claimed, had died for her 'love of dancing', especially the 'strenuous steps of the Charleston'.[114] Later that month the *New York Times* ran a headline stating 'Charleston in Rowboat Costs Lives of Six; Boy Demonstrating Dance Capsizes Craft'.[115] The dangers associated with the dance were played out in a Pathé Newsreel that year, which showed the young dancer Mildred Unger dancing the Charleston on the top of an aeroplane. Although the dance was replaced by new fads of 'the shimmy' and the 'black bottom' in 1926, these sexually suggestive dances never became as universally popular or representative of the era as the Charleston.

Mildred Unger's aerial performance of the Charleston suggested a weightless modernity that was further confirmed by the appearance of a new dance in the late 1920s known as 'the Lindy Hop', named by George 'Shorty' Snowden after Charles Lindbergh's successful transatlantic flight in 1927.[116] The dance extended the Charleston with gravity-defying aerial moves and speed, becoming nationally popular as 'the jitterbug' in the 1930s. Blending the elegant swing style of the big-band sound of Ellington and Henderson with the seemingly effortless tension of a Louis Armstrong 'breakaway' solo, the dance represented American mastery of both the body and the machine.[117] The dance was showcased at the Savoy Ballroom from its opening in 1926 and as one of the few mixed-race dance venues it quickly became the most popular dance hall in Harlem. Wallace Thurman claimed in

Figure 2.3 Film still from *Our Dancing Daughters* (1928) featuring Joan Crawford (© MGM/The Kobal Collection).

1927 that 'When Harlem people wish to dance, without attending a cabaret, they go to the Renaissance Casino or to the Savoy, Harlem's two most famous public dance halls. The Savoy is the pioneer in the field of giving dance-loving Harlemites some place to gather nightly ... The music is good, the dancers are gay, and the setting is conducive to joy'.[118]

Despite the athleticism and enjoyment epitomised by jazz dancing, few saw it as an art form. The commercialisation of jazz and its music led many to search elsewhere for vernacular dance traditions that replicated the pleasures of a pre-industrial age. As a form of expression, jazz dance was also seen as lacking aesthetic qualities; the machine-age movements made it appear as 'play in a Ford factory. Its pounding rhythm is as simple as tightening bolts. It gives very little scope for individual expression'.[119] Industrialist Henry Ford's reaction to the dance fad was to hire dance instructors in his factories to teach square dancing, polkas and waltzes to his employees.[120] Dance teachers also attempted to discourage the Charleston by forging folk dance revivals, even inviting the industrialist as a guest to old-time dances that became termed, somewhat paradoxically, a 'Henry Ford Night'.[121]

The desire to shape and control the dance craze into an art form that expressed ideas and emotions rather than being purely for mass entertainment was most developed in the uplifting 'aesthetic' movement of concert dance in the 1910s and 1920s.[122] Modern dance attempted to find ways to express the same dualistic tensions that characterised the works of the modernist writers and philosophers, seen in the performances by Helen Tamaris of the dance 'Subconscious' (1928) and Martha Graham's dance 'Heretic' (1929), both of which represented the clash between the individual and society that was central to intellectual thought.[123] Graham's style was grounded in pragmatic educational ideals and an experimentalism which she used to explore important issues of the day in works such as 'Immigrant: Steerage, Strike' (1928), 'Poems of 1917: Song Behind the Lines' and 'Dance of Death' (1928).[124]

Classical aesthetic and concert dancing also attempted to forge a modernist aesthetic out of indigenous American traditions. Graham, for example, had her first starring role in the Aztec ballet 'Xochitl' (1920) and by 1930 her choreography had entirely rebelled against formal European classical traditions by including Native American and African American influences.[125]

Conclusion

By 1929 jazz had become the cultural signature of the decade. More than just music, jazz was an 'atmosphere' that crystallised the zeitgeist of 1920s America:

> Always, everywhere, there was jazz; everything that year was enveloped in the hard bright mist of it . . . jazz omnipresent and always carrying the same message of violent escape . . . Everywhere was the atmosphere of a long debauch that had to end.[126]

On one level the cultural and racial shift that this represented appeared revolutionary, but by the end of the decade, black intellectuals were not so sure.[127] The universality and ubiquity of jazz merely concealed a re-inscription of racial divisions that had long dominated American culture. The growth of interest in Harlem by white culture-seekers, for example, made Wallace Thurman complain in 1927 that 'Harlem cabarets were interesting once . . . but their complexion has changed.

The frequenters are almost 95 percent white. Negroes have been forced out of their own places of amusement, their jazz appropriated, their entertainers borrowed'.[128]

Langston Hughes also became disappointed that the vast popularity of black performances did not generate greater racial equality:

> White people began to come to Harlem in droves. For several years they packed the expensive Cotton Club on Lenox Avenue. But I was never there, because the Cotton Club was a Jim Crow club for gangsters and monied whites. They were not cordial to Negro patronage, unless you were a celebrity like Bojangles. So Harlem Negroes did not like the Cotton Club and never appreciated its Jim Crow policy in the very heart of their dark community. Nor did ordinary Negroes like the growing influx of whites toward Harlem after sundown, flooding the little cabarets and bars where formerly only colored people laughed and sang, and where now the strangers were given the best ringside tables to sit and stare at the Negro customers – like amusing animals in a zoo.[129]

The market and opportunity for jazz recording also remained segregated throughout the 1920s. Anecdotes about the racism faced by even the most celebrated black artists illustrated the central paradox that while whites now enjoyed black music and art, they were far from acknowledging or allowing social equality. Examples of prejudice remained profuse: journalist Walter White wrote that on the same night that he received 'wave after wave' of applause from Broadway audiences for his performance in *The Emperor Jones*, the celebrated singer and actor Paul Robeson was refused service in downtown restaurants.[130]

Performers in touring shows encountered similar prejudices in unfamiliar or hostile areas despite achieving high levels of respect on the stage in New York. In order to gain access to performance spaces dominated by whites, black musicians often had to accept second-class treatment or change the way they performed. Claude McKay also noted that behind the 'baroque fantasy of Negro entertainment lies the grim reality of ruthless jobbery' where even top bands were paid less than their white equivalents even when they played the same venues, and although dancing was universally popular across race lines there was not one 'Negro-owned dancing hall in Harlem'.[131] Although radio broadcasting had allowed jazz to be disseminated throughout the nation, white control of the airwaves also threatened to make broadcast music a whites-only affair as the growth of the recording and radio industry centralised power and control into fewer hands and censorship filtered out aspects of jazz that seemed undesirable to white critics. Many musicians who had been central to the evolution of jazz, such as Ferdinand Joseph 'Jelly Roll' Morton and King Oliver, died penniless in the 1930s, having been undercut by agents or replaced by white musicians.[132]

Figure 2.4 Movie theatre showing *The Jazz Singer* (1927) (© Warner Brothers/The Kobal Collection).

Early jazz criticism also relegated black musicians to the obscurity of the margins. In the first serious jazz history *So This Is Jazz* (1926), Henry Osgood admitted that 'Nowhere have I gone into detail about negro jazz bands. There are so many good ones, it would be hard to pick out a few for special mention. None of them, however, are as good as the best white bands, and very rarely are their best players as good as the best white virtuosos'.[133] As late as 1928, Princeton undergraduates worshipped the cornetist Bix Beiderbecke, but were found to possess only one record by an African American musician between them.[134]

Such paradoxes reached their apotheosis in popular entertainment. While *The Jazz Singer* (1927), the first sound movie to reach the ears of a mass audience, addressed certain problems and prejudices faced by the vaudeville performer, the sound era only served to push black performers more fully into the background. In the film, adapted from a popular stage melodrama, jazz represented an archetypal modernity in an ethnically progressive and secular America as a Jewish singer pursues a career in vaudeville against his father's old-world values and prejudices. The film paradoxically illuminated the erasure of black jazz by white performers in popular entertainment in the figure of the minstrel played by Al Jolson, one of the most popular entertainers of the era.[135] Yet, even as it attempted to submerge such ethnic and racial tensions within a narrative of family discord, the film indicated that modernity was indeed embodied by transgressive racial identities and an internalised (if unacknowledged) presence of the despised outcast. Most paradoxical of all, however, was that the film's success helped to usher in an era of sound movies that precipitated the demise of live entertainment, which had been the mainstay for such performers throughout the decade. In one night the movie made old that which was representatively modern by upstaging live entertainment, music and dance with sensational new motion picture technology, changing the face of modern entertainment for the rest of the century.

Chapter 3

Film and Radio

The prevalent image of the 'roaring twenties' as a decade of hedonistic leisure and careless decadence was created and sustained by the expansion of the American film industry at a time of social and moral transformation. As the 'Golden Age' of the silent screen, film art in the 1920s reached new heights of skill and sophistication before entering a period of artistic and representational turmoil with the transition to sound between 1927 and 1931. At the same time the movie industry became big business in the post-war period, where a new connection with the finance industry and corporate practices created ambivalence over its status as culture or art. The only serious threat to the ascendancy of American cinema in this period came from the establishment of a completely new form of art and entertainment: the radio. Going to the movies and listening to the radio became the most popular commercial leisure activities in the 1920s, a fact that raised new concerns about the direction of American culture and the social value and status of such 'mass' arts.

Strenuous efforts in the 1910s had been made to transform the reputation of movies from a low art form made for the masses, viewed in the demoralised atmosphere of the nickelodeon, to an art that created uplift, enlightenment and education among audiences. In a period of mass immigration and industrialisation movies were seen by reformers as a new opportunity to improve urban culture and educate immigrants about American values. Independent directors such as D. W. Griffith had pioneered 'reform aesthetics' that treated serious subjects as art and out of which the feature film had emerged.[1] Griffith's first long feature, *Birth of a Nation* (1915), had not only created a nationwide storm of applause and protest but made America a nation of critics and commentators ascending to the White House itself. The following year, Vachel Lindsay's *The Art of the Moving Picture* (1916) became the first serious cultural criticism of film as an art form in the United States, giving new cultural standing and respectability for the motion picture or photoplay.

In the 1920s this idealism was threatened by the political shift away from the progressive ideals of the reform era and the changing moral and social climate in which movies were made and viewed. Pioneer film historian Lewis Jacobs noted that after the war '[Movies] took up the cause of business, grew cynical, and participated in the repudiation of pre-war conventionality. Like the tabloids of the day, hundreds of films specialized in speed, spice, and spectacle. "Jazz films" by the middle of the period had superseded the last of the pictures in the pre-war tradition, substituting materialism and freedom for the old idealism'.[2] Over the 1920s, the aesthetics of reform were gradually replaced by the aesthetics of pleasure, fantasy and material luxury in which the tension between old and new cultural values was clearly played out.

America's participation in the war had further confirmed that movies could be used to achieve national goals or to change mass opinion. Films had been used to cohere national support for American entry into the war and to raise funds, shown in the efforts by actors and actresses such as Charlie Chaplin, Douglas Fairbanks and Mary Pickford to raise the sales of 'Liberty Bonds', using their status as popular celebrities.[3] While America had continued to perfect film art and streamline production for maximum profit in the relocation to Hollywood, the infrastructure of European countries had been badly damaged by war, making it impossible for them to compete with the economically ascendant American film industry. The expansion of the movie industry meant that film now had an increased role as the main purveyor of American culture, both nationally and internationally. Movies were created and exported on an unprecedented scale and by the 1920s they dominated the world market and were 'suddenly, and actually, exporting not only goods but ideas'.[4]

As the nation shifted to peacetime production, the movie industry similarly shifted into mass production for a flourishing consumer economy. As the Republican Party official who had masterminded Warren G. Harding's election campaign in 1920, William H. Hays recognised the propaganda value of the movies for American government and business. His appointment as President of the Motion Picture Producers and Distributors Association (MPPDA) in 1922 indicated a new connection between the political and ideological goals of the nation's leaders and the motion picture industry.[5] Perceiving the centrality of Hollywood to the creation of stability, 'normalcy' and economic growth in postwar America, Hays became the industry's greatest booster of the period. Even though he later became more firmly associated with censorship than boosterism, he saw no contradiction between movies as culture and movies as big business, and claimed that 'The motion picture is the epitome of civilization and the quintessence of what we mean by "America"'. To Hays it was only in the picture palace that all four of the vital components of any civilisation – industry, art, science and religion – converged.[6] Most importantly, he claimed in 1925, movies were the 'the silent salesmen of American goods'.[7]

Art on a Manufacturing Basis

While defenders of movies attempted to maintain their status as art, industry changes also made this an increasingly commercialised 'Art on a Manufacturing Basis'.[8] Unlike other arts, the film industry depended on a 'constant stream of standard product' that made movie production more akin to a Ford production line than an artist's studio.[9] Fox, MGM, Paramount, RKO, United Artists, Universal and Warner Brothers built huge studios in California between 1915 and 1925 to manufacture their products for maximum profitability. By 1925 the sheer scale and rapid turnover of these factory-like constructions became the subject of a screen short when MGM presented audiences with a filmed studio 'tour' as a prologue to the main feature.

The expansion in production during this era was paralleled by the growth in movie consumption. Box-office receipts increased from $301 million in 1921 to $720 million in 1929, over four times the revenue of all spectator sports and live theatre combined, and attendance revenues doubled from $40 million in 1922 to $80 million in 1928. Companies also sought credit and finance from Wall Street for the first time and investment from business grew from $78 to $850 million dollars between 1922 and 1930.[10] Despite this, the cost of going to the movies remained low, averaging ten to fifty cents per ticket, making such entertainment available to a wider range of audiences than ever before.[11] Robert and Helen Lynd found that in the suburb of Muncie, Indiana, there were nine motion picture theatres operating from 1pm to 11pm, seven days per week, attended by two and three-quarters times the population during the lowest months, and four and a half times the total population during the peak months. Offering two or three programme changes per week, these theatres relied on a quick turnover of films and shorts in order to remain competitive.

Although the feature film was firmly established by the early 1920s, it was never the sole attraction in the silent-movie era. On a typical night at a first-run picture palace in the early twenties movie-goers would be presented with a programme that began with a symphonic overture, was followed by a series of newsreel clips covering the latest events and information, appended with a cartoon or comedy feature, perhaps followed by a live song or dance routine, then an informational or educational film consisting perhaps of a two-reel travelogue or scenic, a modest or elaborate stage show (known as a prologue) and finally the main feature – all of which was accompanied by a live musical performance. After the feature there may have been further musical performances and preview trailers for the next feature to be shown. Variations on this menu might include commercials, serial dramas (35 per cent of theatres ran these in 1922), two-reel short dramas, vaudeville skits, screen 'magazines', jazz instead of classical music, ballet and opera, or a magician instead of a stage show.[12]

In 1922 an exhibitor's poll judged that movies made up only 68 per cent of the total entertainment.[13] The rest of the show consisted of live music, acts and performances that accompanied and often complemented the main feature. Besides this, the majority of feature films were adaptations of novels (popular and classics) or successful Broadway shows and theatrical productions. Offering a wide cultural experience to a huge range of consumers, the picture palace was thus a place of potential education and uplift as well as possible degradation, and not all assessments of the movie house revolved solely around the quality or morality of what was shown on the screen. As one critic commented, despite the 'inane' productions offered by Hollywood, movie houses often exposed audiences to a wide range of 'high' culture at low cost:

A word should be said for the part the movies are playing in the musical education of America. The orchestras and organs which form part of the standard equipment of the better picture houses are not entirely given over to jazz mania. Not infrequently they offer a higher type of entertainment than the screen whose accessories they are.[14]

The fierce competition, rivalry and expansion that characterised the industry at the start of the decade appeared to taint such ambitions for high cultural uplift. Companies appeared to be 'at each other's throats' to find greater outlets for productions and to block those of their competitors.[15] This competition not only led to the release of morally ambiguous films about scandalous or salacious topics but in order to make profits for their investors and stock holders, movie companies built empires of production, distribution and exhibition – a technique later called 'vertical integration' – that ensured the profitability of such a rapid flow of films. By 1924 nearly all of the first-run theatres were owned by a handful of corporations and as chain theatre companies such as First National, Paramount and Loew moved into the movie production business, independent movie producers and exhibitors were virtually driven out. Production companies also merged with, or bought out, theatre chains in order to guarantee an audience for their expensive productions. The theatres that they did not own were forced to block-book a number of films by the same company in order to show the one that they wanted, adding to the variety of monopolistic practices that ensured a return on all films. By 1927 'exhibition had become almost entirely monopolized by chain theatres, all in the hands of the major producer-distributor-exhibitor combinations'.[16] Independent films and controversial subjects were forced into decline by this hegemony so that over the 1920s films about labour, the poor, politics and religion declined in number. By 1922 over 80 per cent of feature films were produced in Hollywood and of the 6,660 feature films made in the era, the majority were Westerns, costume dramas or fantasies, comedies, 'flapper' films or romances.[17]

By 1930 one critic claimed that the movies had become the fourth largest industry in the US and called it the 'amusement octopus': 'It employs more people than Ford and General Motors combined. There are in the neighborhood of 20,000 picture "palaces," with a weekly attendance of close to 100,000,000'.[18] The corporate and commercial imperatives of this industry led some to question the value of the movies as art and culture. In his book *Hollywood: The City of a Thousand Dreams: The Graveyard of a Thousand Hopes: Facts and Fancies of Filmdom* (1928) Jack Richmond argued that it was 'gain, sordid gain' that was the 'driving force behind' the movies.[19]

Critics of the movies contended that the sheer scale of the industry led to low cultural and intellectual values because of the need to appeal to the widest possible audience: because 'every film must be intelligible to everybody', 'it must meet the level of intelligence of every audience which is to see it. The lowest intellectual level, consequently, is that which governs the character of the appeal to be made'.[20] In the mid-1920s the sociologists Robert and Helen Lynd confirmed that people did not go to the movies to be instructed, but instead had a huge appetite for comedy, romance and adventure films. In 1925 the top favourite stars of the inhabitants of Muncie, Indiana were: 'Harold Lloyd, comedian; Gloria Swanson, heroine of modern society films; Thomas Meighan, hero in modern society films; Colleen Moore, ingénue; Douglas Fairbanks, comedian and adventurer, and Norma Talmadge, heroine in modern society films'.[21] Movie theatres were not seen as places to educate and engage with the pressing socio-political issues of the day, but as a place to escape from reality. The Lynds noted that an advertisement for the movies in 1925 encouraged such fantasies by urging audiences to escape 'the cage of everyday existence' and experience 'all the romance, all the excitement you lack in your daily life' by attending the movies.[22] Paramount similarly advertised itself as an 'Escape from Every-Dayland' offering 'adventure, romance, love, comedy and thrilling experience of every kind to millions whose lives would otherwise be monotonous'.[23]

The growth of the luxury picture palace added to the perception that movies were all about escape into fantasy. In 1928 there were 20,500 motion picture houses across the nation operating under fierce competition to attract movie patrons. While many of these were neighbourhood theatres in residential locations playing second-run features accompanied by a small orchestra or simply a solo pianist, the competition between the integrated companies led to the creation of an unparalleled number of elaborately equipped theatres that attracted customers with technological innovations such as air conditioning or theatrical 'atmospherics', high culture in the form of imported European art, elaborate furnishings, military trained ushers, hospitals, lounges and childcare.[24]

Exotic themed theatres, such as the Aztec in San Antonio (1926) or Grauman's Egyptian Theater (1922) and Chinese Theater (1927) in Los Angeles, pandered to sensations of 'foreign' exoticism, while other theatres offered 'atmospherics' or palatial luxury in the style of European gothic architecture. The pinnacle of these was the vast 'Cathedral of the Motion Pictures', the Roxy, which opened in New York in 1927. As the largest and most expensive picture palace ever built it had cost over $12 million and had seating for an audience of 6,200, with room for another 2,000 in lobbies and lounges. The stage alone was large enough for hundreds of performers and dancers to appear together in elaborate Broadway-style shows. The Roxy also had dressing rooms for 200 to 300 actors, singers and dancers, an orchestra platform which could hold a hundred musicians as well as the three organs, which rose majestically out of the basement to stage level at the beginning of a performance, and a team of military trained ushers to politely escort customers to their seats.[25]

The furnishings and décor of the deluxe palace made movie-going a sensuous experience that dissolved 'Puritan strictures', as Lloyd Lewis wrote in the *New Republic*, giving the patron a fleeting taste of unparalleled wealth and sensuality: as 'she strolls voluptuously . . . her feet sink in soft rugs, she is surrounded by heavy Renaissance tables, oil paintings, and statues of nudes . . . attendants bow to her . . . She bathes in elegance and dignity; she satisfies her yearning for a "cultured" atmosphere'. A cross-class fantasy of upward mobility, the deluxe picture palace represented the ascendancy of a new consumer democracy that made every man 'a king and every woman a queen'.[26] The eroticism of the picture palace was matched with the sexualised promotion of feature films with racy or exotic themes, causing one theatre manager to call the theatre 'Valentino Traps'.[27] As the percentage of men in motion picture audiences began to decline in the 1910s (the number of women rose from 60 per cent in 1920 to 83 per cent in 1927) the appeal of the 'cultured atmosphere' operated to attract a rising middle-class and female audience.[28] This in turn sustained a culture of adulation around movie stars that was catered to by growing numbers of fan magazines, which provided movie fans with additional information about Hollywood through their examination of the off-screen activities of the movie stars. Stars' homes and lavish lifestyles mirrored the excess, luxuriance and exoticism of the picture palace and became symbols of the availability of wealth and success promised by American democracy.[29]

The exoticism and eroticism of the picture palace and the glimpses into the luxurious Hollywood lives in magazines were paralleled on screen in a vast number of movies that tackled questions of modern sexual behaviour or fantasies of foreign or forbidden love. With fierce competition in the industry and a climate of changing moral priorities, the end of the war had seen cinemas flooded with numerous provocative titles such as *Sex, Flapper Wives, Ladies of Ease, Gigolo, Reckless Youth, Jazzmania, Kiss Me Again, Seven Sinners* and *Daughters of Pleasure*. Other titles offered fantasies of wealth and class mobility, such as *Extravagance, Success* and *Money Money Money*, leading one observer to claim that '[t]he movies are obsessed with sex, sentiment, and success' and 'pander to the panics and pruriency of the herd'.[30] Although such titles often concealed their moral conservatism, the films explored such ideas as the changing status of women, the generation gap, consumer culture, class transgression and visual desire in increasingly sophisticated ways.

Cecil B. DeMille and Consumer Aesthetics

Changes in attitudes towards marriage and social convention among
the middle classes were most distinctly portrayed in the films of Cecil
B. DeMille, who 'tapped the post-War public imagination' by offering exciting glimpses of illicit modern behaviour, luxury and material
excess.[31] In an overt rejection of Puritanism in the postwar period,
DeMille's social comedies and dramas displayed frequent acts of dis-
robing, washing and enjoying pleasure within palatial bathroom and
bedroom settings that made excessive materialism a sexually energised
screen spectacular.[32] Despite this, his 'jazz age' films *Male and Female*
(1919), *Don't Change Your Husband* (1919), *For Better or Worse*
(1919), *Why Change Your Wife?* (1920), *Forbidden Fruit* (1921), *The
Affairs of Anatol* (1921), *Saturday Night* (1922), *Manslaughter* (1922),
Fool's Paradise (1922) and *Adam's Rib* (1923) gave audiences an excur-
sion into the abandon of social convention only to resolve the tension
between tradition and modernity at the end by making his character's
happiness dependent upon a return to the status quo, albeit one that
was reinvigorated by new sexual expression and experimentation.
As Mary Ryan has noted, movies of the 1920s 'kept sexuality within
traditional bounds, [while] materialistic desires were given bountiful
gratification'.[33]

DeMille's sumptuous sets and lavish interiors created as much sensation as his moral excursions. The success of his movies led Paramount
to advertise DeMille's pictures to exhibitors as a 'Horn of Plenty' out
of which cash literally poured.[34] Yet it was not just the film business
that saw a good return from the director; DeMille's films sustained
consumer desires for the latest goods, styles, fashion and furnishings
to audiences around the world, making him Hollywood's 'architect
of modern consumption'.[35] Just as Hays viewed films as America's
salesmen, others noted that 'The influence of the movies upon
current standards of living is prodigious. The styles of Manhattan and
Hollywood become those of Main Street and Hogg Hollow, in furniture, automobiles, hairdressing, and architecture'.[36]

For working-class women the 'flapper' genre dramatised fantasies of
class mobility and consumer democracy. Films starring actresses such
as Colleen Moore, Clara Bow, Louise Brooks, Virginia Lee Corbin,
Madge Bellamy, Marie Provost and Joan Crawford embodied the
paradox of modern womanhood by depicting characters who defied
tradition and convention only to be contained within the confines of
marriage, or turned into a gender-restricting commodity spectacle.[37]

Figure 3.1 Actress Colleen Moore (© The Kobal Collection).

Colleen Moore's movies, such as *Flaming Youth* (1923), *The Perfect Flapper* (1924), *We Moderns* (1925), *Ella Cinders* (1926), *Her Wild Oat* (1927), *Naughty But Nice* (1927) and *Orchids and Ermine* (1927), showed the negotiation of class and ethnic identity as a transformation or self-improvement narrative that allowed women assimilation into modernity through consumption.[38] *Ella Cinders* (a film based on a popular syndicated comic strip of 1925) was both a parody and a paradigm of the upward mobility that Hollywood represented for the working-class girl. Ella's escape from servitude comes when she accidentally wins a beauty contest and is propelled to Hollywood and, ultimately, marriage to a wealthy football player. This 'shopgirl' fantasy was apotheosised in the real-life and onscreen persona of the most popular flapper of the era, Clara Bow.

Clara Bow and *IT* (Clarence Badger, 1927)

In 1921 a young movie fan fantasising about becoming the next Gloria Swanson entered 'The Fame and Fortune Contest' in *Motion Picture* magazine, a contest that offered the winner a role in a movie. By 1929 the winner of that contest, Clara Bow, had become the first screen sex symbol and one of the most popular Hollywood actresses of the 1920s, receiving 45,000 fan letters each week and endorsing a wide variety of consumer goods.[39] Between 1922 and 1929, Bow's vitality and sexiness defined the liberated woman of the 1920s, while her meteoric rise and the films she starred in became 'a parable about fan culture' that enacted 'a fantastic narrative of female sexual aggression and class transcendence' in the era.[40] *Vanity Fair* magazine saw her as the 'super-flapper of them all — the hyper-reality and extra-ideality of a million or more film-goers'.[41] As a star whose career was virtually over by the end of the decade and who retired in 1933 at the age of 26, her story is also a parable of the rapid acceleration, vertical integration, consumer fetishism and planned obsolescence that characterised the film, fan and fashion industries in the 1920s.

Bow's fairytale rise to Hollywood stardom began inauspiciously with her ghetto birth and unstable upbringing in Brooklyn in 1905. Her mother suffered from mental illness and her father was an abusive alcoholic.[42] Her fantasies of escape from this background were fuelled and propelled by her passion for the movies and she later described how she would spend hours in front of the mirror mimicking her favourite actresses in the hope of one day becoming like them. Bow's propulsion into Hollywood by a fan magazine competition provided the industry with an apparent materialisation of a new success ethic.

In 1927 Bow's success was tied to a new sexual ideal that was manifested in her most popular film, *IT*. In the serialised novelette *IT*, author Elinor Glyn had described a new personal quality that appeared key to success and happiness in the 1920s, 'sex appeal': '"IT" is that quality possessed by some few persons which draws all others with its magnetic life force. With it you win all men if you are a woman — and all women if you are a man'.[43] In a vigorous publicity campaign, Paramount had saturated movie houses and magazines with advertisements asking,

'What is IT?' and later announcing that Bow's next movie would be *IT*. In the movie, Bow starred as Betty Lou, a lingerie salesgirl in the 'World's Largest Department Store', Waltham's. When the owner of the store, Cyrus Waltham, takes a tour, Betty Lou sets her eyes on him and the title card announces the beginning of her quest for possession: 'Sweet Santa Claus. Give Me Him'. The drama then revolves around her attempt to get him to notice her, their growing romance once he does, the breaking down of the class barrier between them through a date on her terms at Coney Island, where they enjoy the pleasures of an amusement ride called 'The Social Mixer', the resurrection of class barriers through various social misunderstandings, and their final reconciliation, as love overcomes their mutual hurt pride.

From the first scene her sexually aggressive persona is established when her 'kinaesthetic' gaze, portrayed through a camera-eye perspective, scans the room where her eyes finally 'lock on' and zoom in on Waltham.[44] In this moment Betty Lou performs on screen the changing experience of female spectatorship in the 1920s, replicating the gaze of the fan fixing on the object of her desires but fulfilling the fantasy further by showing him looking back and finally noticing her. In this way Bow, like other popular movie stars of the day, represented modern femininity as unbounded physical freedom, energy and mobility that contrasted with the demure and selfless heroines depicted on film before the war. Representative of the archetypal flapper, to F. Scott Fitzgerald, 'Clara Bow [was] the quintessence of what the term "flapper" signifies as a definite description: pretty, impudent, superbly assured, as worldly wise, briefly clad and "hardberled" as possible'.[45] Dancing, drinking, smoking and sexually assertive, Bow signified a fast-paced modernity that was often unruly but ultimately appealing.

The excitement generated by *IT* was unprecedented. After seeing the film one girl told reformers; 'Oh to possess what Miss Bow has – that elusive little thing called IT! After seeing her picture by that name, I immediately went home to take stock of my personal charms before my vanity mirror'.[46] Film producer Budd Schulberg wrote that 'Clara Bow became not just a top box-office star but a national institution: The It Girl. Millions of followers wore their hair like Clara's and pouted like Clara, and danced and smoked and laughed and necked like Clara'.[47] Fan magazine descriptions of Bow's 'playgirl' lifestyle provided audiences with an image that confirmed her as a symbol of modern womanhood who was free from traditional restraints.[48] Setting the standard for femininity in the 1920s, Clara's sexual persona was used to sell huge quantities of consumer goods, including cosmetics, hats and red hair dye.[49] 'It' was thereby widely marketed as something that was attainable through consumerism as much as an innate or natural attribute.

The working girl fantasy of escape via consumption and sexual freedom offered fans a response to the restrictions, mechanisation and monotony of labour that was being faced by unprecedented numbers of women who were now in the workforce.[50] Such films offered glamorous social options, physical and social mobility that were unavailable in the majority of working lives and operated to shape 'aspirations in a uniform direction' towards expression through leisure and consumption rather than at work.[51] Despite gruelling schedules to produce over fifty films in the first eight years of her career and her exploitation by the studio she was contracted to, Bow represented the escape from poverty and industrial routine by playing working girls who succeeded by being sexy and self-determined, becoming 'the star system's best advertisement precisely because she perpetuated the illusion of possibility for fans'.[52]

Bow taught a new generation of movie-goers that the way to succeed was to submit to fantasy and desire rather than self-denial and hard work. This illusion, however, could not be sustained into the 1930s, as the flapper figure became a corrupted perversion of the dream of upward mobility at a time of economic depression and the working girl became an increased source of threat and anxiety. Bow also struggled with the transition to sound; her strong Brooklyn accent and a childhood nervous stammer gave her 'mike fright' and the static cumbersome technology reduced the frenetic actress to immobility. As her mental health declined so did her popularity, and she retired in 1933 at the age of 26.

Figure 3.2 Clara Bow in 1926 (© Paramount/The Kobal Collection/Richee, E. R.).

The vibrancy and sexual energy reflected in *IT* was not limited to female screen stars. The new sexuality was epitomised in film spectacles of athletic prowess and physical freedom displayed by popular heroes such as Douglas Fairbanks, whose fantasy epic *The Thief of Bagdad* (1924) presented Fairbanks as a vital and superhuman male whose body actively engaged with exotic foreign landscapes in film spectacles of daring and command.[53] Eclipsing Fairbanks, who represented a healthy athleticism as appealing to men as to women, Rudolph Valentino's highly eroticised tango in a bordello in *The Four Horsemen of the Apocalypse* (1921) began his screen career as the eponymous 'Latin Lover' and screen sex symbol.[54] Like Bow's, Valentino's image was manufactured and sustained by a fan culture that fused his real and screen personae: in films such as *The Sheik* (1921), *Camille* (1921), *Blood and Sand* (1922), *The Eagle* (1925) and *Son of the Sheik* (1926) he played passionate lovers, at times dominating women and at others dominated by them.[55] His rapid ascension to stardom was deeply intertwined with a new cult of the body and the 'optic intoxication' of movie spectatorship, while his premature death in 1926 led to a nationwide outpouring of mass hysteria and a funeral with over 100,000 fans in attendance.

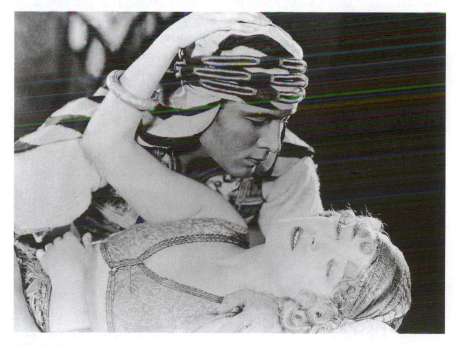

Figure 3.3 Rudolph Valentino and Vilma Banky in *Son of the Sheik* (1926) (© United Artists/The Kobal Collection).

The popularity of onscreen athleticism was deeply intertwined with anxieties over mass urbanisation and the feminising effect of mass culture on the body. As a genre, the Western provided a popular antidote to such concerns where location shooting on vast national parks in California appeared to offer an alternative masculine space free from urban modernity and physical boundaries. Tom Mix became the most popular Western star of the decade by performing horseback stunts that illustrated the hero's unleashed athleticism in that environment, earning him his own elaborate production unit and a salary of $17,000 per week in 1925.[56]

While most Westerns were short films that were made to be included in variety programmes, feature Western melodramas also depicted individual and small group battles for survival within a vast or hostile environment. Epics such as *The Iron Horse* (1924) and *The Covered Wagon* (1923) offered viewers a visual and allegorical dramatisation of the clearly defined tension between modernity and tradition that was central to intellectual thought in the 1920s, whether subsumed in narratives about the battle between the sexes, or in tales of individual struggle within the city, between rural and urban or civilised and primitive. In many cases these themes were combined: the threat of the assertive new woman was explored as a tension between urban and rural that had been a staple of 'reform' melodrama throughout the previous decade. At the height of silent-film expression, F. W. Murnau's *Sunrise* (1927) extended this dialectic by turning such outward or environmental signs of change into a psychological drama of inner conflict that leads a man to contemplate killing his old-fashioned wife to obtain access to modern pleasure and desire. The man's eventual reconciliation with his wife, however, is not depicted as the triumph of a return to tradition, but as a successful accommodation between urban attractions and traditional values. While *Sunrise* is now considered to be the pinnacle of silent film expression and a masterpiece in its own right, many Hollywood films aimed for a similar synthesis and resolution.[57]

As in *Sunrise*, the tension between urban life and the individual was central to the dramatic tension of King Vidor's *The Crowd* (1928). Studies of urban and collective psychology, such as *The City* (1925) by Robert Park or *Group Psychology and the Analysis of the Ego* (1921) by Freud, raised concerns over individuality and agency that are reflected in Vidor's story of the urban 'everyman' who struggles to succeed among the skyscrapers, anonymous offices and mechanical pleasures of New York.[58] In *The Crowd* (see cover illustration) John Sims,

Figure 3.4 Janet Gaynor and George O'Brien in *Sunrise* (1927) (© Fox Films/The Kobal Collection).

played by James Murray, aims to be 'somebody big' but is dwarfed by the city and the pressures of consumer culture to fit in and be like everybody else. Sexual desire is quickly translated into consumption followed by wage slavery as John chooses to marry after a carefree hedonistic romp to Coney Island. As he gradually loses his identity he gains a new one as 'mass' man and comes to terms with his lack of agency. Shot with seven different endings and released with two, *The Crowd* illustrated how the struggle to resolve the tension between the individual and the crowd could result in an artistic ambivalence that was distinctly modern.[59]

Comedies also dealt with the crisis of the individual within hostile or urban environments that literally dwarfed the actor, to comedic effect. Films such as *Manhandled* (1924), starring Gloria Swanson, portrayed a shopgirl literally crushed by crowds in the city. The comedies of Buster Keaton and Harold Lloyd, who, along with Charlie Chaplin, were the most popular comedians of the silent screen, played upon the comedic effects of the individual's negotiation with, transformation within, or triumph over, modernity.

Figure 3.5 Harold Lloyd in *Never Weaken* (1921) directed by Fred Newmeyer (© Hal Roach/The Kobal Collection).

These movies made visual gags out of Ogburn's theory of 'cultural lag', which argued that humans were struggling to keep up with the sum of their inventions. Playing with concepts of time and space, films illustrated surreal perceptions of human fragility that had been created by modernity. A common feature underlying this concern was the frequent contention that '[t]he one characteristic of our present age is SPEED'.[60] Indeed, screens offered material evidence of this change of pace as cameras were hand-cranked before 1925, making the speed of recording variable, while exhibitors and projectionists sped up their machines in order to fit them into a programme, or if the action was too slow or dull. Before 1927, when synchronous sound made regulation of film speed a necessity, audiences may certainly have experienced the movie palace as a further breathtaking example of modernity operating outside of natural time.[61]

Comedies also mocked the material dreams and fantasies of agency that were put forward on screen in parodies of epics or satires of upward mobility such as *Movie Fans* (1923), *Merton of the Movies* (1924) and *Show People* (1928), which reflected on the daydreams manufactured by Hollywood itself. Other films reflected an increasing taste for non-sentimental realist 'photoplays', showing harsh reflections on the recent war in *The Big Parade* (1925), *Behind the Front* (1926), *What Price Glory?* (1926) and *All Quiet on the Western Front* (1930). Materialism was condemned in the lengthiest film of the decade, Erich Von Stroheim's *Greed* (1924) and the crime and corruption that had become prevalent in prohibition culture emerged in gritty gangster movies such as Josef Von Sternberg's *Underworld* (1927), *The Docks of New York* (1928) and *Thunderbolt* (1929).

These films suggested an observational, sociological or scientific role for the movie camera that was becoming increasingly recognised as an anthropological tool in fieldwork that documented disappearing or pre-industrial culture and traditions.[62] A public taste for such screen realism and slower-paced observation was revealed most clearly by a surprise independent hit of 1922, *Nanook of the North*.

Nanook of the North (1922)

While newsreels, 'scenics' and travelogues were regular fare in picture palaces, Robert Flaherty's *Nanook of the North* (1922) created a new genre, the feature documentary. While critics have subsequently unveiled the extent of its narrative dramatisation and falsification, the film blended anthropological observation with techniques of silent melodrama to provide a dramatic and moving account of Inuit, or Eskimo, life that was an unprecedented success.

Flaherty did not set out to be a filmmaker but was a prospector and explorer for a mining company.[63] The growing interest in short travel films and the increasing portability of film equipment allowed him to combine his prospecting with making 'ethnological moving pictures of Esquimo life' that were shown at museums and lecture halls between expeditions.[64] As his obsession with filming began to supersede his interest in mining, he began using his lecture tours to raise funds for a film that would have more narrative thread than the usual observational travelogue, one that focused on one particular Inuit family and showed the significant events in their everyday lives. Finally obtaining funds from the fur company Revillon Frères, he set out in 1920 to film for sixteen months at a subarctic post on the Northeast coast of Hudson Bay in Quebec, Canada.

The star of the film was Allakariallak, a celebrated hunter of the Itivimuit tribe whom Flaherty renamed 'Nanook'. The film showed Allakariallak and tribe performing day-to-day activities such as mending kayaks, making fuel, building an igloo, eating, trading furs at a trading post, going off to hunt in their dogsleds, hunting seal and finally, as narrative tension was increased, sheltering from a storm. The narrative was structured by seasonal changes or natural processes in contrast with the fast-paced industrial routines of the intended film audience, yet parallels and identifications with similar routines in the West are hinted at, either by their absence or in small scenarios such as Nyla, Nanook's 'wife', cleaning her new igloo window made of ice. This combination of difference and identification made Flaherty's documentary unique and accessible.

Such 'glimpses' into apparently natural processes and everyday life, however, relied on some extremely hard labour processes. Flaherty trained and relied on tribe members to sustain the production of the film, as location filming in such extreme weather conditions was an arduous group task that no single person could undertake, yet the labour of Allakariallak and the Itivimuit, who were central to the creation and production of the film, remained unacknowledged and 'Nanook' is represented as an innocent 'noble savage' rather than a technologically savvy film assistant. Equally, Flaherty's insistence on showing hunting methods that were already outdated (the Inuit used guns in reality), the removal of evidence of Western contact and the manipulation of other cultural and historical details have led later film critics to accuse him of inauthenticity, deceit and colonial exploitation.[65]

Nanook's style and subject matter could not have appeared more starkly contrasted with the highly elaborate Hollywood films of the period; indeed a Paramount official rejected it as 'a film that couldn't be shown to the public' and four other companies followed suit, explaining that they couldn't distribute the film as the public 'were not interested in Eskimos' and preferred society films with people in suits.[66] Yet, when Pathé finally exhibited it, *Nanook* confounded all pre-conceived notions of what the audience wanted: the film was premiered at the sumptuous Capitol Theater in New York in 1922 and went on to become a huge international box office success.

As Fatimah Tobing Rony has pointed out, rather than a contradiction the film was a logical continuation of the discourse of ethnographic primitivism that was highly prevalent in all forms of popular culture throughout the early twentieth century.[67] *Nanook*'s popularity was reliant on its specific context within the highly industrialised film production system of the 1920s: to audiences at the time the film portrayed a heroic narrative of the individual (Nanook as well as the independent film-maker) fighting for survival in a harsh and unyielding environment. Flaherty's films personified a popular fascination with the pre-modern or primitive existence of those living outside of Western culture and his attempt to portray that life as unmediated and uncontaminated by modernity was connected to the anthropological critique of Western culture in the 1920s that aimed to highlight the purity of pre-capitalist existence. The drama of Nanook that unfolded provided a metaphor for the threat to traditional culture posed by modernity, a narrative that was ubiquitous in romance, comedy, Western, gangster, horror and adventure movies throughout the nation's movie palaces. That this individual was a brave 'outsider' who succeeded in his quest for survival could only have complemented other ethnic assimilation narratives and success stories that were prevalent throughout the decade.

Nevertheless, complex commercial imperatives and corporate finance drove Flaherty as much as any other film-maker and the film was not as 'pure' as presented. The fur company sponsorship showed up as product placements in a variety of scenes and the film was essentially made 'for viewing pleasure' rather than as a scientific record.[68] A 'Nanookamania' fad also followed the success of the film, represented in the popular Broadway hit 'Nanook' by John Milton Hagen and Herb Crooker in 1922, whose lyrics crooned over Nanook as primitive lover and 'uncultured' Valentino: 'My heart is calling/ Nanook! Nanook!/ . . . Ever-loving Nanook,/ Though you don't read a book,/ But, oh, how you can love'.[69]

The success of *Nanook* led to a generous Paramount contract for Flaherty to film *Moana* (1926), a tale 'of tropical simplicity, portraying a lost Golden Age, a garden of Eden implicitly set in opposition to the troubled world of "civilization"', which Paramount advertised as 'the love life of a South Sea siren'.[70] While Flaherty failed to repeat its success, *Nanook* triggered a spate of 'expeditionary' films such as Merian Cooper and Ernest Schoedsack's *Grass: A Nation's Battle for Life* (1925) and *Chang: A Drama of the Wilderness* (1927).[71] Yet, as William Everson pointed out, the path from *Nanook* led 'more and more to the entertainment feature and away from truthful reportage' and the educational potential of documentary was quickly undercut by the need to draw large audiences into the theatre, a sensationalism that formed the narrative drive of Cooper's and Schoedsack's later fictional adventure, *King Kong* (1933).[72]

Censorship

Although *Nanook* was seen as an educational and informative film and achieved widespread approval as an 'art' film, the prevalence of sex on the screen (increasingly couched in educational films as ethnographic examinations of 'primitive' behaviour) and scandals among Hollywood's actors led to a heightened sense that movie culture corrupted rather than uplifted audiences. Rather than portraying new heights of civilisation, some felt that the movie industry now exported and sold an image of America that was immoral, frivolous and demeaning. The concern went beyond national boundaries, as Peter Odegarde noted:

Almost 90 per cent of the moving pictures of the world are made here, and they go out to Singapore and Zagreb, London and Louvain, Constantinople and Canton. At the gateway to the Garden of Gethsemane, under the shadow of the Sphinx, within a stone's throw of the League of Nations, one can read the posters, Dancing Mothers, The Loves of Sonya, and Forbidden Paradise. The view of American life which they present is at best a distortion. They carry the impression that America is a land of millionaires and mountebanks, of cowboys and Indians, of cigarette-smoking, cocktail-drinking women, and sleek 'stacombed' men. It is a land of divorce and debauchery, bootleggers and brothels. Lust, greediness, infidelity, murder, malevolence, depravity – 'the wide world is invited to believe that the Statue of Liberty holds a red light and that the Tenderloin ends where the West begins.'[73]

For some time the ills of contemporary society had frequently been blamed on the movies but the 1920 deaths of the young actresses Olive Thomas (from a drug overdose) and Virginia Rappe (of whose murder 'Fatty' Arbuckle was accused and later acquitted) set in train a series of concerns over the possible impact of Hollywood lifestyles portrayed on film and in fan magazines.[74] Sociologists Robert and Helen Lynd reported that in 1925 high-school teachers were concerned about the 'early sophistication' of the young caused by movie-going and a judge of the juvenile court listed the movies as one of the 'big four' causes of delinquency.[75] That same year Miriam Van Waters wrote in her *Youth In Conflict* that 'The runaway "Josephine" and her craze for movies, is a case so frequent as to be stereotyped'.[76]

Fearing intrusive censorship by reformers such as George Mundelein, writer of *The Danger of Hollywood: A Warning to Young Girls* (1920), the movie industry created a self-regulating body, the Motion Picture Producers and Distributors of America (MPPDA) in 1922. Under the directorship of Republican Will Hays the MPPDA aimed 'to foster the common interests of those engaged in the motion picture industry by establishing and maintaining the highest possible moral and artistic standards of motion picture production'.[77] The resulting 'Hays Code' became a checklist by which film-makers could ensure that their products were deemed inoffensive and thereby made available to the widest audience possible.

Anxieties over movie culture were connected to rising racial tensions in society, as the industry became increasingly viewed as a 'Jewish monopoly' that was connected to conspiracy theories about Jewish control of the mass media circulating in popular culture: 'Mr. Hays will simply be the hired man of a bunch of rich Jews,' wrote the Reverend Bob Shuler in 1923, while another stated that 'It is a curious paradox that while the Jews are beyond question the largest single group of contributors to, and patrons of, the fine arts in America, the field of mass entertainment shows the peculiar qualities of Jewish solidarity and Jewish business in their least favorable light'.[78]

Fears over the effects of movies on the minds of the masses led reformers to turn to the urban sociologists at the University of Chicago to research the role that movies played in socialisation.[79] Chicago sociologist Robert Park was central to the planning of the Payne Fund Studies that took place between 1927 and 1929 and researchers Frederic Thrasher, Alice Miller Mitchell, Herbert Blumer, L. L. Thurstone, Philip Hauser and Paul Cressey were all faculty or graduates at the University of Chicago. The studies were based on surveys into the impact of movie-going on children's sleep, health, social attitudes and behaviour, as well as examining the moral content of the movies in an attempt to provide scientific data that would show the impact of the movies on the minds of urban youth. Published as a series of volumes in 1933 that were summarised in the popular *Our Movie Made Children* (1933), the studies were used to establish the necessity of increased censorship over the 1930s.[80]

Another way that anxieties over the effects of movie-going were channelled was in the establishment of the Better Films Movement. Reformers argued that the influential aspects of the movie industry could be harnessed for educational and social betterment, holding the First Conference of the National Committee for Better Films in 1925.[81] In *The Public and the Motion Picture Industry* (1926), William Seabury also argued that film-makers should be forced to make pictures that 'promote the moral, educational and cultural development of the people'.[82] High priest of consumer culture Cecil B. DeMille correspondingly made a series of high-budget and sumptuous morality epics with Christian themes – *The Ten Commandments* (1923), *Ben Hur* (1926) and *The King of Kings* (1927). By 1930 it was estimated that 'twenty-five thousand churches in America use the screen as an adjunct to the pulpit [and] [f]ifteen thousand schools, from kindergarten to college, are now making use of moving pictures'.[83] Other critics noted that movies provided immense potential for intercultural understanding in the new global landscape.[84]

Will Hays also claimed that movie culture reflected a national desire for social cohesion within a diverse social landscape and that movies were more than art but 'a great social necessity, an integral part of human life in the whole civilized world'.[85] The potential for education and uplift, as well as entertainment, did not go unnoticed by African Americans, who created and sustained a number of movies by black film-makers that addressed social issues concerning race. The most prolific of these was the controversial and independent filmmaker-entrepreneur Oscar Micheaux.

Oscar Micheaux and 'Race Movies'

Although anti-Semitism filtered into criticisms of Hollywood, racism and segregation remained entrenched both on and off screen within the industry itself. Most picture palaces segregated their audiences into separate seating areas or separate showings, if they allowed entry to African Americans at all, and the majority of Hollywood films portrayed African Americans with demeaning stereotypes.[86] While this was nothing new in the 1920s, the decline of independent, radical and ethnic filmmaking – all of which had served a diverse working-class audience in the 1910s – and the standardisation of the movies as a product of big business meant that racist stereotypes and exclusionary practices were further entrenched as minority film-makers were squeezed out of business. To one screenwriter, Perley Poore Sheehan, the rise of Hollywood onto the world stage was in fact a 'striking development in the history of civilization' and represented the culmination of Aryan migration westwards.[87]

African American groups responded to such white nationalism and cultural hegemony by creating their own productions and representations, most notably with *Birth of a Race* (1918), a response to D. W. Griffith's racist depiction of American history in *Birth of a Nation* (1915). Trends in mass migration and the rise of urban black populations also increased the demand for cinemas to cater to an African American audience, leading one 1920 headline to declare that 'Colored Motion Pictures are in Great Demand'.[88] The opportunities to profit from this new market led to a proliferation of companies purporting to bring about greater racial understanding and offer uplift to African Americans via the screen. Some white companies even disguised their racial origins in order to gain access to the market.[89]

Despite this, a number of African American film companies emerged to cater to growing numbers of African American movie theatres and audiences, including the Colored Players, who produced the all-black films *Ten Nights in a Barroom* (1926) and *Scar of Shame* (1926), and the Renaissance Film Company, who made short pieces on African American-related news stories.[90] 'Moving pictures,' said one journalist in the African American magazine *Competitor*, 'have become one of the greatest vitalizing forces in race adjustment, and we are just beginning'.[91] Of the small black film companies that emerged, Oscar Micheaux, creator of the Micheaux Book and Film Company in 1918, became the most celebrated and controversial. The movies and responses to them show the possibilities and limitations for filmmakers outside of the Hollywood mainstream in the 1920s, especially those who attempted to represent politically and racially explosive issues.

Micheaux began his film career during the 'Red Summer' of postwar race riots and violence that marked the start of the 1920s. His first film, *The Homesteader* (1919), was filmed by an all-black crew and at eight reels or three hours long, was the first long feature made by an African

American. Based on his autobiographical novel depicting the struggles of an African American homesteader trying to make his fortune in the Midwest in the face of racism and corruption, *The Homesteader* received favourable reviews in the black press, despite some objections to certain negative portrayals of African American characters.[92] Micheaux went on to make over twenty more features in the 1920s, all featuring all-black casts and dealing with topics that were central to African American communities, such as racism, passing, lynching, corruption and violence against women: *Within Our Gates* (1920) featured an attempted rape of a mulatto woman by her white biological father and an extremely disturbing lynching scene; *The Brute* (1920) showed racketeering and further abuse of black women; *Symbol of the Unconquered* (1920) exposed the workings of the Ku Klux Klan as well as internalised racism within the black community and passing; *The Gunsaulus Mystery* (1921) was a reworking of the Leo Frank lynching case, while *Deceit* (1922) and *The Dungeon* (1922) were also anti-lynching melodramas; *Body and Soul* (1924) depicted a sociopathic criminal imitating a Church minister, and *The House Behind the Cedars* (1925) was a drama of black passing for white. Unlike the films of the Colored Players, who tried to parallel the entertainment features, detective stories and society dramas of white Hollywood film-makers, Micheaux's films did not back away from negative portrayals of black characters. *Marcus Garland* (1925), a burlesque of UNIA leader Marcus Garvey, as well as *The Spider's Web* (1926), *The Millionaire* (1927), *When Men Betray* (1928), *Easy Street* (1928) and *Wages of Sin* (1929) fearlessly examined black vice, material acquisition and corruption within black communities.[93]

In the subject matter chosen and his methods of promotion, Micheaux courted and created controversy. Not only did his films address issues that raised the spectre of race riots and violence, making white censors fear his films for the stirring effect that they would have on black audiences, black middle-class critics feared that the representation of black villains, vice and corruption would reinforce the white stereotypes that they had worked to counteract and confirm white prejudices about black life. An African American critic of *The Brute*, for example, claimed that it 'magnifies our vices and minimizes our virtues' and that it was the duty of 'race producers to gladden our hearts and inspire us by presenting characters typifying the better elements of Negroes'.[94] Despite the fact that the majority of his silent films have been lost, contemporary critical opinions have remained contradictory: some see Micheaux's films as 'uplift narratives' that conform to 1920s individualism, where his calls for racial solidarity and black self-reliance were in keeping with Harlem Renaissance ideals, while others have seen him as a 'perpetrator and victim of Negrophobia' who used white typologies of race and bourgeois fantasies of capitalist success to structure his works.[95]

These conflicting views of Micheaux highlight the difficulties faced by African American filmmakers and also explain some of the narrative contradictions in his work, as well as his position as an ambivalent role model. The extreme racism that dominated society made it very problematic for black directors to direct or use white actors and film crew for their films, a situation that forced black directors to create falsely monoracial films in which narrative drama and tension between races became displaced or disguised in class or race tensions between black characters. Micheaux also faced repeated censorship that affected his box-office receipts: *Within Our Gates* was banned by state censors in several locations for its controversial depiction of racist lynch mobs and miscegenation, for example.[96] Always the intrepid entrepreneur, he used his role as producer of controversy to further promote his films and often had several different endings to show in different locales, a factor that would also explain the inability to make sustained interpretations of his work. Censorship and antagonism from black intellectuals could also kill a film, as the black press was vital to sustaining audiences and encouraging the middle classes to attend 'race movies', yet aesthetic appreciation remained underdeveloped where films were seen as statements not of the artist but as representations of an entire race of people.

At the same time, white movie companies turning out 'Negro comedies' and dramas that were enjoyed by black and white audiences alike also threatened to out-compete 'race movies' that dealt with serious issues. The central problem for those like Micheaux, however, was the lack of money and credit available to black film producers.[97] Critics' accusations that black films were literally 'poor' imitations of white movies were not unfounded, as banks were less likely to give credit to African Americans for the soaring production, promotion and distribution costs. In 1928 as sound films raised costs to their highest level, Micheaux declared himself bankrupt and turned to white financiers for his sound era films. Although he went on to make another twenty features, few of these addressed the issues surrounding racism, exclusion and black poverty with the force and power of his silent features.

Sound: From Film to Radio

The arrival of sound movies in the late 1920s created a revolutionary shift in cinema aesthetics and provided the industry with a novelty attraction that could be used to market old ideas and formats in new ways.[98] As movie orchestras were gradually made redundant, the screen musical rose to prominence as the most financially successful genre of the late 1920s. Even more successful than *The Jazz Singer* (1927), Al Jolson's next film, *The Singing Fool* (1928), grossed $5 million.[99] Despite the limits of the cumbersome technology and the fact that not all theatres could afford to be equipped for sound in the transitional period, studios clamoured to make further hits. In 1929 alone these included a series of musicals such as *The Broadway Melody*, *The Hollywood Revue of 1929*, *Say It with Songs*, *Broadway*,

Syncopation, Close Harmony, Movietone Follies of 1929, Rio Rita,
Glorifying the American Girl, Broadway, Broadway Babies, Dance
of Life, Broadway Scandals, Gold Diggers of Broadway, On with the
Show, Show of Shows and *Footlights and Fools.*

The coming of sound also necessitated costly adjustments in the
production process and appeared to have ended the silent era ideal
of film as a 'universal', visual or 'hieroglyphic' language. Jesse Lasky
described the adjustments that Hollywood studios now had to make
to retain their hold on the overseas market:

> The American film is shipped to France with the original scenario, and
> various specifications for sets, scenes, costumes and so on. When a par-
> ticular set has been finished, the American replica of the scene is shown
> on the screen for the guidance of the foreign actors, directors and techni-
> cians. Then the scene is filmed, and if it is to be done in all ten languages,
> the various players follow each other in succession, so that with as much
> economy of time, space and labor as is possible, ten different versions of
> the same episode have been screened.[100]

Such films were not only manufactured abroad on a mass scale, as
late as 1929 films were frequently made in both silent and 'all-talking'
versions in order to maximise their distribution, leading one film historian to call the era between 1927 and 1929 'a vast no-mans land of
hybrid productions' that were neither sound nor silent.[101] Directors
and actors were also reluctant to switch to sound. In comparison with
the silents, which relied on highly sophisticated and well-developed
visual story-telling and action, the talkies often seemed slow and dull,
saturated with unclear dialogue that did little for the action and made
only to cash in on the novelty effect of the talkies. Such changes in
production and exhibition proved very costly and companies relied on
further bank loans and stock investments so that when the Depression
hit many overinvested companies struggled to survive in a competitive
climate of increased revenue and lower receipts.

The coming of sound on film coincided with the entry of sound
broadcasting into the home. As the gradual disappearance of orchestras and live musicians from the motion-picture palaces took place,
this entirely new entertainment technology expanded into the musical
silence that was left in the wake of the 'talkies'. If movies appeared to
reflect the speeding-up of culture, radio entertainment appeared to
collapse time and space by making the very air 'alive with the melodies
of composers of all times' and bringing the world into the home.[102]

This sudden ubiquity, proliferation and domestication of American culture was unprecedented in history. Audiences no longer needed to leave their homes in order to enjoy the variety entertainment that was on offer in urban centres, and rural listeners who had previously had infrequent, if any, access to theatres or concert halls could, by the end of the decade, listen to operas, concerts, jazz, news, sporting events, lectures, plays, weather reports, stories and comedy shows on a daily basis. Yet as radio closed the gap between urban and rural, sociologists considered the possible effects of this influence not just in terms of a new cultural homogeneity but as a looming prospect of widespread urban contamination, declaring that 'whatever becomes characteristic of urban centers in one part of the country is rapidly communicated to other parts'.[103]

During the war, radio had been centralised and controlled by government for military purposes but once restrictions were lifted in 1919, the proliferation of radio in civilian culture was astonishingly rapid. Government deregulation at the end of the war left the field open for corporate intervention as companies such as Westinghouse and General Electric, who had played a major role in manufacturing radio equipment for the military, readjusted their focus to peacetime production by expanding into broadcasting and transmission to keep up demand for their products.

In the early 1920s, radios were constructed at home and often listened to with headphones, transmitters were not always good and programming erratic or of poor quality. The announcement of the 1920 Presidential election results over the airwaves and the coverage of the World Series (reported 'live' on air by presenters reading tick-ertape communications as they were sent to them) thrilled amateurs and showed the potential of radio as a fast and exciting new mass medium.[104] The Jack Dempsey–Georges Carpentier boxing match of 1921 became the first live broadcast of an international sports event, followed by the Dempsey–Firpo clash in 1923, all of which served to boost interest and sales to the (mostly male) amateur enthusiasts.[105] Radio shops, radio departments in stores and new radio magazines grew in number to cater to this mass interest, as the assembling of radios became a national preoccupation.[106]

From an amateur hobby and a single broadcasting station in 1920 the number of stations quickly expanded to over 700, broadcasting to 'fifteen million sets, capable of reaching an audience of forty millions' that were listened to by the average family for 850 hours each year.[107] Heralded as revolutionary by its fans, many felt that it was 'going to transform our politics, music, literature, and religion' and that 'no one factor in any art, at any time, has created the right kind of revolution so thoroughly and completely as radio'.[108] Amateurs continued to make their own sets throughout the decade but in 1922, the first pre-assembled radios went on sale, the 'Radiola', presaging the end of radio as an enthusiast's hobby. Even so, most were still powered by a large and heavy battery until the first plug-in radio in the mid-1920s.[109] An aesthetic response to the dialectic between tradition and modernity, radiolas were built to look like a classical piece of furniture rather than a modern machine and were marketed to women for their ease of use and attractiveness in the home, easing the domestication of the new technology.[110]

In the early years the majority of programmes were classical recit-als interspersed with readings or educational talks, but as Chicago became the centre of radio at the same time as the centre of jazz, the airwaves quickly filled with jazz, especially the popular renditions by Vincent Lopez and Paul Whiteman.[111] The introduction of improved loudspeakers from 1925 onwards made listening to music even more enjoyable, as families, friends and neighbours could gather together for popular music hours.[112] As technology improved, broadcasters and listeners became more mobile; the first car radios were manufactured in 1928 and improvements in microphones and transmitters made live broadcasts from non-studio locations possible.[113]

The radio and recording industries thereby played a central role in closing the gap between rural and urban cultures and intensifying the fetishisation of non-urban, 'authentic' or 'primitive' folk culture. As stations began broadcasting in the South, a folk and country music craze swept the nation, beginning with the first appearance of Fiddlin' John Carson on Atlanta's WSB radio in 1922 and followed in 1924 with Chicago's WLS first broadcast of 'The National Barn Dance', a show of live fiddle and square dance music that became an instant hit.[114] A year later, WSM in Nashville, Tennessee, began a similar live variety show called 'The Grand Ole Opry' that was soon being broadcast for four hours every weekend.[115] Popular songs transmitted from these entertainment programmes illustrated the engagement of rural areas with the tension between tradition and modernity in songs about bobbed hair, the Scopes trial, Charles Lindbergh's flight and even Rudolph Valentino's death.[116] Radio boosted the sales of phono-graph records of a new generation of commercial 'old time' musicians, such as Carson, Jimmie Rodgers and the Carter Family, making them nationally celebrated figures. The 'hillbilly' style that developed out of the mix of 'supposedly rustic white Southeastern American musicians with complex patterns of Northern urban industrial commerce' hybridised the old and the new.[117]

It was the founding of the networks or radio 'chains' that made radio a national rather than regional medium. The National Broadcasting Company (NBC) was founded in 1926 and managed to reach an audience estimated at twelve million with its first four-hour broadcast, which included orchestral and opera music as well as comedy by Will Rogers. In 1927, NBC linked up fifty stations across twenty-four states for an all-day live transmission of a Charles Lindbergh celebration parade and medal-giving in Washington DC, an event heard by an estimated 30 million listeners.[118] That same year NBC's example was followed by Columbia Broadcasting System (CBS) and between the two companies, 150 stations were acquired by 1931.[119] The prospect of international broadcasting also changed popular conceptions of speed and distance when in 1926, '[c]oncerts broadcast from a London club and from a New York studio on New Year's night were heard in Europe and in South America' becoming 'the first to half-girdle the globe through relay stations'.[120] Sociologists reported that radio made the world seem psychologically smaller and more interdependent than ever.[121]

The fact that Americans could hear the same information no matter where they lived led to fears that American culture was becoming standardised. Fears grew that the monopolisation of the airwaves could sharply affect political democracy as '[a]gencies of mass impression subject the individual to stimuli of sight and sound that may serve to make him think and act, in some measure, like millions of his fellows . . . [and] [w]ith the concentration of these agencies the control over his behavior is increased'.[122] In 1924 the national conventions of the Republican and Democratic parties were broadcast in all parts of the United States for the first time and two years later radio was playing a significant part in state elections: 'Radio is now in politics. Probably it will never again be out of politics,' stated one contemporary observer.[123] In *The Government of American Cities* (1926) William Bennett Munro reported that 'Literally millions of people hear the voice of the President when he delivers his public addresses, probably more of them than read it in the newspapers'.[124] By 1928 presidential candidates Herbert Hoover and Al Smith were using the radio to make campaign speeches and Hoover's inauguration was later covered in detail.[125]

Although sociologists were wary of the political uses of this persuasive medium, radio did seem to offer exciting new educational possibilities that contained a certain amount of 'cultural leveling: Negroes barred from entering universities can receive instruction from the same institutions by radio; residents outside of the large cities who never have seen the inside of an opera house can become familiar with the works of the masters; communities where no hall exists large enough for a symphony concert can listen to the largest orchestras of the country,' they stated.[126] By 1924, 151 colleges and universities had obtained radio licences and experiments in educational radio and home study classes took place throughout the country.[127] In 1928 the Radio Commission gave permission for the construction of a 'university of the air' broadcasting station in Orange County, California.[128] Other commentators reversed the image of mass audiences duped into low-brow or 'canned' entertainments: 'the taste of the people in music is much higher than was believed, and . . . the radio is going to be the greatest of all forces in the improvement of the general public's taste in music, art, and literature,' wrote one journalist in 1927.[129] Alongside education, the same article argued for the 'striking new possibilities' that radio held for religion, enabling 'the small-town church [to] listen in on the most celebrated pulpit orator'.[130] Radio was seen as a way of reviving traditional religious faith as numerous churches acquired licences and started broadcasting their services. By 1925 religious groups operated seventy-one stations, controlling at least 10 per cent of the nation's total.[131] The tension between the fundamentalists and the liberals played out over the air as radio became an increasingly popular way to preach to, and even heal, communities. As evangelists and revivalists such as Paul Rader, Aimee Semple McPherson and Father Charles Coughlin began broadcasting in the mid-1920s, radio ironically helped to entrench fundamentalism more fully in the isolated parts of the nation that would have appeared backwaters during the live broadcast of the Scopes trial from Dayton, Tennessee in 1925 (see introduction). Writing in the *New Republic* in 1926, journalist Bruce Bliven wrote of the paradox in this evangelical audience whose 'mental mediaevalism [combined with] an astonishing up-to-dateness': 'Its homes are full of electric refrigerators, washing-machines and new-type phonographs, its garages contain 1927 automobiles [but] [i]t utilizes the breath-taking new marvels of the radio in order to hear rigid doctrines'.[132]

By 1927 an editorial in the *New Republic* claimed that the cultural, educational and spiritual possibilities of radio had already ended as radio had become dominated by commercialism and chain ownership, which threatened to eliminate local talent and educational radio programming and had led to a 'timidity of broadcasting in the realm of intellectual and social ideas'.[133] One survey of the programmes of twenty stations found that in the ten smaller stations, 'out of 294 hours 28 were given over to talks, 77 to more or less serious music, and 189 hours were devoted to jazz. For the ten larger stations, out of 357 hours their offering was 56 for talks, 42 for serious music, and 259 for jazz. The proportion is about four hours of syncopation to one of education'.[134] After the mid-1920s shows were broadcast throughout the day and night. In 1925 the health and fitness guru and popular magazine publisher Bernarr MacFadden began a 6.45–8am callisthenics programme in which he promoted his magazines while improving the fitness of the nation. Regular comedy shows and serials began in the late 1920s – notably with *Amos 'n' Andy* in 1929.[135]

Commercialism also seemed to dominate the airwaves as corporate sponsorship became the most popular way of paying for the cost of putting on radio shows. In 1923, for example, the A&P Food Stores sponsored a show with music played by the A&P Gypsies, the first band entirely created by a radio sponsor.[136] Many more followed.[137] While direct advertising was slow to take off, companies sponsored, and even produced, concerts, dramas and shows as a way of indirectly advertising their products.[138] Because of this, corporate brand names became tied to cultural output with names such as the Maxwell House Hour, the Palmolive Hour, the General Motors Family Party and the Eveready Hour, available to a nationwide audience via NBC from 1927.[139]

Radio learned much from the corporate branding that had taken place in the film industry. Despite an understandable fear by movie exhibitors that audiences would stop going to the movies in preference for radio entertainment, before the coming of sound on film the radio often appeared more of a complement to than a competitor of the dominance of the movies. If movies brought new celebrities and ideals into the lives of audiences, radio brought their voices and sounds into the home. Hollywood producers paid particular interest to radio as a means to promote their products and their stars and as early as 1923 Samuel 'Roxy' Rothapfel (owner of the Balaban and Katz chain) broadcast the live vaudeville and solo performances that accompanied the feature film at New York's Capitol Theater.[140] The leading integrated company First National Pictures followed suit, while the larger theatres built their own in-house radio departments. By 1925 Warner Brothers went further and set up their own station – KFWB – in Los Angeles and WBPI in New York the following year, to promote their pictures and stars. Other companies followed and in 1926 Pathé News created a radio tie-in with its twice-weekly news service with an announcer narrating the main stories and features from silent newsreels in a programme broadcast to millions of radio listeners throughout the US, a method copied in MGM's 'teleshorts', broadcast in 1927.[141] In 1927 several production companies announced their intentions to create radio chains to advertise and promote their products, including the Paramount-Famous-Lasky Corporation and MGM-Loew. However, the Federal Trade Commission report in 1927, which censured the 'unfair methods of competition' employed by the movie giants, along with the Radio Act of 1927, deterred companies from operating in an overtly monopolistic fashion.

The coincidence of the success of *The Jazz Singer* (1927) and the headline in the *New York Times* that same year stating 'Radiomovies in Home Forecast by Expert' only heightened the competition between the two media and increased Hollywood's interest in radio programming, exacerbating fears over media monopolies.[142] Universal Studios' founder Carl Laemmle began 'The Carl Laemmle Hour' in 1927 and the appearance of the 'talkies' gave actors and actresses an opportunity to train their voices and adapt their audiences to the sound of a silent screen star. A Hollywood extravaganza, organised by public relations expert Edward Bernays to promote Dodge cars, was broadcast from Douglas Fairbanks' home in 1928 with performances and talks from the leading stars of the day, such as Charlie Chaplin, Norma Talmadge and John Barrymore, all accompanied by Paul Whiteman and his orchestra from New York.[143] In 1929 Paramount began a two-hour Sunday evening show called the 'Paramount Picture Hour', broadcast live from the studio lot.[144] Television had been anticipated as early as 1924, when *Public Affairs* reported that 'the television process whereby photographs can be sent over the wire has been perfected to such an extent that . . . it has been forecast by scientists . . . that it will be possible, eventually, to sit at home and watch motion pictures, or reproductions of stage performances, transmitted via radio with their full musical accompaniment'.[145] By 1930, it seemed, 'the mission of television . . . to bring to the home the panorama of life of the great world outside' had been half completed by the radio, which had 'already brought the opera, the concert stage, the theatre to the fireside'.[146]

Conclusion

The rapid development and consolidation of the movie studio system, the growth of corporate structures and the emergence of the 'talkies' turned movies from a 'universal' to an American art. Film producer Jesse Lasky declared that the motion picture was 'America's major contribution to the arts' and the meeting point of art, enterprise and invention.[147] The development of the movie and radio industries appeared to shrink time and space while creating a vast new arena for culture that had welcome and unwelcome features. Gilbert Seldes, for example, described the chaotic cacophony that radio had brought into the homes of millions of listeners as they turned their dials at the end of the decade:

> Maxwell House Coffee presents old Southern melodies; Mrs. Augusta Stetson talks about God-de; *Collier's Weekly* transposes its forthcoming issue into music and drama; the political situation is summarized by Frederick William Wile; dinner music is broadcast direct from Janssen's Midtown Hofbrau House; Aimee McPherson wishes that she could tell you how lovely Jesus has been to her; specialists speak on recondite subjects which suggest that they have collaborated with Robert Benchley; a lesson in Spanish from the municipality's own station; a plea for Jews to speak Hebrew; how to take care of an Airedale; Al Smith addresses newsboys and can't remember what year this is – waves, voices, personalities crowd each other, interfere with each other; a faint hum of jazz accompanies a Catholic priest; a prize-fight cuts into Bach; as you rapidly turn the dial from one end of the gauge to the other, you hear grunts and shrieks and the wild whistle of static. It is everything that America is interested in; it is America.[148]

Although one observer noted that 'the new age of electrical entertainment which will bring the artist to the public, the lecturer to his audience and the educator to his student body, offers a vast field of opportunity to creative talent', independent artists appeared more straitjacketed and controlled by the demands of the industry, commerce and audiences than ever.[149] As the mass media converged into fewer hands and became reliant on turning a profit for shareholders, artists outside of the mainstream were pushed further into the margins as the success of performers such as Clara Bow created new perceptions of class and social mobility. Similarly, commercialism and materialism had entered the homes of the most remote communities and the appearance of 'canned' and mass-produced entertainment that catered for the broadest audience was received with disdain even among the artists who made a good living from the industry. Without a doubt, however, the cacophony of sound heard from millions of loudspeakers that had simply not been there just a decade earlier fixed the word 'roaring' permanently to 'the twenties'.

Chapter 4

Visual Art and Design

If American culture appeared caught between two worlds in the 1920s, this was a drama that was clearly played out in the visual arts of the decade. Design styles, paintings, photographs and architectural drawings offered visual representation of the tension between past and present as artists looked for harmony and tradition in the fragmented or material landscape of modernity surrounding them. Tradition, however, came in new forms and where movies, phonographs and radio turned culture into big business, visual and graphic artists found new expression in industrial culture. As Lewis Mumford noted in 1922, 'With the beginning of the second decade of this century, there is some evidence of an attempt to make a genuine culture out of industrialization'.[1]

The perception that society had entered a machine age was central to the aesthetics of the decade: the widespread benefits and rewards of new technologies, transportation and modes of production appeared to have materialised in the postwar culture of abundance and the art that emerged celebrated the overturning of hierarchies, traditions and aesthetics. As one writer noted, democracy was machine-made: 'The time is past when any group, class, caste, or clique could hold a monopoly of art, assume the possession of taste and dictate the course of style. Modern distribution of the industrial arts has definitively removed all opportunities for the hierarchic control of art'.[2] The growth in mass production over the decade made high-quality art and the latest designs available to all and the industrial arts emblematic of American freedom and democracy. This perception underpinned the artistic explorations and celebrations of machine-made industrial culture that became the dominant theme in avant-garde art and aesthetics of the 1920s.

The Americanisation of Modernism

While the Armory Show of 1913 had notoriously introduced Americans to modern art, particularly cubism, over the 1920s modernist aesthetics took a decidedly American and vernacular turn. Alfred Stieglitz, the photographer, modern art collector and exhibitor, had been central to a transatlantic modernist interaction even before the show by introducing American artists to the European avant-garde from 1908, when he opened his Photo Secession Gallery at 291 Fifth Avenue in New York City.[3] Not only did Stieglitz gain a new recognition for the 'mechanical art' of photography as a respected art form during this period, he introduced many European artists to New York for the first time. Their encounter with the modern city shifted the centre of modernism gradually away from Europe. By the 1920s the avant-garde gaze was firmly focused on New York.

For most European modernists New York became the centre for art during the war, for not only did the art world continue to exhibit modernist works while Europe was fighting, but the city continued to expand upwards while their urban environments were being razed to the ground. American engineering feats and advanced technology gave speed and motion to everyday life, causing Francis Picabia to declare New York as a 'cubist' and 'futurist' city when he saw it for the first time in 1913.[4] To such artists America came to represent the new, the efficient, the industrial and the rational and instigated a series of works that displayed 'transatlantic fantasies' or 'Américanisme'.[5] These artists not only chose America as a symbol for their aesthetic vision, but in doing so transformed what many considered as appropriate subjects for cultural appreciation, beauty and art. To French modernist Marcel Duchamp in 1915, 'the art of Europe is finished — dead — and . . . America is the country of the art of the future'.[6] The destruction of traditional art and cultural values was perhaps no more apparent than in the celebrated display of an American-made urinal that Duchamp titled *Fountain* at an exhibition of the Society for Independent Artists in 1917.[7] Duchamp's iconoclasm redefined what could or should be considered as a work of art or culture and put the ready-made, mass-produced American object at the centre of the art world's attention, if not its appreciation. What Duchamp illustrated was that America had become art and that art had become American.[8]

The pace of industrial production following the war only accelerated this tendency to use American industrial culture and vernacular expression as a positive symbol of a machine-based democracy. Artists started to produce ultra-rationalised aesthetic representations of the machine age that linked modernity and American mass production more fully. According to the artist Sheldon Cheney, 'The extent of American reliance upon mechanized industry and of the use of industry in everyday life has no parallel in other countries' and the development of an indigenous and authentic American art would address this national landscape.[9] In his book *Port of New York: Essays on Fourteen American Moderns* (1924), Paul Rosenfeld argued that there was a thriving 'new spirit dawning in American life' that indeed ushered in an authentic national art.[10] Even to the 'Lost Generation' of ex-pat American artists such as Alexander Calder, Gerald Murphy, Stuart Davis and Man Ray, who spent much of the decade in Paris, the transatlantic gaze became central to their expression of a particularly American version of modernism.[11] A symbol of cutting-edge modernity, art that examined the industrial landscape of urban America emerged to celebrate the new cultural identity of the confident postwar nation while removing the shackles of European artistic and social elitism. In his *New Backgrounds for a New Age* (1927), a state-of-the-art summary of the artistic, architectural and interior design styles of the 1920s, Edwin Avery Park explained this connection between industrialism and the new Americanism, writing:

> Slowly we are emerging from the doldrums of artistic decadence. And slowly, as the immortal urge to create beauty, latent in man, comes to avail itself of the machine . . . slowly we shall have our own art, no longer a thing of the dead and buried past, nor a new mantle borrowed from our European cousins, but beauty after the pattern of our national individuality.[12]

Park summarised the hope that technology represented when he wrote: 'Surely there is beauty in much we see, in aeroplanes, steel bridges, automobiles, and steamships. There is beauty in scientific precision, in efficiency, in almost anything which may be used to lessen the drudgery, poverty and suffering of human life'.[13] This was more than just business boosterism in an era of intensified capitalist expansion; many artists saw industrial order as harbinger of a better world. Influenced by the French purist manifesto of architect Le Corbusier, *Après Le Cubisme* (1918), which presented a vision of society that functioned with machine-like rationality and harmony, as well as the concepts of the Russian constructivists El Lisitsky and Aleksandr Rodchenko, American artists and designers turned to science and technology to find spiritual meaning and beauty in the rational and functional forms around them.

Precisionism

The desire to depict a new sense of harmony from the indigenous or vernacular American landscape spurred the work of a group of American artists who were at first called 'cubist realists', 'New Classicists' and 'Immaculates', later becoming most commonly known as 'precisionists'. Differing from their European counterparts who shunned realist representation in abstract, cubist, futurist or surrealist art, these American modernists discovered abstraction in realist representations of everyday objects, particularly those associated with the functional or urban industrial environment. Precisionist artists produced geometrically organised art that eliminated almost all surface detailing, even their own brushstrokes at times, and used industrial or architectural themes to evoke the mathematical harmony and order of the everyday landscape, creating 'an aesthetic based upon revealing the pattern, organization, and design beneath the chaos of experience'.[14] Among this loosely conceived group called precisionists and objectivists were Charles Demuth, Preston Dickinson, Charles Sheeler, Georgia O'Keeffe, Peter Blume, Stefan Hirsch, Niles Spencer, Elsie Driggs and Louis Lozowick, whose interpretation of the American scene resulted 'in a highly selective realism, amounting almost to a formal purism'.[15] Precisionism reflected a postwar idealism in art based on the ability of industrialism to create a brave new world where want, dirt and disease were eliminated. These artworks depicted very few people, surface planes were pure, flat, geometric forms, steel was always new, lines always precise with little perceptible decay or even movement. This pristine vision of industrial America offered an ideal of stability, eternity, permanency, order and power beneath the chaotic shifting reality of modern life.[16]

The past, however, was not destroyed by this modern vision of America. Unlike the futurists who were influential over their work, the precisionists continued to engage with and reinterpret historical expression, bridging both 'native tradition and the modern vision'.[17] While the futurist painters had argued in their 1910 manifesto 'to destroy the cult of the past', for the precisionists the new vision was bound tightly to the emergence of an American national aesthetic that re-envisioned and re-examined it.[18] Along with industrial architecture and machinery their work featured American utilitarian objects and designs of daily life such as Shaker furniture, chairs, barns, pioneer buildings and houses. These paintings glorified American self-sufficiency, independence and democracy and further signified a detachment from the class structures and corruption of war-torn Europe. The term 'New Classicism' first applied to their work implied their aspiration to link the ideal past with the industrial present and to build on tradition rather than break from it. Demuth's oil painting *My Egypt* (1927), a depiction of Pennsylvanian grain silos, clearly illustrated this referential link between the landscape of industrial agriculture and ancient civilisation and is archetypal of the referential use of the classical past in the depiction of the idealised industrial new.[19] Although his title can be seen as ironic and the painting as an ambivalent reflection on the present, with its funereal implications a contemplation mortality, it clearly shows that the past was as important to precisionism as the idealized rational future. When asked what he looked forward to by a reporter in 1929, Demuth indeed answered 'the past'.[20] To the precisionists the past offered models that were not yet depleted – they admired and referenced Italian Renaissance art, with its preoccupation with architectural forms and structures and diminishing perspective, even while their work explored a new sense of time and space that had been opened up by scientific enquiry.

The epistemological shift that scientific knowledge provoked was examined in artists' representations of the physical world which explored new modes of observation that destabilised the viewer out of pre-formulated expectations by presenting the familiar and everyday in new and unusual ways. Like modernist poets, most notably William Carlos Williams, with whom they were closely associated, the precisionists aimed for scientific objectivity and precision of expression that would divest their work of formulaic or extraneous expression. Williams' notion of the poem as 'machine made of words' was closely connected to a visual precisionism in his writing: 'For poet read-artist, painter,' he declared in 1921.[21] Through Stieglitz, Williams developed a close acquaintance with the artists Demuth, Sheeler and Marsden Hartley that created a strong intellectual connection between American visual and poetic modernism. While the poets aimed for a use of words that paralleled scientific or technical precision, painters aimed for a poetry of the machine that expressed the emotional relationship between the artist and the landscape. When Williams dedicated his *Kora in Hell: Improvisations* (1920) and *Spring and All* (1923) to his good friend Demuth, in return Demuth visualised Williams' poem 'The Great Figure' in his abstract portrait of Williams titled *I Saw the Figure 5* (1928).[22] Both aimed for expression that was pared of all unnecessary abstraction and ornamentation in which they encapsulated pure meaning and direct communication.

Figure 4.1 Charles Demuth, 1883–1935. *My Egypt*, 1927. Oil and graphite on fiberboard, 35¾ x 30 in. (90.81 x 76.2 cm) (Whitney Museum of American Art, New York; Purchase, with funds from Gertrude Vanderbilt Whitney 31.172).

The art of the precisionists, with their focus on structures and detailed scientific observation, summarised new thinking about the relationship between science and perception or spirituality discussed by Dewey in his essay 'Experience, Nature and Art' (1925), who saw scientific method as 'the sole dependable means of disclosing the realities of existence. It is the sole authentic mode of revelation'.[23] At the same time he showed that 'science is an art' and art was both practice and theory.[24] New art and scientific thought were interlinking ways of expressing the experience of modernity when 'the traditional conception of experience is obsolete'.[25]

The development of the 'machine art' of photography was central to this changing perceptual consciousness and experience of both natural and machine-made objects.[26] By showing enlarged parts of objects or looking at the familiar from new and unusual angles, artists encapsulated Dewey's and Einstein's ideas about contingency and the relativity of space and time. Edward Steichen's *Time/Space Continuum* (1920) presents these ideas as photorealist abstraction – or in other words a reflection of the way scientific realism induces abstract thought. A similar aesthetic underpinned O'Keeffe's close-up abstractions of flowers and shells. Her paintings were undoubtedly influenced by photographs that she encountered once she entered Stieglitz's circle, such as Steichen's *Heavy Roses* (1914), *Pear on a Plate* (1920), *Pears and Apples* (1919) and *Spiral* (1921), or the close-up abstractions and still-life images of Paul Strand's *Bowls* (1915) and *Pear and Bowls* (1916).[27] While machine art appeared opposite to the organic objects precisionists commonly depicted, historian Barbara Zabel has shown that the machine aesthetic still shapes their productions; as organic subjects are deconstructed into their constituent parts the 'resulting abstractions seem to mimic constructive principles of the machine'.[28] Paul Rosenfeld also argued in 1924 that O'Keeffe's work had 'the precision of the most finely machine-cut products' even when depicting natural objects.[29]

Charles Sheeler argued that photography and painting operated symbiotically: 'My interest in photography, paralleling that in painting, has been based on admiration for its possibility of accounting for the visual world with an exactitude not equalled by any other medium.[30] To Sheeler, viewing an object through the lens enabled him to see reality in a new way, a sensation of unique perception that he then attempted to capture in his paintings. A subtitle of one journalist's article in 1926 about Sheeler read 'The Artist Paints with the Cool and Calculated Precision of a Scientist', and explained that 'Sheeler seeks to disengage, with a precision that at times seems almost surgical, the essential forms of his object from all the mere vicissitudes through which it has lived'.[31] Almost in opposition to the futurist aesthetic that attempted to depict speed, photographs froze time and exposed details that were not visible to a transient or flawed human gaze. Showing little movement or activity in a shifting, fast-paced industrial culture, the static and suspended imagery based on this photographic perception produced a sensation of something spiritual and eternal. It is this idealisation of reason and control that differentiates their portrayals of the city and industry from the chaotic and exuberant urban visions of futurism and cubism.[32]

Photographers had been interested in machinery and mass production for some time.[33] Not only was a machine (camera) used to create art (photography), but the industrial object captured on film was transformed into an aesthetically enhanced piece of art for mass consumption. Photos by Ralph Steiner such as *Typewriter Keys* (1921) and *Power Switches* (1928), and Paul Outerbridge's *Marmon Crankshaft* (1923) and *Telephone: Study of Form* (1923) or Paul Strand's *Double Akeley* (1922) and *Lathe, Akeley Shop* (1923) underlay Strand's sense of 'a new Trinity: God the Machine, Materialistic Empiricism the Son, and Science the Holy Ghost'.[34]

In 1927 Strand's trinity came to fruition when Charles Sheeler was hired by a Philadelphia advertising agency to photograph and document Ford's new industrial complex at River Rouge, creating a series of photographs that projected the plant as an idealised space of pure artistic and capitalist production.[35] Sheeler's background made him the perfect choice. From 1923 to 1929 he had worked as a freelance commercial photographer on Condé Nast publications such as *Vogue* and *Vanity Fair*, as well as various advertising agencies, producing photographs that propelled him to explore new subjects in his paintings and leading him towards an even greater photorealism in his art over the 1930s.[36] Along with Steichen, who saw no contradiction between aesthetic and commercial photography, Sheeler's freelance work imported the aesthetic concerns of modernist photography and precisionism into the commercial depictions of spark plugs, typewriters, tyres and soda drinks that he made for a variety of industrial employers.[37]

His worshipful attitude towards Strand's 'trinity' resulted in a celebrated series of thirty-two official photos produced of the River Rouge plant in 1927 that were widely seen throughout America. Albert Kahn's design for the factory not only represented the height of architectural modernity but created for Ford a self-sufficient, self-contained industrial city of 2,000 acres containing 90 miles of railroad track, 27 miles of conveyor belts, 53,000 machine tools in 93 buildings.[38] Every aspect of automobile production was covered, from the making and casting of the steel through to the manufacture of tyres, upholstery and car assembly. This huge city employed over 75,000 employees, though Sheeler's photos depicted few workers and focused on the machinery and the geometric structures of buildings, as seen in *Criss-Crossed Conveyors*. The few representations of workers that appeared showed workers dwarfed among the mammoth machinery, such as *Stamping Press* and *Ladle Hooks*. To Sheeler, Kahn's industrial design was a substitute for the religious expression seen in Gothic cathedrals and was expressive of a new idea of harmony and order based on function. In this respect he accurately reflected the prevailing business attitudes of the day, including President Coolidge's belief that 'the man who builds a factory builds a temple'.[39] Such intersection between the business and religious ethic was explored by Demuth's *Incense of a New Church* (1921), whose somewhat ironic title belied the industrial scene it depicted of smoke rising from factory chimneys.

Sheeler's photographs appeared not just in company literature and advertisements for the new Model A Ford car but in magazines from *Vanity Fair* and *Life* to international art journals such as *Transition* and *Creative Art*. When the photos were featured in an issue of *Vanity Fair* the article declared the Rouge to be 'The most significant public monument in America . . . and American altar of the God-Objective of Mass Production', confirming the widespread idea that industrialism represented a new American spirituality.[40] Terry Smith has noted that the photographs became part of a broader tendency 'toward aestheticising the new corporatist stream in American industry as a whole'.[41] Other photographers such as Margaret Bourke-White went on to produce similarly commercial representations of industrial corporations; her *Niagara Falls Generators* (1928) and *Chrysler Corporation and Electric Furnace* (1929) were equally devoid of the human labour process and presented a hygienic, idealised vision of the machine.[42]

Machine Art Exhibition, 1927

The idealisation of the machine and the ascendancy of American industry provided the key impetus for avant-garde expression over the 1920s. In 1927, however, a number of events presaged the unavoidable ascendancy and presence of the machine in everyday life: Charles Lindbergh's successful transatlantic flight, Ford's move to the River Rouge, sound on film technology and the first national radio network made 1927 the 'fulcrum on which the balance between the old and new tipped with finality in favor of the latter'.[43] Nothing more clearly depicted the utopian idealisation of the machine as an aesthetic object than the Machine Art Exhibition of 1927, a show of over 400 items in a display of 'crankshafts, meat slicers, airplane engines and propellers mingled with representations of skyscrapers in paintings by Charles Demuth and sculptures by John Storrs, geometrical black and white drawings of machinery by Louis Lozowick, along with works by European artists'.[44] Sponsored by the radical arts magazine *The Little Review* and held in Steinway Exhibition Hall in New York, the exhibition synthesised the machine aesthetic and articulated the new relationship between European and American modernism with Duchamp, Léger, Demuth, Sheeler, Steiner and Lozowick all on the board of directors.

Using the show to celebrate scientific rationalism and indigenous American practicality, organiser and editor of the magazine Jane Heap brought together all the world's leading exemplars and exponents of machine art, arguing that 'There is a great new race of men in America: the Engineer. He has created a new mechanical world, he is segregated from men in other activities . . . it is inevitable and important to the civilization of today that he make a union with the artist. This affiliation of Artist and Engineer will benefit each in his own domain, it will end the immense waste in each domain and will become a new creative force'.[45] By bringing together contemporary paintings, drawings and photographs of skyscrapers, bridges, docks, grain elevators, turbines, factories, machines, power plants and cityscapes and simultaneously placing real machines and tools among the display, the show highlighted the elevation of the machine to a work of art. Such ideas also illustrated the shift away from romantic concepts of artistic production by equating the artist with the mechanic or engineer. Stuart Davis, for example, claimed that painting or drawing was like building a machine: a 'picture becomes a thing of construction like any other thing that is made'.[46] 'America is pure practicality and utilitarianism,' he wrote in his journal, and the work of art that represented America most accurately was that which depicted the utilitarian object.[47]

The cover of the catalogue showed a machine design by progenitor of modernist machine art Fernand Léger, while ideas about the future of machine architecture were represented by drawings of a futuristic city by Hugh Ferriss, who later published them in his *Metropolis of Tomorrow* (1929).[48] Hand tools hung on chains from the ceiling and an IBM clock hung on a wall were surrounded by oil paintings such as *Business* (1921) by Demuth and Lozowick's stark black and white geometric paintings and lithographs of American cities *Pittsburgh*, *Chicago*, *Cleveland* (all 1923), *New York* and *Minneapolis* (1925), or abstractions of machine parts such as his *Machine Ornament no. 2* (1927) and *Dynamo* (1925–7).[49] To Sheldon Cheney, the exhibition 'was a first public and critical recognition that the machine and industry, fabled to have strewn the earth with ugliness, might have in themselves the potentialities of a new, hitherto undreamed-of art'.[50]

The transition from European to American modernity that this represented was underscored by Louis Lozowick's essay for the catalogue, 'The Americanization of Art', which stated that 'The history of America is a history of stubborn and ceaseless effort to harness the forces of nature . . . a history of gigantic engineering feats and colossal mechanical construction'. Lozowick saw in the 'intriguing novelty, the crude virility, the stupendous magnitude of the new American environment' material for creative activity 'in extravagant abundance'. [51] Beneath 'all the apparent chaos and confusion' of the American urban landscape, he argued, there was a 'rigid geometry' which expressed a beautiful 'order and organization', visible 'in the verticals of its smoke stacks, in the parallels of its car tracks, the squares of its streets, the cubes of its factories, the arcs of its bridges and the cylinders of its gas tanks'.[52]

Not everyone was convinced that the show accurately represented the vibrancy of machine culture. Journalist Genevieve Taggard argued in her *New Masses* review of the exhibition that it might be interesting to look at meat slicers that were usually watched in delicatessens 'with bored eyes' and that it 'may be that the machine has got to be stopped before we can see it', but the static and sculptural display of machinery at the exhibition lacked the 'dance or drama' of moving machinery and could not compete with the 'comparatively better show' of New York City that the visitor entered into as they stepped out of the exhibition hall.[53]

Despite this, the exhibition indicated a transition away from the trend in ornamental, eclectic or 'decadent' art deco motifs towards a new phase of American streamline design that characterised American architectural and design goals of the 1930s. The celebration of machine efficiency and order had a big impact on industrial design as well as consumer culture. To Cheney the display enabled the artist to 'let his consciousness play over the possibilities presented in the smooth forms, in sheer and gleaming metal surfaces' and 'exposed his soul to the factual realities of the contemporary machine world' heralding the beginning of industrial design as an art expression.[54] Indeed, it was in the same year Norman Bel Geddes opened America's first industrial-design studio and laboratory, followed shortly by designers Walter Dorwin Teague and Donald Deskey. Geddes argued that the industrial aesthetic defined the new spirit of the age, where 'the dominant force is neither religion nor the theatre. It is Industry'.[55] The Machine Art exhibition fuelled further exhibitions and trends in such industrial aesthetics, including two popular machine shows at Macy's department store in 1928, the first featuring 'airplanes, motors, accessories and instruments' and the second incorporating over 5,000 exhibits of 'art and industry' as well as offering organised lectures on machine art, exhibitions that were attended by over 15,000 visitors in the short weeks that they ran.[56]

Skyscrapers and the City

The industrial boom was directly linked to the visible expansion of America's industrial cities. Chicago, where the first skyscraper had appeared in 1885, expanded rapidly in the postwar period, doubling the need for office space and making the cost of land reach a premium. Building upwards rather than outwards was not only cheaper, however, it also gave companies the opportunity to display their success in buildings that in themselves became huge advertisements. Needing new offices, the *Chicago Tribune* created a high-profile international competition in 1922 that led to a very public discussion of skyscraper aesthetics that had lasting impact on skyscraper design for the next decade.[57] American architects John Howells and Raymond Hood won the competition with an eclectic and gothic-style design that spurred huge controversy in the design world, with its cathedral-like jutting buttresses that added no function to the form. While such attempts to accommodate tradition and modernity in design made the resulting skyscraper a controversial compromise, the Tribune Tower competition also released numerous visions of futuristic architecture and cityscapes into the public realm. As the *Tribune* published submitted designs and sought feedback from its readers, the skyscraper took on a new role as public and corporate art and readers were presented with exciting and adventurous blueprints for buildings that were finally erected in urban areas throughout the 1920s and 1930s. Although his design for the Tribune Tower came second, as a result of the competition the Finnish architect Eliel Saarinen moved to America where his visions influenced the design of many urban buildings including those that were to result in the Empire State Building, the Chrysler Building, the Daily News Building and the Rockefeller Center.

While Chicago had been the birthplace of the skyscraper, it was New York that was the symbol of change from old to new over the 1920s.[58] By the middle of the decade New York had become the largest city in the world. Not only was it technologically advanced and undestroyed by the ravages of war, it was symbolic of the aesthetic changes in perception that modernists aimed to convey in their work.[59] Land regulation and the zoning laws of 1916 – progressive legislation that had aimed to prevent tall buildings from cutting out too much light – had led to the development of a unique style of 'stepped-back' skyscraper that diminished in width as it went higher, leading it to be compared to ziggurats or pyramids of ancient civilisations. At the same time, the machine-made soaring lines and flattened planes of the skyscraper made it the key cipher and symbol of modernisation. In 1924 one writer in *The American Architect* declared that 'The Modern Building is a Machine' by virtue of its mode of pre-fabricated steel construction as well as the internal machinery that enabled it to function, such as elevators, pumps, pulleys and wires.[60] As 'machine art', artists and designers celebrated the skyscraper in their work, where the skyscraper and the zigzags it evoked appeared in designs and patterns for modern interior decoration, fabrics, metalwork, woodwork and ceramics, notably in the skyscraper bookcases by Paul T. Frankl and sculptures by John Storrs.[61]

Impressive soaring structures such as the Barclay-Vesey/New York Telephone Building (1922–6), the Delmonico Building (1926), the stunning black and gold American Radiator Building (1924), the Chanin Building (1927–9) and the Park Avenue Building (1927) provided a riotous medley of colour, shape and geometric abstraction.[62] Ornamented with spires or playful references to classical antiquity, topped with glazed terracotta or luxuriously ornamented facades and containing lobbies that were decorated with elaborate geometrical wooden veneering, ironwork, ceramics and bronze work, these were pantheons of the 'modern style' which merged functional machine art with playful references to pre-modern civilisations. The battle for attention between various corporations appeared played out in the emergence of new structures, where buildings such as the Daily News Building (completed 1930) with its geometric strips of white and red brick, competed for visual attention with the shiny decorative structure of the Chrysler Building, completed in the same year.[63]

With the corporate profit motive as the driving force behind the skyscraper and the availability of land limited, the mushrooming of the steel structures became visual symbols of the rocketing economy and dominance of business culture. In a 1925 article titled 'Titanic Forces Rear a New Skyline', the *New York Times* commented that workers were currently building and renovating over a thousand structures to accommodate the expansion in office space caused by the business boom.[64] Towering over churches, schools and museums, the rapid erection of the mass-produced, pre-fabricated, industrially inspired building was a testament to the triumph of the new over past traditions. The skyscraper not only became an extended and hyperbolic advertisement for the company that built it but a further symbol of the commodification of art and culture that delighted some and worried others. As Ann Douglas has noted, the rising skyline, radio broadcasting and aeroplanes transformed the very air into a commodity: 'Netting the sky was part of the imperial ambition of the time, of the invisible but all-powerful American empire taking over the world via its machinery, its media, and its near-monopoly on modernization'.[65]

Appreciation of this landscape of soaring structures or mass-produced objects often came from a distanced or detached viewpoint, most vigorously expressed by artists who were first-generation immigrants born in Europe. To these artists the city represented a living vision of modernist aesthetics, filled with dynamism and unrestricted by the formality of European class and caste traditions. Such transatlantic visions were explored persistently in the futurist-inspired work of Italian-born immigrant Joseph Stella, whose massive five-panel painting *The Voice of the City of New York Interpreted* (1920–2) summarised a superbly hyperbolic futurist vision of New York. Stella's five paintings attempted to represent the city on a symphonic scale, expressing the diversity, hybridity, harmony and beauty of the city in a panoramic movement that took the viewer on a 'tour' from the harbour, across the skyline, through Broadway to the Brooklyn Bridge.[66] In the centre the tallest painting showed the downtown skyscrapers. Placed next to this, the other paintings were 'stepped back' in New York skyscraper style, and represented a panoramic landscape in which he 'translated' and mapped New York for the newcomer and the neophyte. Yet the vibrant colours, design and scale of the paintings paralleled an 'old world' cathedral altarpiece or stained-glass window and bestowed the city with a vibrant spirituality often assumed absent in abstract modernism. As an immigrant who entered the city by Ellis Island in 1906, Stella's painting represents the passage from Old to New as an entry into a technological utopia, ordered, rational, beautiful and geometrically balanced, albeit magnificently detached.[67] As Stella was an admirer of Walt Whitman, whose poetry gained new popularity during the decade, the ambition and scope of his attempt to represent the city resembled the poet's desire to depict America in all its celebratory diversity. Like Stella, other artists attempted to depict the city in art of 'symphonic' dimensions; Paul Strand had been taking still photographs of the cityscape since 1915 and through Stieglitz, had met artist and photographer Charles Sheeler around 1917, who moved to New York in 1919.[68] In an attempt to extend their depiction of the dynamic city, Sheeler and Strand collaborated on what is considered to be the first American avant-garde film: *Manhatta* (1921). [69]

Paul Strand and Charles Sheeler, *Manhatta* (1921)

Although titled *New York the Magnificent* when it opened as a short piece at the Rialto Theater, New York, in 1921, Strand and Sheeler's original title was taken from Walt Whitman's poem 'Mannahatta' in his eclectic and expansive *Leaves of Grass* (1855–91)[70]. The nine-minute film observes the city over a single working day and is divided thematically into sections or scenes introduced by subtitle cards on which appear quotes from Whitman's poetry.

Manhatta begins with the subtitle 'City of the world (for all races are here), City of tall facades, proud and passionate' and shows the city filmed from the water in an approaching Staten Island ferry, replicating the viewpoint of an awestruck immigrant approaching the city in a 'narrative of arrival'.[71] As the title card then reads 'When million-footed Manhattan unpent, descends to its pavements', the ferry is shown docking and commuters flood en masse, with those at the front running to get to work, channelled shoulder to shoulder through narrow gates and bridges into the city. As the commuters disperse, the camera observes them from above crossing through Trinity Church cemetery, dwarfed by surrounding tall buildings and walking along Wall Street. This lingering image replicates Strand's earlier photo *Wall Street* (1915) almost exactly and is just one of many 'citations' or 'quotes' from earlier photographs of the city, including Stieglitz's *City of Ambition* (1910) that captured Manhattan from a ferry-boat.[72]

The camera transfers to one of many aerial views, slowly panning from the top to the bottom of a skyscraper. Unlike the fast-paced movements in the streets below, the only movement here is the smoke rising from chimneys until the camera enters the belly of the city, showing workers digging foundations for a skyscraper and perching precariously on steel frameworks among the geometrical webs of steel and cables, appearing like insects wrestling with huge cranes to move the steel structures that dwarf them. The camera then reverses its downward glance, beginning at the bottom of the skyscraper to pan upwards and show a variety of perspectives with smoke rising from rooftops, to illustrate something more eternal growing from this human industry. The camera eye then turns to the view of the river from the rooftops. The river appears as an artery to the huge organism of the city, with steamships transporting goods essential for the sustenance of a Leviathan. Iron rails then become veins for this organically conceived image, where railways lines and steam trains work symbiotically as a huge transatlantic liner is shown being guided into dock by tug boats.

As the viewpoint shifts to Brooklyn Bridge, human movement is framed by the arches and criss-crossed cables overhead, reminiscent of Joseph Stella's depiction in *Brooklyn Bridge* (1918). The camera turns from the river to an aerial view of the city and, as the title card announces 'where the city's ceaseless crowd moves on, the live long day', the camera roves high up over the roads and train tracks to show overhead views of cars, buses, trains and human traffic moving between the huge buildings. The crowd and cars appear as organic matter moving in a phalanx, while the distance of the camera eye conjures the dispassionate vision of the biologist Jacques Loeb, whose study of ant society informed the sociologist Robert Park's analysis of the city of Chicago in *The City* (1925). As church spires and cemeteries are dwarfed by the skyscraper surroundings, the replacement of the religious with the scientific order is confirmed. The film ends with references to spiritual, organic and eternal depictions of time as the sun sets behind luminous clouds above the river and the skyline.

The use of Whitman's text and the sunset ending appears in the end as an anti-modernist assertion of romantic longing for narrative closure, natural order and structure. Film critic Jan-Christopher Horak has noted that the ending exposes the tension between the 'modernist perspectives and a longing for a universe in which man remains in harmony with nature', causing ambivalent responses to the film.[73] Where some have accused the filmmakers of romanticism, others have accused them of over-rationalisation by focusing on the geometric and aesthetic to present an immaculate city untainted by labour and immigration concerns.[74] Yet rather than eradicating the human, the artists hint at the new unavoidable connection between man and machine and the unemotional camera eye highlights the sense of exile and detachment felt by the outsider, a vision notably created at the height of the 'Red Scare' and during the trial of Sacco and Vanzetti in which the city emerges as a wondrous Moloch, rather than as a harmonious sanctuary.[75] In bearing reference to the earlier city panoramas of both still and moving photography, *Manhatta* becomes a self-reflective panorama that exposed the artists' inability to show the city in its complex entirety. In referring to Whitman and the original Algonquin name for the area – 'Mannahatta' – Strand and Sheeler establish an American genealogy for their modernism while examining the alienation of origins and indigenous expression within the plenitude of social and artistic perspectives.

Although there were similarities with the travelogues and scenics that had become common in movie theatres at the time, the film's use of Whitman's poetry and its concentration on visual patterns, contrasts, poetic motifs and movement created a more symbolic and emotional rendering of the city than these factual or entertainment shorts. Yet, while non-narrative, it was not abstract in the style of later films, such as Fernand Léger and Dudley Murphy's *Ballet Mécanique* (1926), where collage, multiple exposures and other camera tricks were used to abstract effect. However, the focus on geometric patterns and the slowly moving camera eye created a deeply penetrating gaze that lingered long enough to reduce the real to symbolic semi-abstraction – a technique of reduction, condensation, allegory and geometrical fascination that was central to precisionist abstract realism.

Just as Strand had incorporated photographic 'sketches' he had already taken into the film, the movie became a series of sketches for paintings that Sheeler undertook after making the film. In paintings such as *Church Street El* (1920), the viewpoint looks down into the crevasse between the buildings and Trinity Church, replicating the image from the film almost exactly. Other stills from the movie were published a year later in magazines such as *Vanity Fair* and became the inspiration for his paintings *Skyscrapers* (1922) and *Offices* (1922).[76] Sheeler went on to work on ever more photorealist paintings of technological subjects as well as his industrial and commercial photography, while Strand eventually abandoned the machine aesthetic in his art to work on more natural representations. However, their film inspired further attempts to represent the cityscape on film. After *Manhatta*, a number of avant-garde filmmakers made 'city symphonies': Robert Flaherty, whose film *Nanook of the North* was the opposite of the industrial aesthetic explored by Sheeler and Strand, made the two-reel *24 Dollar Island* (1925) about Manhattan, calling it 'a camera poem, a sort of architectural lyric'.[77] Unlike *Manhatta*, which was circulated in Paris art circles by Duchamp in 1922, Flaherty's film was cut to one reel by the directors of the Roxy theatre and eventually used as a background projection for a lavishly staged dance routine called 'The Sidewalks of New York'.[78] Robert Florey's *Skyscraper Symphony* (1929) fared a little better in art cinemas that flourished in the late 1920s, which also showed city symphonies by European experimental filmmakers such as Walter Ruttman's *Berlin: Symphony of a Great City* (1927) and Dziga Vertov's experimental city symphony *Man with A Movie Camera* (1929). With the onset of the Great Depression the city symphony shifted away from idealised visions to more dystopian ones, such as Ralph Steiner's dystopian *The City* made in 1939.

As *Manhatta* showed, the skyscraper could be a symbol of both culture and inhumanity. To writer Stuart Chase the building could metaphorically swallow humanity via its oesophageal elevator shaft:

> The most impressive exhibit in the rebirth of art is of course the skyscraper, a pure machine creation. It consists of a steel skeleton made to mass production, hung about with a curtain of brick. The walls keep the cold out and the heat in, but they sustain nothing. The structure, moreover, could neither be built nor lived in without a machine operating in its esophagus — the elevator.[79]

This ambivalence towards the modern city as contiguously efficient, but also dehumanising, was also reflected in Lewis Mumford's assessment that 'The age of the machine has produced an architecture fit only for lathes and dynamos to dwell in'.[80]

The image of churches submerged beneath business towers in Manhattan only served to confirm that spirituality was swamped and swallowed whole by the new scientific vision of society. Yet although articles such as 'Neglect of Worship and "Machine Age Spirit" Are Causes of Anti-Religion . . .' in the *New York Times* in 1927 confirmed this view, religious bodies quickly picked up on the potential for spiritual expression shown by the skyscraper and embarked on a series of skyscraper churches in a number of cities over the decade.[81] A fundraiser for the proposed 'Broadway Temple' in New York announced 'Restore the Cross to the Skyline' and others declared that the skyscraper church was an excellent way to express worship – like a cathedral, the skyscraper reached towards heaven in a gesture of worship and supplication.[82] On completion in 1924, the $4 million Chicago Temple of the First Methodist Episcopal Church became 'the tallest church building in the world as well as the highest building of any sort in Chicago'.[83]

As Strand and Sheeler had shown, however, the skyscraper fragmented the experience of the city, which could not be represented or experienced as a spiritual whole or totality. To some this dehumanised the cityscape even further as the skyscraper was a 'building that one cannot readily see, a building that reduces the passerby to a mere mote, whirled and buffeted by the winds of traffic'.[84] Lewis Mumford complained that

> For the millions who fill the pavements and shuttle back and forth in tubes, the skyscraper as a tall, cloudward building does not exist. Its esthetic features are the entrance, the elevator, and the window-pocked wall . . . in short, it is an architecture, not for men, but for angels and aviators!'[85]

Stuart Chase concurred with Mumford when he wrote that 'one has to charter a liner or an airplane properly to admire [skyscrapers]'.[86]

Artists, especially photographers, however, were fascinated with new types of observation that aerial viewpoints allowed. The use of aerial photography in reconnaissance missions during World War I had created a new sense of scale and perception that was thrilling to artists.[87] The detail and accuracy of this way of imaging the landscape created new ways of mapping and seeing that were both mechanical and aesthetically pleasing. Hemingway wrote in 1922 that he 'began to understand cubist painting' only when he saw Paris from the window of an aeroplane.[88] Photographer Edward Steichen, who was the chief of the Air Service Photographic Section during the war, stated that aerial photographs 'represent neither opinions nor prejudice, but indisputable facts', offering science and order over the wasteland of wartime chaos and destruction.[89] At the same time, however, 'the defamiliarizing power of the vertical view' meant that photographs taken from the sky at great distances tended to create abstract representations of territory that made the land as strange as close-up perspectives made everyday objects.[90] To the Philadelphian-born Dadaist artist Man Ray, for example, the close-up and the aerial photograph created an abstract rather than a scientific vision. Perhaps responding to Duchamp's abstract photograph *Dust Breeding* (1920), which magnified dust until it had the

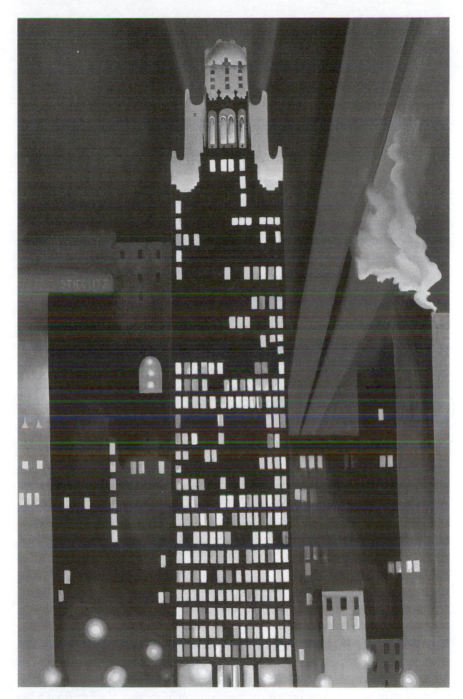

Figure 4.2 Georgia O'Keeffe, *The Radiator Building – Night, New York* (1927) (© ARS, NY and DACS, London 2008).

abstract appearance of an aerial photograph, Man Ray photographed from above the contents of an ashtray that had been emptied into the gutter. Titled *Transatlantic* and *New York* (1920), such photographs offer an ironic reading of both the scientific aerial view and the cityscape in a narrative of randomly produced American waste products.[91]

Georgia O'Keeffe's Skyscraper Aesthetic

New technologies of seeing and perception were central to the paintings created by Georgia O'Keeffe over the 1920s. In 1917 O'Keeffe entered the circle of avant-garde artists surrounding Alfred Stieglitz to begin a prolific career that spanned over six decades. While she is known mostly for her large close-up paintings of flowers, natural objects, rural buildings and desert landscapes she was equally fascinated by intellectual ideas concerning formal structures and the perception of time and space. Her close encounter with the art and photography produced by Sheeler, Strand, Demuth and Steichen propelled her to relentlessly pursue what Sheeler described as the precisionist goal to 'reduce natural forms to the borderline of abstraction'.[92] As their work from this period showed, however, these artists were fascinated by the non-natural formations of the cityscape as symbols to express both an exaltation and an anxiety over the new scientific vision of the world.

O'Keeffe's move from Texas to Manhattan in 1918 began a sexual and artistic revolution in her life and work. Not only did she begin an affair with the married Stieglitz and become closely connected with New York's avant-garde writers and artists, her encounter with Manhattan during this period forced her to reconsider ideas of time, space and visual perception that would shape the rest of her artistic career. O'Keeffe and Stieglitz moved to the thirtieth floor of the newly built Shelton Hotel, the tallest hotel building in New York in 1925, a building of the utmost modernity that aimed to 'eliminate all horizontal lines and leave only the soaring verticals'.[93] O'Keeffe had watched the building go up over the past two years and the move inspired her to try and 'paint New York'. Skyscraper living changed her experience of nature and reality, a sensation that she hoped to represent in her art from this period: 'When you live up high, the snow and the rain go down and away from you instead of coming toward you from above,' she wrote.[94] Her desire to paint the urban environment, however, was discouraged by Stieglitz, who saw the subject matter as a male sphere: 'I was told it was an impossible idea – even men hadn't done too well with it. From my teens on I had been told that I had crazy notions so I was accustomed to disagreement and went on with my idea of painting New York'.[95]

In a series of over twenty paintings undertaken between 1925 and 1929, O'Keeffe depicted the city that had become her home. Beginning with *New York with Moon* (1925), she went on to explore the city from a variety of perspectives in paintings such as *Shelton Hotel, New York No.*

1 (1926), *City Night* (1926), *New York – Night* (1928), *The Shelton with Sunspots* (1926), *East River from the Shelton* (1927–8), *Ritz Tower – Night* (1928) and *The Radiator Building – Night, New York* (1927).[96] Her decision to paint the urban was in defiance of the gendered prescriptions of art in the machine age, where the perception of an artist as 'engineer' or operator of a machine (photographer) coded art as a male pursuit. At the same time the move was also part of her engagement with a growing body of critics (encouraged by Stieglitz) who interpreted her work through a prism of Freudian ideas relating to gender and sexuality – in which her work was taken to represent private, interior, feminine spaces rather than the public buildings and spaces surrounding her. In painting this 'male' subject matter using the photographic aesthetic of her male contemporaries she rejected the privileged patriarchal gaze and connected her aesthetic to a female repossession of the cityscape. Particularly symbolic was the vision of the city at night where electricity and lighting now enabled unaccompanied women to roam freely for the first time. As a young woman in the 1910s, O'Keeffe had discovered that 'I can't live where I want to – I can't do as I want to – I can't even say what I want to' and only painting 'was nobody's business but my own'.[97] By painting the city she was reasserting her refusal to live by such restrictions and answering those critics who forced women into interior, domestic or sexually defined spaces.

O'Keeffe's 'mapping' or portraiture of the city was also a response to the restrictions she encountered as a female artist. As well as orchestrating a gendered critical response to her art, Stieglitz took almost 400 photos of O'Keeffe between 1917 and 1929, many of which were various close-up portraits of parts of her body such as hands, neck, breasts and torso. As art exhibitor as well as photographer, Stieglitz arranged and displayed these images, alongside her paintings, in exhibitions that created a composite portrait depicting an 'abstract language of womanhood' that placed her in a separate sphere to her male equivalents.[98] In a parallel with the aerial photography that had changed ideas about modern vision, Stieglitz mapped O'Keeffe's body in an attempt at reconnaissance, or deeper knowing, of feminine expression.

In *The Radiator Building – Night, New York*, O'Keeffe returned the male gaze and playfully challenged the sexualised interpretations of her work and artistic vision, as well as reflecting on the limitations women encountered in the 'scientific' age of liberated sexuality and freedom.[99] As Vivien Fryd has pointed out, the painting can be interpreted as an abstract 'portrait' of Stieglitz that responds to his creation of her sexualised biography and the portraits that he made of her in the 1920s. In *Radiator Building*, O'Keeffe reflected ironically upon such representation and scientific knowing: the building was the latest in design and technology – a 'King' of skyscrapers with its black facade topped and gilded with a 'crown' that was wired for stunning illuminations – yet, to the right of the building O'Keeffe placed the words 'Alfred Stieglitz' in bright red where the words 'Scientific American' had appeared on a billboard. This overlay reversed the visual possession coded within Stieglitz's 'building block' portraiture and reappropriated the urban patriarchal aesthetic by making Stieglitz the object of construction and scrutiny.[100]

Questioning the basis of scientific knowledge that was so deeply linked with masculine rationality and omniscient vision, her depiction of night illuminations such as lamps and floodlights showed that halos of light distract and create abstractions, obscurities or visual distortions, as much as they reveal. The bright illuminations create deep planes of flat darkness that make it impossible to view the surrounding visual field, indicating that such technology can reveal only partial truth. Windows, too, only offer the illusion of vision; while seeming to reveal what is inside, the eye strains to make sense of the shapes and forms that are hinted at rather than revealed. The fallibility of the observing human eye as well as the mechanical eye of the camera lens is also captured in *The Shelton with Sunspots* where the position of the sun created the optical illusion that it had taken 'a bite out of one side of the tower'.[101] The sunspots that dot the painting highlight the fragile position of the viewer not as an omniscient all-seeing eye but as one part-blinded and creating illusions rather than seeing reality.

O'Keeffe's paintings thereby articulated the complex social and psycho-geography of the intellectual New Woman of the 1920s. Her urban paintings reflected ambivalence towards the city, offering a tantalising illusion of freedom but hiding a menacing and controlling male modernity in which the female artist sits in shadow gazing upward at the phallic skyscraper. Despite this, her encounter with the urban also triggered her exploration of alternative female spaces and points of view in her large flower paintings that displayed an assertive female sexuality and rejected Victorian ideologies of separate spheres and the passive or virginal female. O'Keeffe's 'nature' paintings were closely connected to the new way of seeing that was inspired by her urban experience, illustrated by her claim that the inspiration for painting large flowers was to 'make even busy New Yorkers take time to see what I see of flowers'.[102] Although she abandoned urban landscapes when she abandoned Manhattan in the early 1930s, O'Keeffe's urban paintings from the 1920s are crucial to understanding her place in precisionist circles as well as the connection between visual art and new scientific thought as a basis for American modernism.

Popular Culture and the Machine Aesthetic

While scientific rationalism underlay modern art theories, art in the 1920s was more a complex synthesis of high and low culture, past and present, European and American. The blending of traditional and modern was most visible in the ubiquitous international design style that spanned the decade and beyond: art deco. The style reached its apotheosis at the Paris-based Exposition Internationale des Arts Décoratifs et Industriels Modernes in 1925, a showcase exhibition for modern styles in architecture, fashion, furniture, sculpture, ceramics and metalwork. Despite America's role as a symbolic referent in European modernism, it did not exhibit at the French fair. One government representative in Paris even declared that 'American manufacturers and craftsmen had almost nothing to exhibit in the modern spirit'.[103] Despite this, the exhibition had a huge impact on the American design landscape when selections from the exposition were put on show at the Metropolitan Museum of Modern Art in 1926 and then went on tour around the country at various locations. To Edwin Park the exhibition had 'made New York blaze forth in this galaxy of new color, these strangely designed fabrics and window dressings', and once the designs became popular, the mass manufacturing of the art deco styles increasingly blurred the boundary between commercial, popular and 'high' art.[104]

While the exhibition was a catalyst to the popular spread of modernism, art deco offered a perfect visual analogue of the tension between old and new culture. To art historians Charlotte and Tim Benson, 'the fascination of the style lies precisely in its confrontation of new values with old'.[105] Influenced by cubist and futurist art, incorporating overlapping planes, simplification of natural forms, collage and juxtaposition, or references to speed, streamlining, industry and technology, art deco styles were also peppered with exotic or traditional references and decorations such as geometric patterns and themes from ancient Aztec, Egyptian, Assyrian, African or Mayan cultures. Art deco was thereby eclectically modern and playfully classic.

Art deco quickly became a symbol of luxury and sophistication and Hollywood incorporated the style in movie sets and designs. Leading actresses expressed their modernity and exoticism by purchasing and displaying the style in their clothing and houses, styles that were quickly transformed into cheaper versions for mass consumption.[106] Although art deco objects were often machine produced, incorporating new materials such as plastics, pressed glass and chrome, some leading modern artists saw art deco design as an influx of wasteful and superficial styling that created a chaotic 'melange' or 'infection of ornament' that went against the aesthetic goals of American utilitarianism and industrial streamlining that better represented national design values.[107] Despite this, art deco themes and styles appeared in a multitude of arenas and even purists allowed themselves the luxury of decoration if they could see function in the form.

In common with art deco, many avant-garde artists also included an eclectic and irreverent use of popular influences in their work. The painter Stuart Davis charted such influences on his own work when he wrote that the things that made him want to paint were:

American wood and iron work of the past; Civil War skyscraper architecture; the brilliant colors on gasoline stations, chain-store fronts,
and taxi-cabs; the music of Bach; synthetic chemistry; the poetry of
Rimbeau [sic]; fast travel by train, auto, and aeroplane which brought
new and multiple perspectives; electric signs; the landscape and boats of
Gloucester, Mass.; 5 & 10 cent store kitchen utensils; movies and radio;
Earl Hines hot piano and Negro jazz music in general.[108]

While most of Davis's inspirations were the products of a machine
culture, the melange of influences he listed were far from the ordered,
rational or controlled visions of the precisionists. In contrast to their
machine efficiency, his juxtaposition and accretion of mass-produced
influences depicted a playful but absurd industrial wasteland more in
keeping with the eclecticism and ambiguity of dada and surrealist art.

Jazz music fitted perfectly into this conglomeration of mechanical
and natural influences and was, Davis believed, the musical equivalent
of cubism.[109] The role of African aesthetics within European modernism had been highlighted in the previous decade by shows of African
art alongside European avant-garde that Stieglitz had shown in his 291
gallery, but it was in the 1920s that jazz became particularly associated
with the new modern styling and art.[110] Symbolising youth, energy,
urbanism, dynamism and a rejection of tradition, jazz was both
manufactured and natural, urban and primitive, the music of mechanical precision, speed, syncopation and movement: purist architect Le
Corbusier even called New York City 'hot jazz in stone and steel',
illustrating the connection between a new sense of time, space and
rhythm in architecture with that in music.[111]

Jazz was referenced in visual art and design in a variety of ways,
from figurative scenes of Harlem or dance halls, depictions of instrumental forms or dancers, to abstractions representing the polyphony,
repetition or variation of jazz through colour. In his abstract painting *Jazz* (1919), for example, Man Ray used a collage aesthetic to
reference harmonic syncopation, as well as mechanical references
to timing, measurement and syncopated beat in his photographic
abstract *Admiration of the Orchestrelle for the Cinematograph*
(1919).[112] John Marin, Joseph Stella, Charles Demuth, Arthur Dove,
Stuart Davis and Aaron Douglas also explored the connection
between art, music and national identity in their works over the
1920s. Jazz was a metaphor for the urban fragmentation of experience that they 'conducted' into harmonic symphonies on canvas
and film. Joseph Stella, for example, used sound as a reference in the

title of his series *The Voice of the City of New York Interpreted*, which presented 'the city's colossal skyscrapers blended together in a symphony of lights'.[113] Arthur Dove's musical paintings *George Gershwin – Rhapsody in Blue part I and II* (1927), *Primitive Jazz* (1929), *I'll Build a Stairway to Paradise – George Gershwin* (1927), *An Orange Grove in California – Irving Berlin* (1927), *Improvisation* (1927) and *Rhythm Rag* (1927) portrayed jazz as abstract movement and colour in an attempt to 'illustrate' realistically the inventiveness, speed and restlessness of the music.[114]

For African American artists the Harlem Renaissance also provided a lively art and literary scene that created both work and inspiration. Dignified images of African subjects worked to counteract prevailing stereotypical 'old Negro' images such as the minstrel, 'Aunt Jemima' or the downtrodden slave that had been common in nineteenth-century illustration.[115] In his essay 'Enter the New Negro', Locke argued that it was central for the progress of African Americans to 'be seen through other than the dusty spectacles of past controversy. The day of "aunties," "uncles" and "mammies" is equally gone. Uncle Tom and Sambo have passed on,' he insisted.[116] Counteracting such comic and grotesque caricatures, German-born artist Winold Reiss's portraits 'Harlem Types' in the *Survey Graphic* illustrated African American faces with detailed precision and dignity and his Viennese style provided significant impetus for Harlem Renaissance artists to blend the geometric art deco style with folk art influences.[117] Reiss's portrait *Langston Hughes* (1925) depicted a serious Hughes with a book, drawn against an abstract geometric background of urban scenes and floating musical scores. Jazz was treated carefully and respectfully in these works in an attempt to avoid the proliferation of new demeaning stereotypes. New images of successful, educated, wealthy or fashionable middle-class African Americans were also created in the hundreds by James Van Der Zee, his studio portraits of African Americans in smart clothes and dignified poses providing visual evidence of the ascendancy and respectability of the urban African American, while his street photographs documented the vibrant African American life in Harlem in all its diversity.

African American intellectuals emphasised the influence of African art on European modernists to show the centrality of African-derived aesthetics to modern art and explored new ideas about the contribution of African Americans to modern civilisation.[118] Images created by Harlem Renaissance artists were vital in creating the new negro identity where African Americans could be seen both as modern and as bearers of ancient culture and civilisation.[119] Locke argued that 'in a powerful simplicity of conception, design and effect, [African Art] is evidence of an aesthetic endowment of the highest order'.[120] This idea was visually encapsulated in illustrations such as Aaron Douglas's 'Ancestral' in Locke's The New Negro (1927), which incorporated modernist abstract geometric designs taken from African masks and shields that were arranged around African figures. Douglas's illustration for the September 1927 cover of Crisis also portrayed an Egyptian figure holding a massive sphere towering above a geometric landscape that included skyscrapers and smoke stacks. In such images it is the African who is a progenitor of modern culture – both builder of and heir to American civilisation.

Aaron Douglas's illustrations for the African American magazines Opportunity and Crisis incorporated a jazz iconography that used flat black and white geometric abstractions to show abstractions of trumpet shapes, saxophonists, drummers and dancers surrounded by zigzags or sunbursts in a highly modern stylisation. Such 'jazzed' visual aesthetics were employed in illustrations such as Invincible Music: The Spirit of Africa (1925), Play de Blues (1925), Music (1925), The Judgement Day (1927) and Charleston (1929), as well as illustrations for Locke's The New Negro, Langston Hughes' poetry in Opportunity (October 1926), James Weldon Johnson's Gods Trombones: Seven Negro Sermons in Verse (1927) and the cover illustration for Carl Van Vechten's controversial novel Nigger Heaven.[121]

Fearing an overly restrictive and bourgeois tendency in the Harlem intellectuals' desire to control the images created of and by African Americans, younger artists such as Gwendolyn Bennett, Richard Bruce Nugent and Archibald John Motley Jr, as well as Douglas, looked to new avenues for expressing a diverse African American identity more freely. Illustrations for the breakaway magazine Fire!! (1926) gave some older black intellectuals cause to fear that '[v]ulgarity has been mistaken for art' and that the old stereotypes had reappeared.[122] Vulgarity, however, was just another term for everyday life to the Chicago artist Motley, who was typically influenced by the urban jazz culture surrounding him. The first African American artist to have a solo show in New York in 1928, Motley's figurative paintings such as Blues (1929), showing dancers in a nightclub surrounded by jazz musicians, Cocktails (1926), showing the black middle classes being served by a waiter, and Tongues (1929), a revivalist church scene, served to capture moments of African American daily life in an unprecedented way.

Commercial Art and the Art of Commerce

Although Stuart Chase claimed that 'whenever a promising painter, sculptor or writer, begins to use his talents for a brisker turnover in soap, teaspoons and silk stockings, the world stands to lose an artist, even as the bank stands to gain a depositor', commercialism and economic growth provided income and source material for a number of artists whose artworks increasingly reflected upon America's growing consumer culture.[123] The boom in magazine subscriptions and the creation of new publications, such as *Vanity Fair* and the *New Yorker* in 1925, was a boon for illustrators who exaggerated or satirised the culture of prosperity. The popular illustrator and cartoonist John Held became the most famous illustrator of the period, whose dancing flappers on the covers of *Life, McClure's, Collier's* and many others defined the image of youth, in particular the flapper, for the decade. Held's drawings portrayed the freedom and mobility of young women in angular line cartoons that gently satirised the clash between the morals and lifestyles of an older generation with the jazz age.[124] Ralph Barton also achieved success with his black and white cartoons and caricatures of popular figures such as writers, famous actors and actresses in *Vanity Fair* and *Life*. His cartoon *Filming the Ultimate Super-Nonpareil-Ultra-Cylopean-Ten-Billion-Dollar-Art-Spectacle-Masterpiece Feature With the Stupendous All-Star Cast*, which appeared in *Life* magazine in 1923, satirised Hollywood by showing all of the famous actors and actresses of the day trying to squeeze into one film set to create the biggest film spectacle of all time.

The huge growth of the advertising industry in the postwar period alongside new advertising strategies incorporating Freudian theories of human drives created new roles for the artist, illustrator, photographer and designer. Consumer objects could be made 'new' and alluring by the techniques that had been developed by avant-garde artists to create art from ordinary objects. Edward Steichen began as an art photographer in Stieglitz's Photo-Secession group but after the war became the most highly paid advertising photographer of the decade, working for the J. Walter Thompson agency and Condé Nast at *Vanity Fair* and *Vogue*, creating iconic images of 1920s consumer culture such as his *Art Deco Clothing Design* (1925) and *Douglas Lighter* (1928).[125] As Roland Marchand has noted, examples of cubism, vorticism, futurism, impressionism and art deco were regularly visible 'not through visits to galleries or even through art magazines' but in the pages of mass-market magazines such as *Ladies' Home Journal* and the *Saturday*

Evening Post where 'the newest work of such photographers as Edward Steichen, Charles Sheeler, Margaret Bourke-White and Anton Bruehl' were used.[126] Offering the combination of classical aesthetic values and machine-made modernity, Paul Outerbridge also combined art and commerce in his photographs of commodities for *Vogue* and *Vanity Fair*. His photos aestheticised and fetishised consumer objects such as *Jello Mold in Dish* (1923) or accessories such as handbags, shoes, stockings and perfume bottles in *Gloves, Mask and Fan* (1924) or *Mannequin* (1927), making him popular among the advertising agents as well as the surrealists when he visited Paris in 1925.[127] Surrealist artist Man Ray also undertook significant contracts in advertising and became well known for his fashion photos and portraits.

Artists saw in advertising a new form of American expression that encapsulated the cacophony of modern times and overthrew traditional cultural concepts and hierarchies. In his essay 'The Great American Billposter' (1922), Matthew Josephson saw the role of the artist as a composer of folklore out of machine civilisation and the cacophony and detritus of consumer culture.[128] Advertising agents concurred and described advertising as 'a humble picture gallery for millions who never see the inside of an art museum'.[129]

The avant-garde concurred with such assessments, creating art that addressed the new role of consumer objects or mass marketing techniques in everyday life. Murphy's billboard-sized oil paintings showed everyday objects such as his *Odol* (1924), an oil painting of a can of disinfectant with the slogan 'it purifies' on the side. In *Razor* (1924) he depicted ubiquitous and fashionable objects of mass production that were associated with the latest in modernity and masculinity: a Gillette razor, a box of 'Three Stars' matches and the first Parker Pen, enlarged to huge dimensions and arranged geometrically in a flat style on the canvas. A rich playboy and friend of F. Scott Fitzgerald, Murphy celebrated consumption in *Cocktail* (1927) and the transatlantic experience of modernity in another huge oil painting *Engine Room* (1922), made following a visit to an engine room of a transatlantic ocean liner. Originally titled *Turbines*, the painting was not an accurate rendition of a working machine but a composite image that reified the machinery in the abstract. American mass production was similarly depicted by Stuart Davis in his oil paintings *Bull Durham* (1921) and *Lucky Strike* (1921 and 1924), which placed mass-produced objects of everyday life – newspaper, pipe, Lucky Strike tobacco and Zig-Zag papers – into an arrangement representing the experience of an everyday encounter between the American mass-produced object and its mass-mediated consumer.

The booster spirit in art belied a deep ambivalence towards mass culture and the machine. Just as T. S. Eliot's *The Waste Land* had shown, the modern was a scene of haunting references to a lost classical culture that was now enmeshed with mass-market detritus removed from a logical context. Advertising culture in particular revealed the absurd logic of the visual landscape as signs became blank references to ephemeral objects that had already disappeared. In his photos *Always Camels* (1922), *Lollipop* (1922), *Rival Shoes Billboard* (1924), *Vanderbilt Garage* (1924), *Billboard* (c. 1926–9) and *Nehi Billboard in a Field* (1929), freelance advertising photographer and avant-garde filmmaker Ralph Steiner depicted huge advertising signs in realist abstraction. Like the huge billboard eyes of Doctor T. J. Eckleberg in Fitzgerald's *The Great Gatsby*, the billboards photographed by Steiner symbolised the shallow promises of a consumer culture that hovered over the industrial wastelands.

The New York avant-garde incorporated this illogical landscape into their work and in doing so both endorsed and undermined the mechanistic and commercially driven vision of art. By placing machines into irrational Dadaist abstractions in collages and paintings they changed the semantic meaning and purpose of the object and highlighted the absurdity of mechanised logic and rational thought. Man Ray, for example, hinted at the mechanisation of human and the humanising of the machine by placing a photograph of an eye on a metronome in his *Object to be Destroyed* (1923).[130] Such work remained committed to the idea of the artist as engineer, as an assembler of objects on the page, an idea that was especially relevant to Man Ray's production of 'rayographs', ghostly images of objects placed on photosensitive paper and exposed to light. Despite this, the artist/engineer was more fond of placing a spanner in the works than creating a rational order or logical sequence. The rayograph *Clock Wheels* (1925), for example, showed a variety of gears placed in unworkable abstract relationships to each other.[131] Other rayographs captured industrial objects such as combs, needles, lightbulbs, and drills in similarly decontextualised and impractical relationships. Utilitarianism also appeared undermined by *Gift* (1921), a flat iron to which Man Ray attached a series of tacks like a spine down the middle, thereby creating an inefficient machine incapable of doing the job that it was intended for. In *Rebus* (1925) he detached a component of a gun and placed it upright in a 'sculpture' that looks uncannily similar to a piece of African art, a work that both mocks the art world and shows the 'mass produced object as a modern fetish'.[132]

Like Man Ray, Gerald Murphy's oil painting *Watch* (1925) also undermined ideas of logical scale and time by magnifying the inside of a pocket watch in an unworkable abstraction of mechanisation, an exaggeration that according to Zabel 'critiques the control' of 1920s efficiency experts, making it 'an ambivalent testament to the postwar summons to order'.[133] Similarly his *Portrait* (1928–9) showed a mechanically deconstructed self with parts of a disproportionately enlarged eye, a foot, lips and a head intersected by the lines of rulers, a painting of painful dissection that shows destruction behind the mechanised vision of the human.

Other paintings provided comment on the construction of human identity by consumer culture. Stuart Davis argued that 'I do not belong to the human race but am a product made by the American Can co. and the New York *Evening Journal*', an idea that emerged in his 1921 collages of human figures constructed of consumer detritus surrounded by popular advertising slogans.[134] Arthur Dove's collage *The Critic* (1925) illustrated the figure of the cultural critic as a 'dehumanized product of the machine age' constructed out of newspapers and turned into an automaton with wheels/roller skates on his feet. His *Miss Woolworth* (1925), a collage of a woman made out of cheap consumer items available at the Woolworth chain store, such as gloves, flowers, stockings, insoles, a mask, a watch, ring, a brooch and a necklace, illustrated the construction of female identity out of consumer products. Dove titled his collage of chintzy mass-produced furniture covers, wood veneer and a page from a bible *Grandmother* (1925), another examination of mass-produced identity that reflected on tradition and sentimentality as a mass-manufactured commodity.[135]

Zabel has argued that such representations illustrated the avant-garde's irreconcilable goals of embracing and resisting machine-age culture. Indeed, ambivalence over industrial culture was visible beneath the smooth surfaces of much precisionist art and presented a visible tension in many of the art works, where the machine effaced the self-sufficient human past for an efficiency that rendered people subservient to, or dependent upon, the machine. The sociological photographs taken by Lewis Hine of industrial workers in the 1920s highlighted this tension between glorifying and vilifying industrial culture. In his *Power House Mechanic Working on a Steam Pump* (1920), the worker is dwarfed by the machine, his body is almost incorporated into it and his musculature and stance make him its mechanical equal, almost like an additional cog. The beauty of the machine is precisionist in detail

Figure 4.3 Lewis Hine, *Power House Mechanic Working on a Steam Pump* (1920) (© The Art Archive/National Archives Washington DC).

and abstraction, yet while the human is dignified by his adjacent position he remains trapped inside.

The isolation and alienation of human identity within industrial culture was most overtly depicted in the realistic scene paintings of Edward Hopper. Hopper was fascinated with the American industrial landscape and its incursion into the small towns and rural spaces of America, shown in paintings such as *Freight Cars at Gloucester* (1928) and *Box Factory, Gloucester* (1928). In opposition to the celebration of speed, dynamism and the consumer plethora, his works displayed a curious stasis and sense of unfulfilled desires. His paintings and etchings from the 1920s highlighted a deep insecurity beneath suburban and industrial change in which the human figure appears isolated in desolate surroundings or deserted landscapes, surrounded or trapped within an architecture of commerce and industry. In *Sunday* (1926) a single figure is shown sitting in front of a row of clapboard shops, almost but not quite in the gutter, and in *Manhattan Bridge Loop* (1928) a small single figure is shown walking against the backdrop of an industrial landscape, only just visible in a shadow on the left.

Industrial anomie is paralleled by sexual alienation in *Night Windows* (1928), a painting showing a partial figure of a single woman shown undressing with her back turned in an illuminated apartment window, creating a disturbing sense of urban voyeurism in the viewer. *Automat* (1927) also places the viewer in the position of a stranger watching a young woman sitting alone in an industrialised, automated cafeteria. Despite her overt modernity, the new woman in these images is lonely rather than liberated, vulnerable rather than assertive and sexually dominant, exacerbating 'awareness of the estrangement and isolation that has been fixed, forever, in time'.[136] In *The Drug Store* (1927) the fallible human body is only hinted at in the form of an Ex-Lax advert in the illuminated pharmacy window on an isolated street corner, deserted by people. Hopper's paintings thereby highlighted the anti-rational subconscious beneath the surfaces of machine-age modernism and that positioned the human even further from the machine environment surrounding them. As such, Hopper's America is very different from the precisionists with whom he is often associated; his landscapes and buildings show little nostalgia for the utilitarian past, and there are no glorified skyscrapers or modernist dynamism. To Hopper, there is little joy in the radically altered modernist vision, only detachment and isolation, where the urban and suburban main street are places of lack rather than community, a depiction that also appeared in the literature of Sinclair Lewis and Sherwood Anderson. While industrial artists celebrated the functional and utilitarian, Hopper mourned the emotional and spiritual losses of transient industrial culture .

Conclusion

American artists of the 1920s turned to the industrial and the indigenous to express a unique American vision that separated their art from its modernist European roots and asserted a forceful American identity based on self-sufficiency, utilitarianism and functionalism. The expanding commercial realm, the visible expansion of the city upward, and ideas about perception coming out of science and technology had a huge impact on the development of this new visual landscape. To many artists, the machine became an object of beauty and spirituality, capable of freeing humans of physical labour and toil and releasing them for higher pursuits. Artist and critic Edwin Park could thereby write of the most 'impelling beauty' of 'a dynamo room where in terrific silence tremendous, shining, encased engines perform an unseen task. Here is beauty . . . which seems above all things modern, animate with a mysterious spiritual significance'.[137] Such visions glorified production as a way of lifting humans out of the primitive need for survival into the realm of the cultural and spiritual.

Yet the dynamo and the machine, as Henry Adams, Eugene O'Neill and others also explored, opened up the doors to a vertiginous modernity and monstrous alienation that seemed to reach its apotheosis when the Wall Street Crash closed the factory gates and unemployment set in. Although Sheeler continued to pursue the industrial aesthetic more furiously, by 1929 many of his contemporaries such as Georgia O'Keeffe, Arthur Dove, Paul Strand and Edward Weston had turned their gaze from industrial to natural subjects, while others returned to figurative representations to better document the inhumanity and waste of industrial overproduction. The ideal of society and democracy based on technological fantasies began to diminish as the Depression became entrenched and people appeared ousted by the machines they had celebrated. By the 1930s, public, social-realist art that was created for the people and often by the people became a prevailing goal. Social and documentary art of the 1930s reintroduced the human into the visual landscape and the machine fantasy of the future did not recuperate until the New York World's Fair of 1939, whereupon it was abruptly interrupted by the outbreak of war. However, even before the Wall Street Crash had turned such machine dreams into nightmares of overproduction and technological unemployment, the alienation of the individual and the absorption of the avant-garde into what later became termed 'the Culture Industry' – with its incessant demand for the new in order to preserve the old power structures – had already been anticipated in artistic reflections on the erosion of traditional values and their replacement with a transient, commercial, mass-produced modernism.

Chapter 5

Consumption and Leisure

The expanding corporate landscape visible in soaring skyscrapers and advertising art produced an image of the 1920s as a decade of unremitting prosperity and machine-made pleasure. This booster landscape was sustained and manufactured by a dominant business ideology that entered into all aspects of social and political culture. Yet it did not begin in prosperity but with a serious economic crash as Harding was taking over the presidency. The transition from a wartime economy led to the collapse of wholesale prices, rising unemployment and a decline in business profits 'from 8 billions in 1919 to less than a billion in 1921'. The crash caused more than half of all companies to go into debt and commercial failures to increase from 6,500 to 19,700.[1] Such economic instability was disastrous for business and labour and, in the grip of the 'Red Scare', Warren G. Harding promised to correct and return the volatile economy to 'normalcy'. Harding blamed the problems on excessive government expenditure in war and over-dependency on unstable European markets and worked to replace these with a deregulated, laissez-faire, corporate-run economy based on low government spending, low taxes, trade tariffs and the widespread availability of credit to stimulate consumption and wealth. Declaring in his campaign speech that there should be 'Less Government in Business and More Business in Government', Harding appointed the millionaire banker Andrew Mellon to head the treasury on his appointment in November 1920.[2] Mellon cut federal spending and dramatically reduced taxes for the wealthy, while business was left to operate unhampered.[3]

It was a policy that appeared to be paying off by the time that Calvin Coolidge became President in 1923. By 1925 the frugal Coolidge, who had adopted Harding's policies but had distanced himself from the subsequent corruption scandals that had emerged, confidently announced that 'the chief business of the American people is business . . . We make no concealment of the fact that we want wealth'.[4] Whether wealth flowed because of their policies or because of a postwar production boom, the economy revived from the 1921 slump and, with only slight contractions in 1924 and 1927, boomed until October 1929.'

Figure 5.1 'Calvin Coolidge plays for Big Business' (© The Art Archive/Culver Pictures).

Once wartime restrictions on construction were lifted the expansion in domestic, commercial and public building works fuelled a whole range of further industries.[5] As well as increasing demand for labour and raw materials, new home ownership propelled the sales of household appliances and furnishings, as demand for modern bathrooms, telephones, electricity, lighting and heating increased. The electrification and modernisation of houses created a consumer boom in fridges and other electrical appliances such as electric irons, stoves, washing machines, toasters, kettles and curling irons, all of which were made more cheaply by an intensification of mass production and bought in unprecedented quantities. The role of the consumer in economic life came under increasing scrutiny by social scientists who noted that this significant social shift from making a living to *buying a living* introduced new factors into the economic equation.[6]

The newly established radio industry entered the market and expanded in value from $54 million to $177 million between 1923 and 1925 alone.[7] Economist Stuart Chase noted that in this period the sales of '[m]otor cars, telephones, radios, rayon, refrigerators, chemical preparations – particularly cosmetics and cleaning compounds, and electrical devices of all sorts have skyrocketed'.[8] The fashion and synthetic textile industries expanded as the demand for cheap ready-to-wear clothing increased, while the new popularity of cigarettes and make-up among women led to further exponential increases in consumption. To nearly everyone, however, it was the massive expansion in the automobile industry that presented the most dramatic revolution in the social and economic landscape. To Stuart Chase the automobile was the single largest force in the abundance of the decade and its proliferation helped to give the decade the 'visible appearance of a prosperity in which everybody seemed to share'.[9] Economist Leo Wolman noted in 1929 that 'It would be difficult to find anywhere in economic history so swift and pervasive a revolution' as the expansion in production and use of the motor car over this period: 'In 1910 there was one automobile to every 265 persons in the country; in 1917 one to every 22; in 1919 one to every 16; and on July 1, 1928, one to every 6'.[10] Such growth had boosted a variety of other industries and businesses, from highway construction to the expansion of filling stations, roadside diners and motels. Accelerating the speed of social change, the automobile led to new, sometimes troubling, social behaviour. Not only did the auto make living in newly built suburbs possible, creating a flight from the city by wealthier citizens, activities such as 'auto-camping' and automobiling became popular leisure pursuits among the less wealthy. Most noted of all, however, was the way the automobile became the locus of increasing sexual freedom and a private leisure space for youth outside of traditional social control.

Between 1923 and 1929 industrial production increased by a huge 40 per cent as a result of these technological and industrial conditions. The increased availability of credit and instalment payment plans for the consumption of everyday goods meant that many Americans were able to get mortgages, as well as buy houses, cars, washing machines, refrigerators and radios without saving for them first. While credit wasn't new, its widespread use as a way of selling mass-produced goods was. Over the decade the volume of consumer debt increased from $3.3 billion to $7.6 billion, a rise of 131 per cent, household debt doubled and home mortgage debt tripled.[11] By the end of the 1920s half of all households had one or more payment instalment plans. As consumer credit became more available many noted big changes in social attitudes to debt and saving; sociologist Robert Lynd found that the desire to possess an automobile had 'unsettled the habit of careful saving for some families' and that it was no longer uncommon practice to mortgage a home in order to purchase one.[12] In fact two-thirds of all new cars were purchased on credit. Movies even began to depict the 'perils and pitfalls' of the new credit culture in pictures such as *Charge It* (1921) and *Keeping Up with Lizzie* (1921).[13]

When, in 1926, it was announced that, with an income of $90 billion, the United States had reached 'the highest standard of living ever attained in the history of the world', the Coolidge years of prosperity were widely accepted as a sign of universal national progress and democracy.[14] In his election speech only twelve months before the Wall Street Crash, Herbert Hoover, Secretary of Commerce since 1920, claimed that the Republican policy was a self-evident success that had led to the greatest degree of well-being in the world and that America was 'nearer to the abolition of poverty, to the abolition of fear of want, than humanity has ever reached before'.[15]

The pay-off for this increased productivity and efficiency was visible in the increasing availability of leisure time. Coolidge saw this as a sign of machine-made progress, for where technology had 'steadily reduced the sweat in human labor' the 'hours of labor have lessened; our leisure has increased'.[16] Not only had Americans devised solutions to traditional problems of labour, housing, health and education, the increasing leisure hours that machinery made available had released humans from toil for more cultural pursuits, a victory that seemed to lead to a new and higher phase of civilisation.

By 1929 the boosting of business culture had attained the status of a new orthodoxy. As ex-stockbroker turned historian, James Truslow Adams noted in *Our Business Civilization* (1929): 'It is assumed that spiritual and intellectual progress will somehow come also from the mere accumulation of "things," and this assumption has become a sort of American religion with all the psychological implications of religious dogma'.[17] Belief in the success of the capitalist ethos went deep: in 1928 even muckraker and future communist Lincoln Steffens stated that big business was 'producing what the Socialists hold up as their goal: food, shelter and clothing for all'.[18]

Adams and Steffens were surrounded by a proliferating ideology of business that was particularly visible in the outpouring of books celebrating corporate culture as the highest achievement of civilisation. In *Business the Civilizer* (1928), marketing executive Earnest Elmo Calkins argued that business values had attained the highest goals of civilisation and had done more to promote peace, spiritual and social satisfaction and well-being than any previous form of government: the 'world gets civilized just as fast as men learn to run things on plain business principles,' he claimed.[19] Business and industrialism had enabled the arts and science to flourish and businessmen displayed their culture and learning through endowments and trusts that further helped civilise society. To Calkins, a civilisation based on business values represented the zenith of American democratic culture.

Not everyone agreed with this assessment. The new business dogma ushered in a host of difficult questions about the relationship between capitalism, culture and the role of consumption. In entering a 'money and credit age', argued economist Stuart Chase, America had allowed the businessman to emerge 'as the dictator of our destinies . . . he has ousted the statesman, the priest, the philosopher, as the creator of standards of ethics and behavior, and has become the final authority on the conduct of American society'.[20] Adams observed that America had become 'almost wholly a *business man's civilization*' and noted that the profit motive underlying cultural change was 'at war' with the traditional, financially disinterested, spirit of art and progress.[21] Not only did business 'facts' about prosperity conceal the gulf that had grown between the rich and 'average' American, he argued, but business idealism had turned the idea of attaining culture into something by which to profit further, rather than as a means towards spiritual and intellectual growth and fulfillment.

Writers confirmed and satirised the adoption of culture as a part of business capital. Former advertising copywriter William E.

Woodward wrote several novels mocking the advertising industry and business culture: *Bunk* (1923), *Lottery* (1924) and *Bread and Circuses* (1925). F. Scott Fitzgerald noted that successful cultural production was shrouded in business rhetoric: 'a successful program became a racket [and] I was in the literary racket,' he noted.[22] In Sinclair Lewis's *Babbitt*, the commercial 'artist' and poet Chum Frink proposes business sponsorship of a civic symphony orchestra, even though preferring jazz himself, saying:

> Culture has become as necessary an adornment and advertisement for a city today as pavements or bank-clearances. It's Culture, in theaters and art-galleries and so on, that brings thousands of visitors to New York every year . . . The thing to do then, as a live bunch of go-getters, is to *capitalize Culture*; to go right out and grab it.[23]

As Jackson Lears has noted, advertising agents like the fictional Frink began to see themselves as poets of the new corporate uplift and harbingers of a cultural modernity that merged avant-garde and commercial culture. Copywriters were described as 'agents of aesthetic progress' and the Shakespeares or Marlowes of their day by advertisers, a view supported by avant-garde writers such as Matthew Josephson, who saw them as pioneers of the terse and vigorous modernist style in literature.[24]

While fiction writers explored the possibilities and limits of a culture based on business rhetoric, the lifting of taxes on advertising outlays in 1919 led to huge investment and a rapid escalation of the marketing industry. The notable change in output was matched by changes in style, as the theories of Freudian psychoanalysis were applied to marketing campaigns. Much to the chagrin of observers like Chase, adverts switched from providing information about products to appeals directed at unconscious sexual drives, neuroses or social anxieties. The leading public relations expert in America, Edward Bernays, also happened to be Freud's nephew and had drawn on his uncle's ideas to develop techniques for 'democratic social engineering' during the war, later turning his attention to consumption and public opinion. In *Propaganda* (1928) he argued that this 'conscious and intelligent' manipulation of the unconscious habits and actions of the 'the masses' was a way of organising chaos and restoring democracy.[25] Since Hugo Munsterberg's *Psychology and Industrial Efficiency* (1913), American psychologists had provided advice and guidance about the psychology of workplace management. None, however, had applied this to advertising or consumption in the way Bernays suggested. Freudian analysts, he argued, had revealed that human thoughts and actions were often 'compensatory substitutes for desires' that had been suppressed; the intelligent public relations expert could manipulate the behaviour of these people by channelling those desires into consumption. Such public relations experts were, to Bernays, social engineers, who manufactured or engineered behaviour based on scientific rationalism in order to create social, political and financial stability.[26] In his *Public Opinion* (1922), Walter Lippmann called such new techniques of persuasion and social control the 'manufacture of consent', arguing that its use as a tool of popular government called for a reassessment of the idea of democracy itself.[27]

Marketing professionals now saw the findings and discoveries of social science professionals and psychologists as useful tools for dovetailing business with social reform goals, and led them to believe that real social progress could emerge from such an organised business civilisation. In this spirit, leading behavioural psychologist John B. Watson gave expert advice to the J. Walter Thompson company from 1920, becoming a vice-president in the company from 1924. Other business professionals were encouraged to update their knowledge of the latest scientific theories by consulting magazines such as *Industrial Psychology Monthly*, which began publication in 1926.

Despite these attempts to rationalise advertising along scientific lines, many felt that Bernays' propaganda techniques could potentially harm the gullible masses as much as guide them, by forcing them to buy unscientifically. Chase, for example, considered advertising 'the life blood of quackery'.[28] In *Your Money's Worth: A Study In The Waste Of The Consumer's Dollar* (1927), written with F. J. Schlink, he exposed the fraudulent claims and malign selling practices of advertisers and salespeople, in the first exposé of modern advertising techniques.[29] The psychological selling of goods gave them 'dubious' new uses that could not be proven or tested, he argued, forcing masses of unwanted goods upon unwitting consumers with false promises. While the book established the need for the national regulation of the advertising industry and helped produce a growing consumer-rights and trading-standards activism, many continued to fear the threat to democracy implied in the manipulation of the masses by unelected profit-motivated business forces.[30] To these intellectuals 'business' and 'culture' were contradictory terms.

Shattering the illusion of business uplift from 1923 were ongoing investigations into the 'Teapot Dome' affair, a high-profile scandal involving senior Harding officials in accusations of fraud and graft. Alongside the exposure of other corrupt dealings between business and government, confidence in those entrusted to run the nation appeared falsely placed.[31] Not only did the expansion of consumer credit and materialism lead to rises in loan sharks and illegal finance companies that placed people into the hands of shady dealers or gangs, stock market racketeering also increased as inexperienced investors joined the speculation game.[32] One *New York Times* article in August 1929 called such investment scams Wall Street's 'financial "speakeasies"', a term that hinted at the proliferation of a new and unregulated underground business culture that was pulling many businesses into the morass of the underworld. Indeed, prohibition-fuelled profiteering that sucked corporate, federal, state and police officials into an unregulated Darwinian struggle, brought into question the very possibility of a civilisation based on business.

The Culture and Business of Prohibition

Although twenty-three states had already been 'dry' since 1914, when the Eighteenth Amendment and Volstead Act came into effect in January 1920, the sale, transportation and manufacture of alcohol, though not its consumption, was made illegal throughout the entire United States. From one perspective prohibition appeared a victory of the rural, small-town conservatism of the southern states against the urban, ethnic North and a victory of moral uplift against cultural degeneracy. It was, however, also a victory for the forces of modernisation who had worked to adjust social organisation with industrial culture. The central role of the Women's Christian Temperance Movement in both the suffrage campaign and prohibition linked the two with the ideology of the New Woman, in which alcohol consumption was connected to the abuse of women in the home, poverty and the corruption of the working class. The race 'modernisers' in the eugenics movement also saw alcohol as a 'racial poison', a significant factor in 'race suicide' and the degeneration of civilisation as discussed by Stoddard and Sanger.[33] Great hopes lay in the ban.

Initially introduced to control alcohol consumption in wartime by the Democrat government, it was ironically the free-market Republicans who oversaw its implementation and who became associated with the dry crusade. As David Kyvig has pointed out, this was an apparently anomalous policy at a time of business deregulation that 'set a new standard for governmental intervention into personal lives'.[34] To many free-market businessmen, however, the law supported both the moral and the practical requirements of modern industrial culture. While all other business controls were loosened, strict control over the liquor trade was seen as a coherent part of wider industrial control over the working class and operated along-side other controls such as anti-unionism, anti-communism, 'efficiency drives' and welfare capitalism – all characteristics of labour control in the era. John Rumbarger notes that during this period 'most reformers and wealthy capitalists believed the transformation of American society into a productive order based upon capital concentration and a truly stable, reliable working class, required the creation of a liquor free social environment' where the working class were 'capital' or stock to be improved.[35] In a world where everyone was operating machinery or dependent on those who did, drinking was not only seen as potentially lethal but wastefully inefficient. In *Prohibition, an Adventure in Freedom* (1928) Harry Warner quoted teetotaller Ford as saying 'Booze had to go out when modern industry and the motor car came in. Only on one condition can the nation safely let it come back, that is, if we are willing to abolish modern industry and the motor car'.[36]

Despite this, the unenforceable law unleashed an alternate business culture that existed in a Jekyll and Hyde relationship with modern capital and legitimate business. As Andrew Sinclair has written, in 'politics and in business, in labor unions and employers' associations, in public services and private industries, prohibition was the golden grease through which organized crime insinuated itself into a position of incredible power in the nation'.[37] The problem ranged from the corruption and criminality of ordinary citizens to the corruption of federal agents, state officials and police departments – making it hard to decipher who was on which side of the law, who were victims and who were perpetrators. In order to catch bootleggers, federal agents used methods of entrapment that breached the boundaries of legality, and the official method of preventing industrial alcohol from being drunk by adding toxic denaturants led to further deaths and poisonings. Bootleggers created lethal mixes of industrial alcohol with essences such as juniper to create 'gin' or whisky-like brews that were sold in bottles with counterfeit labels, emulating mainstream marketing strategies to promote their 'authentic' products. Civilians turned against federal agents when innocents were gunned down in the crossfire with lawbreakers and bootleggers became local heroes by offering jobs and welfare to poor and immigrant communities, while black-market activities enabled uneducated or immigrant men to make a good living outside of the emasculating restrictions and repetitive tedium of either the labourer or the white-collar worker.[38]

Prohibition had opened up a new interstitial space between legitimate and non-legitimate business activities. By 1929 the police commissioner of New York City estimated that there were 32,000 nightclubs and underground leisure speakeasies. Such a climate made drunkenness a badge of social prestige and conspicuous consumption or a sign of individual valour against conformity and puritan repression. In reverse of the original goals, the law made people drink more in one go, drink more of poor quality and speed up their drinking in the fear that it might run out at any moment.

In this topsy-turvy moral environment a further paradox arose as mass production and technology made crime easier. The underworld was modernised and made efficient by machine guns and fast getaway cars, turning gangsters into machine operatives whose role on the 'production line' turned their leaders into self-made tycoons. To these men the business of prohibition provided an alternative form of upward mobility and success in a world where the gap between the rich and poor was wider than ever. Leading Chicago gangster Al Capone invested his gains in legal businesses and portrayed his activities as public service. His philanthropy made him a local hero when he gave food and coal to the poor or donated money to charity. 'Everybody calls me a racketeer,' he said, but 'I call myself a business man'.[39] Capone's corporate-style vertical integration paralleled the business models 'of the robber barons and trusts, with the elimination, through terror or murder or price cutting, of all rivals'.[40] The 1929 St Valentine's Day Massacre established Capone as the dominant leader of the Chicago underworld and revealed the hidden violence behind such business methods but he still evaded prosecution and it was only in 1931 that he was prosecuted, not for violence or bootlegging, however, but for the businessman's crime of tax evasion.

New sociological models of human behaviour and criminal psychology were developed in studies of immigrant and gang culture by Chicago sociologists. Frederic Thrasher's *The Gang* (1927) described gangland as 'interstitial', or a space that intervenes between one thing and another.[41] To crime writer Dashiel Hammett this space became a place in which the unwanted or unseen detritus and waste of capitalism gathered; a space he paralleled with the subconscious mind as it enacted the repressions of civilisation. In *Red Harvest* (1929) the city is a social and moral wasteland ('Poisonville') in which the mindless destruction of gangland killings mirrors the mechanical destruction of humanity on the production line. As his 'Continental Op' investigates this underbelly of capitalist culture the latent subconscious or primitive drives that are released are barely contained beneath a thin veneer of civilisation, a social dialectic that was replicated within the individual as a battle between the ego and id.

While Herbert Hoover called prohibition 'a great social and economic experiment, noble in motive and far-reaching in purpose', the plan was not only failing but had paradoxically contributed to further cultural decline. The experiment had gone so badly wrong that by 1933 demands for repeal even came from those who had formerly supported it.[42] Despite this it was the Great Depression that gave impetus to the nullification of the law. 'Wets' partly blamed the economic collapse on prohibition by arguing that not only had it furthered rural poverty by curtailing the brewing industry and lessening the demand for grain but that the loss of government revenue in liquor taxes and the cost of law reinforcement had also weakened the federal coffers. In the end, it seemed, it was a business argument that hammered the final nail into the 'dry' coffin.

While prohibitionists such as Irving Fisher argued that the 18th amendment had helped to create current prosperity levels and had added an additional $6 billion to the national income, the emergence of a deregulated black-market economy proved costly to federal and state governments.[43] The results of such a failure provided troubling parallels with legitimate but cutthroat business operations in a time of decreasing union protection for workers, for while it could not be denied that the free market had created huge prosperity the uneven distribution of that wealth into the pockets of the few was creating a potential disaster. By 1929 the richest tenth of the nation received almost 40 per cent of the national income, leaving well over half of the country's households in a condition of economic hardship and living below the 'decent standard' drawn up by the Bureau of Statistics.[44]

Not everyone ignored the inequalities that had arisen in the economy. In *Prosperity: Fact or Myth* (1929), a book completed just before the Wall Street Crash, Stuart Chase attempted to look behind the dogma of prosperity 'to find out what this period of alleged prosperity has meant to the man on the street, and to his family'. His popular book disclosed what economic studies were starting to reveal about the nature of business prosperity: real wealth had been generated but it was not spread evenly and the reality was a widening gulf between the rich, the middle-income and the poor, between urban and rural populations all of whom were reliant on an unstable credit economy to sustain rising modern standards of living. As one lecturer noted just four months before the Wall Street Crash: 'This myth of prosperity if believed will lead to inevitable catastrophe. America's prosperity is for only 24 per cent of the people, and this percentage owns all the wealth of this country'.[45]

The harshest reality behind the myth lay in the farming depression that hit rural communities for the entire decade. From 1920 the price of staple crops had plummeted while high interest rates on wartime loans, taken out in order to mechanise and increase farming efficiency, had increased the cost of production and distribution. Mechanisation and scientific innovations that made farming more efficient also created surpluses of food and labour, leading to markets flooded with cheaper agricultural products and the 'technological unemployment' of manual labour. Wage labourers, tenant farmers and sharecroppers were already trapped in a cycle of debt peonage that a series of natural disasters such as drought, crop diseases and poor harvests made even worse. Rural communities had become increasingly indebted and by 1929 more than 40 per cent of the total farm population living on low-value farms '[had] not improved their standards of living in the period under review, and [appeared] to have sustained such standards as they have by the use of a vast mortgage indebtedness'.[46] The crisis in rural areas, in which almost 50 per cent of Americans still lived, created a deep divide through the culture of prosperity.

While the urban working classes fared better overall than the rural poor, gaining from the low food prices that afflicted farmers, as well as rising wages and the expansion of corporate welfare, unemployment remained a prominent spectre and unskilled industrial labour made almost as few gains as farm workers. As industries relied increasingly on the unpredictable retail of fashions, fads and trends, the certainty of regular work and profits diminished. In most industries closures, shutdowns and reliance on casual labour were common tactics for making savings in slow periods or to weaken union activity and keep wages down.[47] Not only were unions weakened in this period, working conditions were increasingly strenuous and subject to increased control by 'efficiency experts' and corporate managers. Many industrial workers failed to benefit from expanded production or consumption as technology made fewer workers necessary and depressions in the cotton, woollen and coal industries held down prices and wages, leading to industrial unrest in the coal and railroad industries in 1922 and in textiles in 1929. To these workers the 'electric' revolution in households was sustained at the expense of the miners by cheap coal and low wages, while the production of cheap ready-to-wear fashions came at the cost of low wages in southern mills.

Such imbalances and potential instabilities were addressed in a number of publications that eventually contributed to the regulation of the economy by the New Deal government in the 1930s. Rather than criticising excessive spending, William Trufant Foster, an educator and former student of John Dewey, and businessman Waddill Catchings developed a theory of underconsumptionism as the root cause of economic problems, a theory that predicted the Wall Street Crash and gave them added credence in the 1930s. They wrote a series of books to address the inadequacies of the free market based on unregulated consumption: *Money* (1923), *Profits* (1925), *Business Without a Buyer* (1927) and *The Road to Plenty* (1928) which argued for a greater balance in the distribution of industrial prosperity by controlling and regulating the flow of money. In this way a form of rationalised and universal consumption would balance production. One way of doing this was through a federal advisory board consisting of economists, business leaders and planners who would create financial regulation through a government-sponsored public works programme.[48]

None of these ideas questioned private ownership of businesses, capitalism or the importance of increasing profits and competition. Rather, stabilising and regulating the capitalist economy was central to these planners and reformers, who increasingly focused on the panacea of a reformed and educated consumer. Chase's *The Tragedy of Waste* (1925) was concerned with controlling the waste and inefficiencies of consumerism and the unregulated commercial market in order to make corporate culture stronger and more scientific. Chase's exposure of the myths behind prosperity and the unregulated market in *Prosperity: Fact or Myth* was indebted to the findings of the most influential study made of work, consumption and leisure in the 1920s: Robert and Helen Lynd's *Middletown* (1929).

Middletown (1929)

Economic and social balance was central to the social ideals of Robert Lynd and Helen Merrell Lynd, who undertook fieldwork in Muncie, Indiana, for *Middletown: A Study in Contemporary American Culture* (1929), the first statistical and social analysis of the 'average' or ordinary aspects of American life. Unlike other social scientists at the time, the Lynds consciously set out to select the most 'middle-of-the-road' place for their study, somewhere with 'no outstanding peculiarities or acute local problems that would mark it off from the mid-channel'.[49] They relied on the philosopher John Dewey for their methodology and even their choice of a Midwestern location, who saw the Midwest as a 'common denominator' or 'mean' that 'held things together and [gave] unity and stability' to America.[50] They further sought the most average city in that region, a place with a small, homogenous population of mainly white native-born Americans that was as representative as possible of 'traditional' America. In this context they hoped to illustrate what had happened to typical Americans in the crucible of industrial modernity.

The study compared life in the small Midwestern city of 1925 with how it had been in the 1890s, charting growth and social change in order to illustrate the impact of modernity on society and behaviour. The Lynds' aim to record only 'observed phenomena' and create a dynamic and 'functional study of the contemporary life of this specific American community' accorded intellectually with pragmatist philosophy and experimentalism, as well as the work of the economist-sociologist Thorstein Veblen, whose *Theory of the Leisure Class* (1899) had earlier explored the social and psychological trends of consumer modernity.[51] Rather than imposing their beliefs on the community, the researchers undertook a modern self-reflective approach, openly questioning their methodologies as they proceeded and claiming to show the reader 'where the ice is thin'.[52] In the appendix 'Note on Method', details were given about the way that data was collected so that the reader could judge how representative or accurate it was for themselves. Information was gathered from a number of extensive personal interviews and reports from representative individuals using lengthy questionnaires rather than outside observations. Research staff entered into and became part of the community, living locally in rented accommodation and attending dinners, meetings, rallies and parties and then writing up a record of this experience. Census data, surveys, city records, business reports, local histories, local newspapers and the minutes of various meetings provided additional statistical information, while diaries, scrapbooks and casual conversations provided more anecdotal or personal perspectives. As trends became apparent the researchers tested various hypotheses on their chosen groups to see if a common standard or average type could be drawn up. From this data *Middletown* emerged.

Divided into six main 'life activities': 'Getting a Living', 'Making a Home', 'Training the Young', 'Using Leisure', 'Engaging in Religious Practices' and 'Engaging in Community Practices', it was the first attempt at a cultural or anthropological examination of everyday life in an entire American city and subsequently became the most celebrated sociological study of the 1920s. While a comparison of the years 1890 and 1924 structured the book, making it an extensive documentation of the dialectic between traditional and industrial culture, the most interesting comparative aspect of the research emerged in the lived experience of class differences that underlay American 'normalcy'. The study was unique in the way that it examined income differentials, social and religious beliefs, diets, education, leisure, group memberships and common activities in various class, age and gender groups of ordinary people. Offering detailed descriptions of the minutiae of lives, what people read, what their houses looked like, what art they had on their walls, whether they had carpet or linoleum, servants or machines, their working and their leisure activities, the book illustrated the varying class experience behind consumer homogeneity. While they found little unrest or agitation, this method exposed the network of consensual and habitual activity that kept capitalism functioning effectively even when its rewards were unevenly distributed.

Although the Lynds exposed the class difference behind industrial culture, they also discovered an increasing standardisation in attitudes and behaviour among all groups that gave them cause for concern. Where people had once made and built the things they used, money was now earned by business manipulation in a credit economy that forced the working class into mechanical servitude to a money-making culture. Where the citizen of 1890 had dreaded the stigma of debt, the Lynds showed that in 1925 they now blindly accepted the expansion of a credit economy in order to keep up a common standard of living and purchase new technologies and home comforts that had not been available in the past. This standardisation extended into their leisure, which had become passive and mechanised, centred around mass arts such as the movies, narrow club membership, conspicuous consumption and automobile ownership. Art and music were more likely to be passively absorbed in standardized ways than created locally or performed spontaneously, and while people read more – being better educated and having greater access to an increasing number of publications – the literature they read tended to be intellectually light, escapist or salacious, published in serials and motion picture magazines. This was not cultural balance but conformity to the mean.

While this unthinking conformity caused H. L. Mencken to praise the book as a confirmation of his views on the stupidity of rural America, a review he titled 'A City in Moronia', Lynd did not dislike Middletown or its people.[53] What bothered him was the hegemony of business culture and the lack of checks and balances over its chaotic development. Although the Lynds argued that 'no effort was being made to prove any thesis', the book was clearly not as value-neutral or objective as the described goals suggested. The book began as an enquiry into community religion funded by Rockefeller's Institute of Social and Religious Research and Robert Lynd had been training to be a Presbyterian minister before he switched to social science as a substitute for his ethical social goals. *Middletown* was consequently peppered with moral questions about the direction of American society that was based on an idyllic vision of the 1890s set against the pecuniary and materialistic business culture of the 1920s. To Lynd the fundamental goal of social science was the improvement of culture; his functionalist vision meant that he had no qualms manipulating his information in order to shake people out of their conservative habits, taking limited selections from newspaper reports and diaries from the 1890s at face value, while pointing out the media hypocrisies and manipulations of contemporary business culture. Richard Wightman Fox has pointed out that 'Lynd never acknowledged the irony that *Middletown* was produced through the philanthropy of the very corporate leader whose outrageous neglect of oil workers Lynd had graphically detailed' in 1923.[54] Both the lack of objectivity and the change in focus caused the original sponsors to refuse publication of the final report.

As a former publisher and journalist, Lynd had little trouble getting his study published and despite his despair about the reading habits of middle-brow Americans, when the book came out it became a surprising bestseller.[55] While they rejected the dominant Chicago School theory of group conflict, the gentle critique of ordinary life under industrial change ultimately depicted a disturbing portrait of a nation that had submitted unwittingly to the shallow materialism and goals of consumerist and capitalist 'normalcy' in sacrifice of the pioneer past. Underlying his critique was the point that by choosing to delegate their choices to business authorities and by ordering their lives around money, Americans were losing the self-reliance, community values and independence that had long been the basis of their democratic cultural heritage.

The Business of Leisure

Like many of their contemporaries, the Lynds felt that the arrival of the 'highest standard of living' was a business chimera that covered up the new problems and inequalities it had spawned. This tendency was most notable in the vast expansion of commercialised leisure. While the Lynds approvingly noted growing leisure time and the appearance of a 'vacation habit' among the inhabitants of Middletown, the more money and leisure that was gained, the more degraded, 'canned' or commercialised their activities became. This was as worrying to the social scientists as the imbalance between production and consumption, for if leisure no longer offered the opportunities for self-culture and civilisation, then prosperity seemed a pointless achievement once basic human needs were catered for. Throughout the 1920s reformers argued that the new leisure hours released by technological advances should be directed into healthy activities led by experts and used scientifically and efficiently. By targeting leisure, reformers believed that positive social change could happen without disturbance to the operations of capitalism on which it relied. Such leisure should be free of business culture and commercialism, away from industrial crowds and workday stresses, in order to operate effectively as a balancing mechanism.

Industrialists also became increasingly interested in meeting union demands for lower hours as a way of improving workers' productivity even further. Over the 1920s paid vacations for workers were becoming an increasingly accepted practice as a way of rejuvenating workers for industry as industrialists accepted arguments from the play reform movement that workers' leisure functioned as a way of recharging and storing up energy for greater efficiency later. Although the percentage of workers receiving paid or company vacations remained low, some employers now encouraged or even continued to pay wages during short vacations. As Cindy Aron has noted, this benefited employers and productivity only if the time was used wisely, a concern that led to increasing interference in the non-working time of industrial employees.

Movie receipts, radio, book and magazine sales as well as the proliferation in domestic tourism, automobiling and travel all indicated that not only did people have more time and money, they increasingly spent it 'spending'. A government report in 1929 noted that not only was leisure itself a 'consumable' but that 'people can not "consume" leisure without consuming goods and services, and that leisure which

Figure 5.2 Coney Island Beach Scene, Brooklyn, New York, c. 1920s (© The Art Archive/Culver Pictures).

results from an increasing man-hour productivity helps to create new needs and new and broader markets'.[56] The changing class dynamics of leisure visible in the crowds of workers attracted to the commercial amusements of Coney Island and the growth of spectator sports such as football and baseball were more often cause for concern rather than celebration. As the numbers of vacationers and day-trippers increased, so did the spectre of revolution, chaos and mob rule, as well as fears that standardisation, passivity and conformity would lead to a breakdown in democracy and social order. Writers like James Truslow Adams argued that free time should be a space in which individualism and freedom was stimulated and crowds resisted, for the 'road of conformity is merely the road back to savagery'.[57]

Both social scientists and industrialists increasingly believed that commercialised leisure left workers fatigued and dissatisfied and aimed to promote leisure pursuits as an opportunity for rest or self-improvement that would enable them to become better workers: one 1923 company newsletter told workers to 'Make yourself 100% efficient by getting out into the open and living the natural life for the next two weeks'.[58] Yet, concerns about self-cultivation in leisure were not just applicable to the working masses; as Adams pointed out, the primitive debauch of consumer culture particularly applied to successful businessmen who 'may live in a palace, ride in the most luxurious cars and fill his rooms with old masters and the costliest manuscripts which his wealth can draw from under the hammer at Christie's but if he cares more for riches, luxury, and power than for a humanely rounded life he is not civilized but what the Greeks properly called a "barbarian"'.[59] To Adams the business ethic of increased consumerism militated against real leisure opportunities and civilisation: 'our prosperity can be maintained only by making people want more, and work more, all the time,' he stated, and where business focused on profits it remained blind to culture and aesthetics.[60] In the end, he asked, can 'a great civilization be built up or maintained upon the philosophy of the counting-house and the sole basic idea of a profit?'[61]

Balance through Leisure

Intelligence and health tests on soldiers after the enactment of universal conscription during World War I had created a 'composite portrait' of the average man as physically and mentally 'unfit' for modernity that became a pervasive concern.[62] Sociologist William Ogburn argued in *Social Change* (1922) that proper adaptation to the new pace of society was vital, as Americans were now lagging behind the technologies they had invented and could not be happy or successful until they had achieved balance and adjustment to it. One of the first to combine Freudian thought with sociological research, Ogburn claimed that 'nervous disorders, hysteria, morbid compulsions, anxiety-neuroses, paranoia, melancholia' and manic depression were all evidence of 'psychological maladjustment occasioned by cultural influences'.[63] Others feared that society would revert to barbaric atavism if cultural lag was not overcome. Director of the Rockefeller Foundation Raymond B. Fosdick stated in *The Old Savage in the New Civilization* (1928) that humanity was in 'unique peril' from cultural lag, asking is 'man to be the master of the civilization he has created, or is he to be its victim?'[64] As the inadequacy of staying 'average' was revealed, a flurry of cures promoting personal efficiency techniques emerged in self-help publications that merged social science theories with pop philosophy and psychoanalytic thought.

Psychological health, efficiency and balance became increasingly paralleled with health in the wider social and political system. A stream of publications advised on using psychoanalysis for business, family and individual success. In 1923 the appearance of the magazines *Psychology: Health, Happiness, Success* and the *Psychological Review of Reviews* gave voice to a rising number of lay and popular analysts dedicated to the popular use of psychology as a form of cultural uplift. Psychologist Joseph Jastrow wrote a daily syndicated newspaper column that appeared in more than 150 newspapers titled 'Keeping Mentally Fit' that was eventually published as *Keeping Mentally Fit: A Guide to Everyday Psychology* (1928) and *Piloting Your Life* (1930).[65] Books by non-analysts such as Joseph Ralph's *How to Psycho-Analyze Yourself : Theory and Practice of Remoulding the Personality by the Analytic Method* (1921) popularised Freudian ideas and provided cheap DIY therapy for those clamouring to succeed in this new climate. Samuel Schmalhausen's *Why We Misbehave* (1928) and *Sex in Civilization* (1929) offered guidance for those troubled by the tension between traditional morality and new sexual attitudes and Andre Tridon's *Psychoanalysis and Love* (1923) scandalised many moralists by describing humans as rutting animals. Orison Swett Marden's *Masterful Personality* (1921) played on desires to control others, writing that 'You can compel people to like you'.[66] The most popular self-help book of all became Émile Coué's *Self-Mastery Through Conscious Autosuggestion* (1922) that claimed health and happiness could be achieved through the repetition of mantras such as 'Day by day, in every way, I am getting better and better'.[67]

While the ideal of achieving balance between work and leisure became a popular antidote for breakdown and dysfunction on an individual and social level, such nostrums often confused spiritual with corporate success. Frederick Lewis Allen noted that the veneration of business and its association with religion was 'the most significant phenomenon of the day', a phenomenon encapsulated in *Moses, Persuader of Men*, published by the Metropolitan Casualty Insurance Company, a booklet that claimed 'Moses was one of the greatest salesmen and real-estate promoters that ever lived . . . a Dominant, Fearless, and Successful Personality in one of the most magnificent selling campaigns that history ever placed upon its pages'.[68] Advertising executive Bruce Barton's popular book of the life of Jesus, *The Man Nobody Knows: A Discovery of the Real Jesus* (1925), paralleled the story of Christ's ascendancy from poverty to great leadership with modern business achievements, adding a modern spin to theology by claiming that Christian parables were examples of the greatest advertisements ever made. To Barton the story of Christ represented the greatest achievement story of all and a model of executive leadership for all businessmen. Barton led a 'new class of secular priests conveying the gospel of consumption to the nation's anxious flock of consumers' thereby helping to overturn traditional protestant morality concerning abundance and excess.[69] A mixture of pop psychology and Christian thought, such rhetoric provided the ultimate booster salve to any concerns or moral ambivalence about the culture of abundance, business and consumption.

The commercial success of such pop psychology led to the proliferation of other self-help tendencies including popular parlour games such as 'Know Your Type' and personality tests in popular magazines. In 1920 Emanuel Haldeman-Julius began The Little Blue Books publishing company to cater to the demand for self-instruction and self-help among the less wealthy and by 1928 he had sold over 20 million books. His own history of the enterprise, *The First Hundred Million* (1928), became a self-help bestseller, and his mass production of all types of instructional learning earned him the nickname 'the Henry Ford of Publishing'.[70] The creation of the Book-of-the-Month club in 1926 and the appearance of the first *Reader's Digest* in 1921 further helped consumers to make informed choices about their leisure-time reading, providing consumer efficiency alongside cultural uplift.[71] Given such commercialism it was not surprising that by the end of the decade intellectuals noted a degradation in American psychology that called into question the link between individual success and wider social improvement.[72]

While mental adaptation to modernity was important, new ideas about the physical presentation of the self were also prevalent in popular advice and self-help instructions. To Lorine Pruette and Harry Elmer Barnes in *Women and Leisure: A Study of Social Waste* (1924), women were more at danger than men from the potential degeneration caused by inefficient use of leisure and more attention should be given to this urgent cause. The elimination of household tasks by machines or efficiency techniques, such as those taught by C. W. Taber's *The Business of the Household* (1922) or Christine Frederick's *Efficient Housekeeping or Household Engineering* (1925), had left middle-class, educated women in danger of having too much leisure at their disposal. To Pruette, women in 'part-time jobs are growing fat and intellectually flabby [and] their minds are going soft like their bodies'.[73] Women were also responsible for 90 per cent of all consumption, a fact that tied their leisure or free-time pursuits closely to goals for national efficiency in consumption.[74] Women's leisure thereby came under increasing scrutiny by management and efficiency experts, for, as the chief consumers and educators of the nation's youth, women were central to the success of civilisation.

Most advice, however, defined success differently according to sex. For men it mostly entailed keeping or getting ahead in business; for women, it was finding and keeping the right mate and sustaining the needs of a family. Such advice helped women navigate the uncharted path from Victorian morality to sexual expression but also involved the promises of consumer goods to maintain their youth and allure or keep their family healthy. Anxieties were generated in an increasingly competitive market for relationships, highlighted by competitions such as the first Miss America contest held in 1921, where women were encouraged to compare themselves to flawless Hollywood stars whose promotion of products caused cosmetic sales to skyrocket 'from less than $17,000,000 in 1914 to $141,488,000 by 1925'.[75]

Paradoxically it was during this period of unprecedented excess and increasing automobile travel that exercise and dieting became fashionable. Active leisure pursuits were recommended for both sexes as ways to streamline the body and overcome the physical attributes of cultural lag that were manifested in flab or weakness. Fads for dieting and body shaping emerged as understanding of the science of food increased and made vitamins and calories part of a common vocabulary. The most popular non-fiction book of the 1920s was Lulu Hunt Peters' *Diet and Health, With Key to the Calories*, that advocated slimming or 'reducing' by counting calories and slow eating. This was the first diet book to encourage women to scientifically manage their diets in order to streamline their bodies. Diets became big business as celebrities revealed their secrets to slimness in popular magazines and eating fads such as the 'Hollywood Eighteen Day Diet' of 585 calories per day or the 'Medical Millennium Diet' which consisted of slow chewing and daily enemas became popular. Changes in dress styles and the popularisation of swimsuits and leisure clothes that exposed more of the body led middle-class women to try and streamline their bodies into the new angular and boyish shapes that had become symbolic of efficient modernity and control. By 1923 an article in the *Woman's Home Companion* noted that: 'Once fat was an asset: now it's a liability, both physical and esthetic'.[76] This was also true of men who, despite the growth in popularity of spectator sports such as football, baseball and boxing, feared the results of passive leisure and sedentary work on their waistlines. Using leisure to engineer and develop a new self was further promoted by the bodybuilding craze set in train by Charles Atlas, who won the 1922 'Most Perfectly Developed Man' contest. Following his success he made a fortune marketing his training programme to feeble or flabby acolytes.[77]

A variety of other fads, crazes and pastimes that 'performed' displays of endurance, speed, deprivation or physical excess seemed to test the capacity of human strength as well as the tolerance of social reformers. Crazes for flagpole sitting, mountain climbing, marathons, long-distance flying, high-altitude stunts and all types of record-breaking were fuelled by national media attention in movie houses and newspapers. Daring stunt pilots or 'barnstormers' gave popular shows that were regularly featured in movie houses and women performed impressive physical feats that illustrated a new daring and female strength: pilot Amelia Earhart set the women's altitude record in 1922 and Gertrude Ederle became the first woman to swim the English Channel in 1926.

Such successes encouraged others to attempt feats of endurance and skill, all of which provided advertising opportunities for promoters who sponsored the winners. Of all the bizarre contests that became fads and entertainment in the decade – among them skipping derbies, ball-bouncing records, yo-yoing, gum chewing marathons, peanut pushing, staying awake, egg, doughnut or spaghetti eating – flagpole sitting and marathon dancing became the most popular. Alvin 'Shipwreck' Kelley began his flagpole sitting career in 1924 in a thirteen-hour sit as a publicity stunt for a Hollywood movie theatre. He and copycat rivals seeking to break his record quickly became a national phenomenon that continued throughout the decade. In one year Kelley managed to sit on a pole for 145 days, while his non-stop record was 49 days in Atlantic City, a feat witnessed by more than 20,000 spectators who watched him eat, shave, have his hair cut and catnap on the pole. By 1928 he was able to charge $100 a day for his performance, plus a share of the receipts, a wage that fuelled further competitors to challenge him.[78]

Kelley may have taken inspiration from a new fad that had taken off in 1923 when Alma Cummings won the first dance marathon contest in the US. Cummings had danced for twenty-seven hours non-stop in a New York ballroom, wearing out six partners and several pairs of shoes, an achievement that led to a national craze for record-breaking endurance dancing.[79] Within three weeks the record for non-stop dancing had risen to ninety hours and ten minutes and, by 1928, dance marathons lasting at least a week and with big prizes were being held throughout the nation. By pitting men against women, the individual against the clock, allowing audiences a popular vote and turning working-class dancers into amateur celebrities, marathon dances embodied, performed and tested the new frontiers of recent social, work and gender transformations.[80] Such popular performances played out the possibilities and dangers of the efficiently trained mind and body and explored the boundaries of excess, balance and control in machine culture. While reformers opposed such trivial, exhausting and dangerous 'time wasting', shows like Kelley's replayed the drama of the frontier and the precariousness of existence in a hostile environment. Such performances were a form of self-manufacture in which 'time wasting' turned into individual triumph over adversity and anonymity. The heroism of such feats and their symbolic value to the nation reached an apotheosis in 1927, when a barely known aviator turned personal endurance into a national public celebration.

Charles Lindbergh's Transatlantic Flight (1927)

When twenty-five-year-old aviator Charles Lindbergh flew alone across the Atlantic in the single-engine *The Spirit of St. Louis* on the first non-stop solo flight from New York to Paris in 1927, his achievement became a national symbol of epic proportions. Since 1919 aviators had sought the prestige and $25,000 prize money that Raymond Orteig had offered for the first non-stop transatlantic flight, and numerous lives had been lost in the attempt. The danger of the trip was considered so great that Lloyds of London gave odds of 10 to 1 against any successful attempt and later refused all bets on Lindbergh as too great a risk.[81] Six pilots had lost their lives in the attempt in 1926. Just a fortnight before Lindbergh's attempt, two French aviators, Nungesser and Coli, had left Paris for New York but were still missing, while others died later trying to repeat his success. So when the young and relatively unknown Lindbergh took off in the single-engine *Spirit of St. Louis* with a packet of sandwiches, some water and his passport, few believed he would be seen again.

Lindbergh's flight was certainly a feat of courage and endurance. He had not slept the night before and had to keep himself awake for an additional thirty-three and a half hours while he navigated alone over vast stretches of sea and ice. Yet despite the gruelling physical and mental challenges he faced during the flight, Lindbergh was completely unprepared for what faced him when he landed in Paris. The whole world, now connected by telephone, telegraph and radio, had waited for news of the aviator and by the time the pilot landed, a crowd of 150,000 had gathered at the airfield to catch sight of him. As the crowd surged and grabbed at him the hysteria was palpable, recorded by a laconic entry into his flight log that read: 'Fuselage fabric badly torn by souvenir hunters'.[82] From that moment, Lindbergh was catapulted into world fame and placed under a constant media spotlight. As excitement snowballed around the world he finally returned to New York to a rapturous homecoming reception in New York City attended by more than four million hero-worshippers. Within a few weeks Lindbergh had become the most famous and most photographed man in the world.

His celebrity was soon accompanied by numerous requests for appearances, product endorsements and new fashion trends. Shoes, hats, pants, bread, toys, games and cigars appeared bearing 'Lindy' logos or incorporating plane propellers in their design.[83] 'Lindy' could sell anything. Movies about aviation proliferated with titles such as *Won on the Clouds*, *Cloud Riders*, *Wings* and *Flight* and movie moguls offered vast sums in order to get Lindbergh to star in pictures, most of which the shy airman rejected.[84] His flight was the spur for the emergence of an additional American icon when Walt Disney made his first Mickey Mouse cartoon, *Plane Crazy* (1928), a comedy of Mickey's failure to emulate his hero Lindbergh. Fitzgerald wrote:

> In the spring of '27, something bright and alien flashed across the sky. A young Minnesotan who seemed to have nothing to do with his generation did a heroic thing, and for a moment people set down their glasses in country clubs and speakeasies and thought their old best dreams. Maybe there was a way out by flying, maybe our restless blood could find frontiers in the illimitable air.[85]

This emotional response to Lindbergh's success came to represent 'a mass ritual in which America celebrated itself more than it celebrated Lindbergh'.[86] In such materialistic, cynical and corrupt times, Lindbergh signified the return of innocence, the revival of the frontier spirit, the triumph of the individual and the glory of the machine. The American ambassador in Paris wired President Coolidge immediately to tell him that 'we could not have found a better type than young Lindbergh to represent the spirit and high purpose of our people'.[87] Lindbergh's success revived traditional notions of individualism unconnected with the selfishness or greed of the corporate-minded era. The *Chicago Tribune* ran a cartoon titled 'The Pioneer Spirit Still Survives' showing a covered wagon in one panel with Lindbergh taking off in the next, while reports of his success claimed that he had conquered a 'new frontier'.[88] This frontier spirit contrasted with the moral and cultural vacuum that had plagued the nation and the media quickly latched on to Lindbergh's act as a symbol of promise in a 'grubby world', as one journalist wrote at the time.[89] To one journalist he was 'US personified. He is the United States'.[90]

The symbol of Lindbergh became cathartic because it offered a solution to the tension between tradition and modernity. By flying from New York to Paris he created 'a bridge between the two great nations' that linked old and new worlds and his story of individual survival counteracted the sense that individual acts were impossible in an era of mechanisation and mass production.[91] His success was both man- and machine-made: President Coolidge congratulated his airplane as the 'silent partner' who 'represented American genius and industry'.[92] Counteracting prevalent fears of

Anglo-Saxon 'race suicide', the blonde, blue-eyed Lindbergh also came to represent fantasies of Nordic ascendancy. A lifelong believer in eugenics, Lindbergh was himself convinced that all of the world's problems could be solved by the scientific breeding of the race.

Around this single man a structure of mythic values cohered that synthesised the contradictory and conflicting views about the American past and present. Emblematic of both pastoral and industrial visions of America, he became a paradigm of dualist tensions of the 1920s, something he acknowledged in his autobiography:

> I loved the farm, with its wooded river and creek banks, its tillage and crops, and its cattle and horses. I was fascinated by the laboratory's magic: the intangible power found in electrified wires, through which one could see the unseeable. Instinctively I was drawn to the farm, intellectually to the laboratory. Here began a conflict between values of instinct and intellect that was carried through my entire life, and that I eventually recognized as inherent in my civilization.[93]

In light of the conflict he represented, it is not surprising that the mythic structure surrounding Lindbergh collapsed. After the kidnap and murder of his baby son in 1932 he left America to live in England and in an ambassadorial role for the American aviation industry in 1936 he was honoured by the Nazis. His refusal to condemn the regime and his later spokesmanship for the isolationist anti-war 'America First Campaign' called his politics, his patriotism and his status as all-American hero into question.

Despite his fall from grace he continued to be a pulse of the times: a man who befriended both the first man to fly a plane and the first man to walk on the moon. Although his success provided a catalyst for the growth of the air, space and missile industries, he remained ambivalent about his achievements and became a committed conservationist who worked to preserve threatened animal and native populations around the world. Like Henry Ford, he paradoxically spent much of his later life using his success and wealth to seek out the peace and order of pre-industrial simplicity.[94]

Conclusion

The collapse of the mythic structure around Lindbergh was presaged in the collapse of business culture in late 1929. The unsustainable excesses and paradoxes of business civilisation, reflected in pursuits that turned social anxieties and tensions into popular performance and display, began to strain as the stock market nose-dived from unprecedented altitudes in the autumn of 1929. Up until then, like the risk-taking Lindbergh, gambling was surrounded by an aura of heroic individualism and masculinity that counteracted the conformism, consumerism and control of modern industrial culture. Walter Lippmann even commented that the unplanned activities of businessmen were 'more

Figure 5.3 *New York Times* headline reporting Charles Lindbergh's successful transatlantic flight (© The Art Archive/Culver Pictures).

daring' and 'revolutionary' than the liberal progressives who called for control.[95] In this climate the rise of stock market speculation also took on the spirit of a game, for, as Chase noted: 'The stock market possesses a double function. It provides a field for investors, and a super roulette wheel for gamblers'.[96] As competitions turned contest winners and record-breakers into overnight success stories, so too, it seemed, had business speculation. Frederick Lewis Allen reflected on the widespread popularity of such speculation in *Only Yesterday*:

> Across the dinner table one heard fantastic stories of sudden fortunes: a young banker had put every dollar of his small capital into Niles-Bement Pond and now was fixed for life; a widow had been able to buy a large country house with her winnings in Kennecott. Thousands speculated – and won, too – without the slightest knowledge of the nature of the company upon whose fortunes they were relying, like the people who bought Seaboard Air Line under the impression that it was an aviation stock. Grocers, motormen, plumbers, seamstresses, and speakeasy waiters were in the market. Even the revolting intellectuals were there: loudly as they might lament the depressing effects of standardization and mass production upon American life, they found themselves quite ready to reap the fruits thereof. Literary editors whose hopes were wrapped about American Cyanamid B lunched with poets who swore by Cities Service, and as they left the table, stopped for a moment in the crowd at the broker's branch office to catch the latest quotations; and the artist who had once been eloquent only about Gauguin laid aside his brushes to proclaim the merits of National Bellas Hess. The Big Bull Market had become a national mania'.

While it seemed that everyone was playing the business game, with roughly 4 million out of the total population of 120 million owning stock, most investments were actually concentrated in very few hands.[97] The unequal distribution of wealth created by business deregulation, cuts in federal spending and tax cuts for the rich had been concealed behind an unprecedented growth of consumer credit. In his inaugural speech of March 1929 President Hoover uttered total confidence in the system, saying that he had 'no fears for the future of our country' that was 'bright with hope'.[98] Yet despite the return of political isolationism after the war, American banks had become entwined in a global economy that made them reliant on European debtors' ability to repay extensive loans or purchase mass-produced goods, while the severe depression of 1920–2, downturns in 1924 and 1927, the market collapse in Florida of 1926 and the ongoing agricultural depression all provided warning signs that the economic system was not as robust as such rhetoric maintained.[99]

As stock speculation became frenzied, the Federal Reserve Board issued a warning in early 1929 that their member banks should not make loans for speculative purposes and raised interest rates to deter speculation further. It was already too late: as building contracts declined and consumer spending fell from a 7.4 per cent rise in 1927–8 to a 1.5 per cent rise in 1928–9, production slowed and commodity prices fell. Despite these signs the stock market continued to rise by buying 'on margin' – using loans to buy further stock – causing prices to double or triple in just a few months. From September 1929 the stock market started to falter, leading to huge falls on 19 October and a further severe drop on 24 October. Confidence was briefly restored as a group of bankers created a $240 million reserve fund to help balance the market but their efforts appeared fruitless when on 28 and 29 October the stock exchange plummeted again. Within the month $30 billion had been lost and the Dow Jones average had declined from $364.90 to $62.70 per share, destroying investor and business confidence.[100]

While the 1929 Wall Street Crash was not the only cause of the Great Depression, the economic realities of the decade had been far easier to ignore in the speculative environment of business prosperity that claimed uplift for all but offered no security or equality.[101] In the end the Crash highlighted the instability of a political system based solely on business ideals, in which the seemingly 'solid plateau of values was nothing but arrant nonsense'.[102] By 1930 the ideals of a business civilisation had collapsed and intellectuals like Chase and Dewey had their views of 'pecuniary' business culture cruelly confirmed. Dewey reflected on the inability of collective enrichment to lead to the elevation of civilisation in his *Individualism Old and New* (1930), blaming a 'perversion of the whole ideal of individualism' on 'the practices of a pecuniary culture'.[103] Such observers now called for new collectivist ideals based on a planned economy in which the insecurity of random stock market 'orgies' and boom and bust cycles would become a thing of the past.

A political cartoon of 1931 depicting a farmer, a worker and an 'honest businessman' at a poker game, demanding a 'new deal' from dishonest speculators and politicians, depicted the transition from big business 'games'.[104] The social scientist replaced business leadership as Roosevelt's New Deal Government aimed to remove insecurity and risk-taking, replacing it with a system of social security that would balance out the inequalities of capitalist culture. This formula aimed not to destroy the faulty system, but to get it working again, for, as Chase wrote, 'The going financial structure, my friends, is as temperamental as a cigar lighter. Sometimes it works and sometimes it doesn't'.[105]

The Cultural Legacy of the 1920s

In his popular summary of the decade, published in the early years of the Depression, Frederick Lewis Allen showed readers that what they now took for granted as part of everyday modern life was part of a truly remarkable transformation that had taken place over the 1920s. The citizen of 1919 could hardly have imagined the changes, he asserted. Common, everyday experiences that ordinary Americans took for granted by 1931 would have seemed exotic and extraordinary only six months after the armistice, he wrote. Imagining the daily routine of 'Mr. and Mrs. Smith' in May 1919, Allen noted that they would not have heard of vitamins, tabloid newspapers, Babe Ruth, Jack Dempsey, the Chrysler automobile, traffic congestion and speed restrictions. Prohibition and votes for women were ratified but not yet law, smoking and drinking among the female population was unusual and frowned upon, and F. Scott Fitzgerald had 'yet to confront a horri-fied republic with the Problem of the Younger Generation'.[1] Although the Smiths enjoyed the movies, the luxurious picture palace was in its infancy, as was the celebrity culture of the movie star that would manifest itself in the mass hysteria at Rudolph Valentino's funeral in 1926. Most significantly the radio age had not yet started, a technical innovation that made popular culture out of the intellectual trends, music, opinions and events of the era.

Such changes made the culture of the 1920s more national and more mass-mediated than ever before. Yet while Allen's lively assessment of the decade set the tone of the many evaluations that have followed, the tendency to conflate image with reality entrenched some truisms at the expense of understanding others. After the Wall Street Crash, the 'post mortem' of the decade quickly began as writers, artists and historians rushed to dissect the years that had led to such catastrophic economic results. The image of wild spending sprees, carefree hedonism and unremitting prosperity that had been promulgated by business and advertised through the media at the time solidified in the hardship of the Great Depression that ensued. In 'Echoes of the Jazz Age' (1931) F. Scott Fitzgerald wrote that he already looked back on the era with a nostalgia for the 'gaudiest spree in history', even though the image was, both at the time and since, a delusional 'flimsy structure' built around the perceptions of the 'upper tenth of the nation [who were] living with the insouciance of grand ducs and the casualness of chorus girls'.[2]

While the fictions and dreams generated by businessmen, politicians and writers about the 1920s take much significance from the comparative and sobering relationship with the decade that came after, such comparison also tends to make the two decades appear more divided by economic and psychological chasms than they really were, a conceit in which the similarities are dismissed as cultural hangovers rather than continuities within a wider sweep of social and intellectual change. The hint in Fitzgerald's essay that contemporary perceptions had actually rested on a 'flimsy structure', woven from longings for progress and cultural nostalgia, provides a salutary lesson here. Seen as a discrete unit of time, bookended by war and depression, the 1920s gave the perfect impetus to 'decadisation' itself as a way of understanding and ordering the history of the twentieth century.

However, the concept of the decade which 'represents thinking about time in a punctuated, discontinuous manner' in many ways constitutes a historical 'disremembering', which has been seen to contribute 'to an abbreviated historical attention span'.[3] For example, Jason Scott Smith has noted that this 'decimal-oriented chronological marker' imposes an artificial historical structure that has become an intellectual shorthand with which rapid changes in short periods of time can be discussed. This shorthand acquaintance with history tends to take precedence over other modes of historical perception and is itself a continuation of the trend towards rationalisations of time and motion that gave meaning, order and organisation to an otherwise chaotic experience of modernity in the late nineteenth and early twentieth centuries.

As Smith explains, the tendency to reorganise temporal perceptions into manageable units was a legacy of ideas about time and progress that came to fruition within the intellectual climate of the 1920s, making it 'the first decade truly to legitimate a ten-year span of time as a historic category'.[4] In this way the 1920s laid the intellectual and cultural foundations that legitimised such formulations of history as 'the decade'. As Smith has shown, in retrospective and nostalgic post mortems by intellectuals and historians such as Walter Lippmann and Frederick Lewis Allen, 'the idea of the decade in American culture' was propagated as a way of reconstructing faith in historical progress during the 1930s.[5]

While Smith sees the use of the decade as an organising principle as a triumph of cultural 'style' over social and political content, in this series David Eldridge and Graham Thompson have both noted the problematic way in which a conception of 'the decade' simulates a temporal order that does not easily map onto the category or idea of 'culture' either.[6] To Eldridge, 'determining the cultural legacy of any given decade can become something of a parlour game, observing those aspects which have survived into the present-day'.[7] It tells us something about the history of such periodising, then, to learn that Allen's hugely popular bestselling book about the 1920s was turned into a popular parlour game called 'The Only Yesterday Game', that was marketed to those in the 1930s who became 'experts in nineteen-twentiana'.[8] This piece of cultural trivia exposes the way that the idea of the historical decade itself performed the function of helping Americans negotiate complex structures and changes in the wake of events that had led to the economic crash.

Despite the problems involved, the flimsy structure of the decade as a way of examining – or concealing – shared events over a short period of time has proved surprisingly robust as a way of linking with subsequent events in history. Accepting its limitations, this shorthand mode of interpreting history has proved useful as a tool for exploring cultural continuities far more often than the rigid criticism of the discontinuous ten-year unit of time has allowed. Observers in the 1930s, for example, structured the cultural legacy of the decade as a critique of an unregulated economy that served to support New Deal transformations.

Later critics have also held up the 1920s as a way of examining the shortcomings and problems of their own time. Comparisons made between the postwar 'Red Scare', political disillusion, consumerism and materialism of the 1920s with similar developments in the 1950s, for example, reflect more on the contemporary era than they reveal about the 1920s. These reflections, however, also create a multilayered perception of history as an accretion, something continuous rather than disrupted by a 'snapshot' decade view. Such views add cultural resonance to nostalgic backward glances at the 1920s in the 1950s, for example, in which a film musical such as *Singin' in the Rain* (1952) can

be seen to expose the deception and artful construction of both eras'
mass-mediated fantasies of cultural 'realities'.

The Manichean tendency of 1920s culture, with its varieties of
paradox, ambiguity and dualist tensions, have led to many other comparisons with subsequent decades. The sexual liberation of the New
Woman, Garveyism and the New Negro of the Harlem Renaissance
have found parallels in second-wave feminism, black nationalism and
the black arts movement of the 1960s. Likewise, Irene Thomson has
examined the legacy of the 1920s in the 1970s, comparing the similarities such as the public withdrawal from activism, the rise of feminism,
high divorce rates and the popularisation of Freudian psychology.
As Thomson's work has shown, however, such close examination
exposes nuanced differences that are far more revealing about cultural
change than overt but surface similarities indicate.[9] As such, cultural
reproductions of the 1920s in the 1970s, such as E. L. Doctorow's
Ragtime (1975), Ishmael Reed's *Mumbo Jumbo* (1972) and the most
famous film adaptation of *The Great Gatsby* (Coppola, 1974), can be
best examined not by their relation to actual history but in relation
to how that history has subsequently and subtly shifted as a cultural
emblem.

Perceived similarities between the 1920s and the 1980s further
illustrate the impact of the nostalgic glance on subsequent events. As
Gregory Bergman noted in 1986, both Republican Presidents of those
decades, Coolidge and Reagan, instituted deregulatory, anti-statist
policies and both eras witnessed a resurgence in the religious right
and fears of moral and family breakdown.[10] As the historian Robert
McElvaine has noted, Ronald Reagan was twelve years old at the time
that Coolidge ascended to the presidency and his subsequent nostalgia for his boyhood era led him to 'publicly [praise] his predecessor
for cutting "tax four times"'.[11] Whether 'normalcy' or 'Reaganomics'
actually gave rise to the nihilism behind the cultural productions of
the Lost Generation and Gen Xers, or whether this also led to the
emergence of the flapper or the yuppie, are perhaps moot points – the
significance lies more in the way each era emphasised such shared
fantasies of individualism, agency and consumer democracy through
cultural productions.

While all of this deals only with surface interpretations and popular
cultural perceptions, the cyclical reappearance of the 1920s as iconic
shorthand for a variety of social and cultural changes or problems has
perhaps become its greatest cultural legacy. Indeed, the decade repeat-
edly acts as a mirror in which contemporary viewers regard their own

reflection. Anxiously looking back at the Wall Street Crash in 1986, Bergman noted that:

> A recent New York Times article, headed 'Economists Fear That History May Repeat Itself,' reported that fear of a new depression is a topic of daily conversation among Wall Street executives. It went on to list a number of striking similarities between the economic situation which preceded the crash of 1929 and our situation today. These included the booming stock market, slow economic growth, inflation, and the increasing use of credit to finance speculative investment.[12]

Cultural debates over the role of mass culture, business, religion, consumer credit, education, health, race and gender in the first decade of the twenty-first century continue to provide startling parallels with those fermented in the crucible of the 1920s. That Bergman's comments over twenty years ago could have been written today confirms the point that while 'decade thinking' does create short attention spans, residual cultural memory of the 1920s will haunt us for far longer.

Notes

Introduction

1. F. Scott Fitzgerald, 'Echos of the Jazz Age' (1931), reprinted in Loren Baritz (ed.), *The Culture of the Twenties* (New York: Bobbs-Merrill Co., Inc, 1970), p. 414.
2. Lawrence Levine, 'Progress and Nostalgia: The Self-Image of the Nineteen Twenties', in Lawrence W. Levine, *The Unpredictable Past: Explorations in American Cultural History* (New York: Oxford University Press, 1993), pp. 189–205.
3. Henry Adams, *The Education of Henry Adams: An Autobiography* (New York: Houghton and Mifflin Co., 1918).
4. Thorstein Veblen, 'Dementia Praecox', *The Freeman* (21 June 1922), reprinted in Baritz (ed.), *The Culture of the Twenties*, p. 29.
5. Sean Dennis Cashman, *America in the Twenties and Thirties: The Olympian Age of Franklin Delano Roosevelt* (New York: New York University Press, 1989), p. 511.
6. Alan Bilton and Philip Melling (eds), *America in the 1920s: Literary Sources and Documents* (Robertsbridge, UK: Helm Information, 2004), pp. 249–50.
7. African American journalist and NAACP leader Walter White documented the lynchings and mob violence in his *Rope and Faggot: A Biography of Judge Lynch* (New York: Knopf, 1929).
8. William E. Leuchtenburg, *The Perils of Prosperity: 1914–32* (University of Chicago Press, 1993), p. 39.
9. Warren Harding, 'Return to Normalcy' (1920), in Cynthia Rose (ed.), *American Decades Primary Sources: 1920–1929* (Detroit, MI: Gale Publishing, 2004), p. 262. The original recorded speech is available at: http://lcweb2.loc.gov/ammem/nfhtml/nfexpe.html
10. Malcolm Cowley, *Exile's Return: A Literary Odyssey of the 1920s* (New York: Penguin Books, [1934] 1994), p. 215.
11. Reprinted in Baritz (ed.), *The Culture of the Twenties*, p. 414.
12. Ibid.
13. Ibid.
14. Barbara Haskell, *The American Century: Art and Culture, 1900–1950* (New York: Norton, 1999), p. 153.

15. Lewis Mumford, *The Golden Day* (New York: Boni and Liveright: 1926), pp. 275–6.
16. Ibid., p. 282.
17. Harold Evans Stearns, *Civilization in the United States* (New York: Harcourt, Brace & Co., 1922), p. vii.
18. Warren Susman, *Culture as History* (Washington, DC: Smithsonian Institution, 2003), p. 137.
19. Clarence Hooker, *Life in the Shadows of the Crystal Palace, 1910–1927: Ford Workers in the Model T Era* (Bowling Green, OH: Bowling Green State University Popular Press, 1997), pp. 83–4.
20. Terry Smith, *Making the Modern: Industry, Art, and Design in America* (Chicago: University of Chicago Press, 1993), pp. 15–159.
21. Antonio Gramsci, 'Americanism and Fordism', in *Selections From the Prison Notebooks* (London: Lawrence and Wishart, 1971), p. 303.
22. Mumford in Stearns, *Civilization in the United States*, p. 13.
23. The museum site is online at: http://www.hfmgv.org/village/default.asp. Historic preservation was all the rage for industrialists in the 1920s; oil magnate John D. Rockefeller also began the restoration of Colonial Williamsburg in 1926.
24. Cashman, *America in the Twenties and Thirties*, p. 5.
25. Baritz (ed.), *The Culture of the Twenties*, p. 415.
26. Cowley, *Exile's Return*, p. 93.
27. Lewis Mumford, *Story of Utopias* (New York: Boni and Liveright, 1922), p. 17.
28. See John Dewey, *Reconstruction in Philosophy* (New York: H. Holt & Co., 1920). Dewey's publications over the 1920s included: *Human Nature and Conduct: An Introduction to Social Psychology* (1922); *The Public and its Problems* (1927); *The Quest for Certainty* (1929); *Experience and Nature* (1929); *Individualism Old and New* (1930).
29. Dewey, *Reconstruction in Philosophy*, p. 211.
30. John Dewey, 'The Need for a Recovery of Philosophy' (1917), in Louis Menand (ed.), *Pragmatism: A Reader* (New York: Vintage Books, 1997), pp. 220, 228, 231.
31. Ibid., p. 229.
32. Ibid., p. 232.
33. George Cotkin, 'Middle-Ground Pragmatists: The Popularization of Philosophy in American Culture', *Journal of the History of Ideas* 55.2 (1994), 283–302. See also Laura M. Westhoff, 'The Popularization of Knowledge: John Dewey on Experts and American Democracy', *History of Education Quarterly* 35.1 (1995), 27–47.
34. See Dewey's book on this subject, *The Quest for Certainty* (New York: Minton, Balch, 1929).
35. Martin Bulmer, *The Chicago School of Sociology: Institutionalization, Diversity and the Rise of Sociological Research* (Chicago: University of Chicago Press, 1984), pp. 29–32. See also J. David Lewis and Richard L. Smith, *American Sociology and Pragmatism: Mead, Chicago Sociology, and Symbolic Interaction* (Chicago: University of Chicago Press, 1980).
36. Bulmer, *The Chicago School of Sociology*, p. 200.
37. On anthropology and ethnography as intellectual anxiety over culture see Paul R. Gorman, *Left Intellectuals and Popular Culture in Twentieth-Century*

America (Chapel Hill, NC: University of North Carolina Press, 1996), pp. 95–107.

38. Warren Susman stated that '[b]y 1922 an exceptional and ever-growing number of Americans came to believe in a series of changes in the structure of their world ... based on the extraordinarily rapid accumulation of both new knowledge and new experience', which led to increased awareness of, as well as anxiety over, the changing face and pace of modern culture. Susman, *Culture as History*, p. 106.

39. Preston William Slosson, *The Great Crusade and After: 1914–1928* (New York: Macmillan, 1931), p. 384.

40. Ibid., p. 383.

41. Available online at http://www.vintagetooncast.com/2006/11/einstein-theory-of-relativity.html. The impact of Einstein's theory on ethics and beliefs was discussed in James Truslow Adams, *Our Business Civilization: Some Aspects of American Culture* (New York: A. and C. Boni, 1929), p. 73.

42. Paul A. Carter, *Another Part of the Twenties* (New York: Columbia University Press, 1977), p. 74.

43. David J. Rhees, *Public Images of Science In America: Science News-Letter, 1922–1929*, available online at http://scienceservice.si.edu/essay/.

44. Alfred B. Kuttner, 'Nerves', in Stearns (ed.), *Civilization in the United States*, p. 434. Freud was first translated into English by A. A. Brill in 1913. For Freud's influence in this early period see Frederick Hoffman, *Freudianism and The Literary Mind* (Baton Rouge, LA: Louisiana State University Press, 1957), pp. 44–80. For a thorough discussion of the history of Freud's influence in America see Nathan Hale, *The Rise and Crisis of Psychoanalysis in the United States: Freud and the Americans, 1917–1985* (New York: Oxford University Press, 1995) and Hendrik Ruitenbeck, *Freud and America* (New York: Macmillan, 1966).

45. Baritz (ed.), *The Culture of the Twenties*, p. 35.

46. Sigmund Freud, *The Future of an Illusion*, ed. James Strachey (Garden City, NY: Anchor Books, 1964), p. 2.

47. Stearns, *Civilization in the United States*, p. 136.

48. Frederick Hoffman, *Freudianism and The Literary Mind* (Baton Rouge, LA: Louisiana State University Press, 1957), p. 251.

49. Carolyn Kitch, 'Family Pictures: Constructing the "Typical" American in 1920s Magazines', *American Journalism* 16.4 (1999), 57–75.

50. 'Is Freudianism Destined to Live?', *Current Opinion* (September 1920), 355-7; George Sylvester Viereck, 'Freud: Columbus of the Subconscious', *Forum* (March 1925), 302–12; Cornelia Stratton Parker, 'The Capital of Psychology', *Survey* (15 August 1925), cited in Gary Dean Best, *The Dollar Decade: Mammon and the Machine in 1920s America* (Westport, CT: Praeger, 2003), pp. 2–5.

51. Hale, *The Rise and Crisis of Psychoanalysis*, p. 27.

52. For the popular reception of Freud's ideas see Hoffman, *Freudianism and the Literary Mind*, pp. 44–77.

53. Stearns, *Civilization in the United States*, p. 434.

54. Lucy T. Benjamin and David N. Dixon, 'Dream Analysis by Mail: An American Woman Seeks Freud's Advice', *American Psychologist* 51.6 (1996), p. 461.

55. Hale, *The Rise and Crisis of Psychoanalysis*, pp. 91–3. For an excellent introduction and collection of primary documents concerning the trial see Douglas

Linder, *Illinois v. Nathan Leopold and Richard Loeb: An Introduction*, at http://www.law.umkc.edu/faculty/projects/ftrials/leoploeb/leopold.htm.

56. Hale, *The Rise and Crisis of Psychoanalysis*, pp. 89–91.

57. Ann Douglas, *Terrible Honesty: Mongrel Manhattan in the 1920s* (New York: Farrar, Straus and Giroux, 1995), p. 21.

58. Freud, *The Future of an Illusion*, p. 25.

59. 'Religion Doomed', *New York Times* (27 December 1927), p. 6.

60. Shailer Matthews, *The Faith of Modernism* (New York: Macmillan, 1924), pp. 22–3.

61. Charles H. Lippy, 'Religious Liberalism, Fundamentalism, and Orthodoxy', in Mary Kupiec Cayton et al. (eds), *Encyclopedia of American Cultural and Intellectual History*, Vol. 1 (New York: Scribner's, 2001), pp. 713–22. For a general survey of religion in the decade see Lynn Dumenil, *The Modern Temper: American Culture and Society in the 1920s* (New York: Hill and Wang: 1995), pp. 169–200.

62. George M. Marsden, *The Shaping of Twentieth Century Evangelicalism, 1870–1925* (New York: Oxford University Press, 1980), p. 159.

63. Harry Emerson Fosdick, 'Shall the Fundamentalists Win?', *Christian Work* 102 (10 June 1922), pp. 716–22.

64. John Thomas Scopes, *The World's Most Famous Court Trial: State of Tennessee v. John Thomas Scopes. Complete Stenographic Report . . . Including Speeches and Arguments of Attorneys* (New York: Da Capo Press, [1925] 1971), p. 5.

65. Cited in Sheldon Norman Grebstein (ed.), *Monkey Trial: The State of Tennessee vs. John Thomas Scopes* (Boston: Houghton Mifflin, 1960), p. 195.

66. Lawrence Levine, cited in Edward J. Larson, *Summer for the Gods: The Scopes Trial and America's Continuing Debate over Science and Religion* (New York: Basic Books, 1997), p. 39.

67. Bryan cited in Grebstein, *Monkey Trial*, p. 164.

68. Darrow cited in Grebstein, *Monkey Trial*, p. 164.

69. Larson, *Summer for the Gods*, pp. 140–203.

70. Scopes, *The World's Most Famous Court Trial*, p. 87.

71. Grebstein, *Monkey Trial*, pp. 158–9.

72. Ibid., pp. 20, 195.

73. H. L. Mencken, 'The Monkey Trial: A Reporter's Account' (1925), online at http://www.law.umkc.edu/faculty/projects/ftrials/scopes/menk.htm.

74. John Dewey, 'The American Intellectual Frontier' (1922), reprinted in Bilton and Melling (eds), *America in the 1920s*, pp. 98, 96.

75. Ibid., p. 98.

76. Carter, *Another Part of the Twenties*, p. 79.

77. Stanley Cobden, *Rebellion Against Victorianism: The Impetus for Cultural Change in 1920s America* (New York: Oxford University Press, 1991), pp. 136–56. See also Dumenil, *The Modern Temper*, pp. 235–49.

78. Michael E. Parrish, *Anxious Decades: America in Prosperity and Depression 1920–1941* (New York: Norton, 1993), p. 119.

79. Ibid., p. 118.

80. Rolf Lunden, *Business and Religion in the American 1920s* (New York: Green wood Press, 1988), p. 60. See also R. Laurence Moore, *Selling God: American Religion in the Marketplace of Culture* (New York: Oxford University Press, 1995).

81. Shailer Matthews, 'Business – Maker of Morals' (1927), cited in Lunden, *Business and Religion*, p. 36.

82. Susan Nance, 'Mystery of the Moorish Science Temple: Southern Blacks and American Alternative Spirituality in 1920s Chicago', *Religion and American Culture* 12.2 (2002), 123–66; Susan Nance, 'Respectability and Representation: The Moorish Science Temple, Morocco, and Black Public Culture in 1920s Chicago', *American Quarterly* 54.4 (2002), pp. 623–59.

83. See Randall K. Burkett and David W. Wills, 'African American Religious History, 1919–1939', http://www.amherst.edu/~aardoc/Biblio.html. See also Randall K. Burkett, *Garveyism as A Religious Movement: The Institutionalization of a Black Civil Religion* (Metuchen, NJ: Scarecrow Press, 1978).

84. John White, *Black Leadership in America* (London: Longman, 1985), pp. 83–104.

85. Stanley Cobden, *Rebellion Against Victorianism: The Impetus for Cultural Change in 1920s America* (New York: Oxford University Press, 1991), pp. 74–90.

86. Marcus Garvey, *The Philosophy and Opinions of Marcus Garvey*, ed. Amy Jacques Garvey, [1923] http://www.wordowner.com/garvey/.

87. W. E. Burghardt Du Bois, *The Souls of Black Folk* (Chicago: A. C. McClurg & Co., 1903). Available online at http://www.bartleby.com/114/2.html.

88. Lothrop Stoddard, *The Rising Tide of Color Against White World-Supremacy* (New York: Charles Scribner's Sons, 1920), pp. xxix, xxxii.

89. Ibid., p. 61.

90. Ibid., pp. 219–21.

91. Ibid., p. 255.

92. For a detailed discussion of the rise of anti-immigration and the passage of the acts see David J. Goldberg, *Discontented America: The United States in the 1920s* (Baltimore, MD: Johns Hopkins University Press, 1999), pp. 140–66.

93. Grant Overton, *American Nights Entertainment* (New York: D. Appleton & Co., 1923), p. 381.

94. Ibid., p. 382.

95. 'Shall the Negro be Encouraged to Seek Cultural Equality?', *Report of Debate Conducted by the Chicago Forum. Affirmative: W. E. B. Du Bois; Negative: Lothrop Stoddard, March 17, 1929* (Chicago: Chicago Forum Council, 1929). See also Jane Kuenz, 'Black No More: George Schulyer and the Politics of Racial Culture', Victor A. Kramer and Robert A. Russ (eds), *Harlem Renaissance Re-Examined*, (Troy, NY: Whitston Publishing Co., 1997), p. 202.

96. See Daylanne K. English, *Unnatural Selections: Eugenics in American Modernism and the Harlem Renaissance* (Chapel Hill, NC: University of North Carolina Press, 2004).

97. Laban Carrick Hill, *Harlem Stomp: A Cultural History of the Harlem Renaissance*, (New York: Little, Brown, 2003), pp. 56–7.

98. *Survey Graphic* special edition, *Harlem: Mecca of the New Negro* (March 1925) available online at http://etext.virginia.edu/harlem/.

99. Alain Locke, *The New Negro: Voices from the Harlem Renaissance* (New York: Simon and Schuster, [1925] 1997), p. 8.

100. Ibid., p. 15.

101. Douglas, *Terrible Honesty*, p. 332.

102. Barbara Foley argues that Locke's formulation of the New Negro was a retreat from radical class-based politics into 'cultural romanticism'. See Foley, *Spectres of 1919: Class and Nation in the Making of the New Negro* (Urbana, IL: University of Illinois Press, 2003).
103. Locke, *The New Negro*, p. xix.
104. Ibid., p. 10.
105. Dumenil, *The Modern Temper*, pp. 98–144.
106. Stearns, *Civilization in the United States*, p. 135.
107. Ibid., p. 145.
108. Ibid.
109. Ibid., p. 182.
110. Ibid., p. 438.
111. Kathleen M. Blee, 'Women in the 1920s Ku Klux Klan Movement', *Feminist Studies*, 17.1 (1991), p. 67. See also Kathleen M. Blee, *Inside Organized Racism: Women in the Hate Movement* (Berkeley, CA: University of California Press, 2002).
112. Blee, 'Women in the 1920s', p. 73.
113. Daniel J. Kevles, *In the Name of Eugenics: Genetics and the Uses of Human Heredity* (Cambridge, MA: Harvard University Press, 1999), p. 90.
114. Margaret Sanger, *The Pivot of Civilization* (New York: Brentano's, 1922).
115. The law was not repealed until 1974. See Kevles, *In the Name of Eugenics*, p. 100.
116. John Dewey, in Albert Einstein et al., *Living Philosophies* (New York: Simon and Schuster, 1931), p. 33.
117. Baker Brownell, *The New Universe: An Outline of the Worlds in Which We Live* (New York: D. Van Nostrand, 1926), p. 290.
118. Krutch, 'The Modern Temper' (1927), reprinted in Bilton and Melling (eds), *America in the 1920s*, pp. 132, 134.

1. Fiction, Poetry and Drama

1. Willa Cather, *The Professor's House* (London: Virago Press, [1925] 2003), p. 150.
2. See Douglas, *Terrible Honesty*, p. 41.
3. Malcolm Cowley, *Exile's Return: A Literary Odyssey of the 1920s* (New York: Penguin Books, [1934] 1994), p. 9.
4. Krutch reprinted in Baritz, *The Culture of the Twenties*, p. 371. Cowley, *Exile's Return*, p. 9.
5. George Santayana, *Character and Opinion in the United States: With Reminiscences of William James and Josiah Royce and Academic Life in America* (New York: Scribner's, 1920), p. 172.
6. Douglas, *Terrible Honesty*, p. 23.
7. F. Scott Fitzgerald, *The Crack Up* (New York: New Directions, [1945] 1962), p. 20.
8. Sigmund Freud, *Beyond the Pleasure Principle*, trans. James Strachey (New York: Norton, 1961), p. 30.
9. Thomas Stearns Eliot, *The Waste Land* (New York: Boni and Liveright, 1922).
10. Frederick Hoffman, *The Twenties: American Writing in the Postwar Decade* (New York: Free Press, 1965), p. 78.

11. John Dos Passos, *One Man's Initiation: 1917* (New York: George H. Doran Co., 1922), p. 86.
12. Dos Passos, *One Man's Initiation*, p. 113.
13. John Dos Passos, *Three Soldiers* (New York: George H. Doran Co., 1921), p. 201.
14. Ernest Hemingway, *The Essential Hemingway* (London: Arrow Books, 2004), p. 333.
15. Quoted in Ronald E. Martin, *American Literature and the Destruction of Knowledge: Innovative Writing in the Age of Epistemology* (Durham, NC: Duke University Press, 1991), p. 216.
16. Ernest Hemingway, *The Essential Hemingway* (London: Random House, [1947] 2004), p. 7.
17. Alan Trachtenberg and Benjamin DeMott (eds), *America in Literature*, Vol. 2 (New York: John Wiley and Sons, 1978), p. 1917.
18. Claude McKay, *Home to Harlem* (Lebanon, NH: Northeastern University Press, [1928] 1987), p. 156.
19. Alain Locke, *The New Negro*, p. 14.
20. Alan Locke, 'Harlem', *Survey Graphic* (March 1925), p. 629. Available online at http://etext.virginia.edu/harlem/LocHarlF.html.
21. Ibid.
22. Jessie Fauset, 'Nostalgia', *The Crisis* 22 (August 1921), pp. 154–8.
23. Sterling A. Brown et al. (eds), *Negro Caravan* (New York: Dryden Press, 1941), p. 368. Available online at http://cai.ucdavis.edu/uccp/wearyblues.html.
24. F. Scott Fitzgerald, *The Great Gatsby* (London: Penguin Books, [1926] 2000), p. 106.
25. Ibid., p. 114.
26. Ibid., p. 79.
27. Ibid., pp. 8, 106.
28. Ibid., p. 9.
29. Ibid., p. 170.
30. Ibid., p. 26.
31. Ibid., p. 131.
32. Hearst began building his castle in California in 1919; it was a patchwork of architectural styles from Roman, Greek, Egyptian, Gothic and Medieval Spanish. Like Ford, Hearst didn't just recreate buildings but dismantled and imported originals from around the world and had them reconstructed on his land.
33. Fitzgerald, *The Great Gatsby*, pp. 171–2.
34. Gertrude Stein, 'Composition as Explanation' (1926). Available online at http://academic.evergreen.edu/curricular/fopa/theatre/texts/stein.htm.
35. Ezra Pound, *Machine Art and Other Writings: The Lost Thought of the Italian Years*, ed. Maria Luisa Ardizzone (Durham, NC: Duke University Press, 1996).
36. See Lisa M. Steinman, *Made in America: Science, Technology and American Modernist Poets* (New Haven, CT: Yale University Press, 1987).
37. Gertrude Stein, *The Making of Americans: Being a History of a Family's Progress* (The Dalkey Archive Press, [1925] 1995), p. 3.
38. Ibid., p. 186.
39. Thomas Stearns Eliot, *The Sacred Wood* (London: Methuen, 1920), online at http://www.bartleby.com/200/.

40. T. S, Eliot, 'Tradition and the Individual Talent' [1919], published in *The Sacred Wood*.
41. Marianne Moore, *Selected Poems* (New York: Macmillan, 1935), p. 99.
42. Carol Donley, '"Springtime of the Mind": Poetic Responses to Einstein and Relativity', in Dennis P. Ryan (ed.), *Einstein and the Humanities* (New York: Greenwood Press, 1987), p. 119.
43. See Cecilia Tichi, *Shifting Gears: Technology, Literature, Culture in Modernist America* (Chapel Hill, NC: University of North Carolina Press, 1987), p. 267.
44. Archibald MacLeish, 'Einstein', in *Collected Poems* (Boston: Houghton Mifflin, 1985), p. 143.
45. William Carlos Williams, *Selected Poems* (New Directions, 1985), pp. 44, 55. An archive of recordings (including 'To Elsie') is available at http://writing.upenn.edu/pennsound/x/Williams-WC.html.
46. Pound, *Machine Art*, p. 81. On Pound's interest in science and mathematics see Ian F. Bell, 'The Poundian Fourth Dimension', *Symbiosis* 11.2 (October 2007), pp. 61–84.
47. Frederick J. Hoffman, 'The Technological Fallacy in Contemporary Poetry: Hart Crane and MacKnight Black', *American Literature* 21.1 (March 1949), 94–107.
48. Langston Hughes, 'The Negro Artist and the Racial Mountain', *Nation* 72 (23 June 1926), p. 693.
49. Oliver M. Sayler, 'Training the Playwright of the Machine Age', in Oliver Sayler (ed.), *Revolt in the Arts: A Survey of the Creation, Distribution and Appreciation of Art in America* (New York: Brentano's, 1930), p. 175.
50. Mardi Valgemae, *Accelerated Grimace: Expressionism in the American Drama of the 1920s* (Carbondale, IL: Southern Illinois University Press, 1972), pp. 73, 91.
51. See Constance D'Arcy Mackay, *The Little Theatre in the United States* (New York: Henry Holt, 1917); Oliver M. Sayler, *Our American Theatre* (New York: Brentano's, 1923); Weldon B. Durham (ed.), *American Theatre Companies, 1888–1930* (New York: Greenwood Press, 1987). On black little theatre see Yvonne Shafer, *American Women Playwrights, 1900–1950* (New York: Peter Lang, 1997), p. 159.
52. Carme Manuel, 'A Ghost in the Expressionist Jungle of O'Neill's *The Emperor Jones*', *African American Review* 39 (Spring 2005), 67–85. For a vast collection of scholarship and original documents from the era see the Eugene O'Neill electronic archive at http://www.eoneill.com/.
53. W. David Sievers, *Freud On Broadway: A History of Psychoanalysis and the American Drama* (New York: Cooper Square Publishers, [1955] 1970), pp. 104–5.
54. Ibid., p. 98.
55. Ibid., p. 115.
56. See Tamsen Wolff, '"Eugenic O'Neill" and the Secrets of *Strange Interlude*', *Theatre Journal* 55 (2003), p. 221.
57. Hoffman, *The Twenties*, p. 256.
58. Eugene O'Neill, *The Collected Plays of Eugene O'Neill* (London: Jonathan Cape, 1988), p. 806.
59. Adams, *The Education of Henry Adams*, at http://xroads.virginia.edu/~HYPER/hadams/eha25.html.

60. Mardi Valgemae, 'Civil War among the Expressionists: John Howard Lawson and the "Pinwheel" Controversy', *Educational Theatre Journal* 20.1 (March 1968), pp. 8–14. See also Dennis G. Jerz, *Technology in American Drama, 1920–1950: Soul and Society in the Age of the Machine* (New York: Greenwood Press, 2003).

61. Elmer Rice, *Elmer Rice: Three Plays* (New York: Hill and Wang, 1993), p. 61.

62. Elmer Rice, *The Subway: A Play in Nine Scenes* (New York: S. French, 1929), pp. 94–5.

63. Valgemae, *Accelerated Grimace*, p. 94.

64. Ibid., p. 92.

65. Ibid., p. 88.

66. Ibid., p. 87.

67. For other types of drama such as vaudeville see Arthur Gerwitz and James J. Kolb (eds), *Art, Glitter and Glitz: Mainstream Playwrights and Popular Theatre in 1920s America* (Westport, CT: Praeger, 2004).

68. Sinclair Lewis, *Main Street: The Story of Carol Kennicott* (New York: Harcourt, Brace and Howe, 1920), p. 265.

69. Ibid.

70. Sinclair Lewis, *Babbitt* (New York: New American Library, [1922] 1961), p. 5.

71. Ibid., p. 8.

72. Ibid., p. 16.

73. Raegis Michaud, *The American Novel To-Day: A Social and Psychological Study* (Boston: Little, Brown, 1928), pp. 145–6.

74. H. L. Mencken, 'Sahara of the Bozart' [1917], reprinted in Huntington Cairns (ed.), *The American Scene: A Reader* (New York: Alfred Knopf, 1977), pp. 157–8.

75. Ibid., p. 160.

76. In fact, Mencken provided succour to these magazines and the Southern renaissance. See Richard H. King, *A Southern Renaissance: The Cultural Awakening of the American South* (New York: Oxford University Press, 1980), p. 14.

77. Richard Gray, *A History of American Literature* (Malden, MA: Blackwell Publishing, 2004), p. 464.

78. Paul V. Murphy, *The Rebuke of History: The Southern Agrarians and American Conservative Thought* (Chapel Hill, NC: University of North Carolina Press, 2001), p. 29.

79. All quotes from Hoffman, *The Twenties*, p. 174.

80. For the influence of 'The Waste Land' see Murphy, *The Rebuke of History*, p. 12.

81. John Tyree Fain and Thomas Daniel Young (eds), *The Literary Correspondence of Donald Davidson and Allen Tate* (Athens: University of Georgia Press, 1974), p. 189.

82. Religion was central to the agrarians who saw it as the path towards moral unity. See Murphy, *The Rebuke of History*, p. 55.

83. Susan V. Donaldson, 'Introduction', *I'll Take My Stand: The South and the Agrarian Tradition* (Baton Rouge, LA: Louisiana State University Press, 2006), p. x. Paul K. Conkin, *The Southern Agrarians* (Knoxville: University of Tennessee Press, 1988); Richard Gray, *Writing the South: Ideas of an American Region* (New York: Cambridge University Press, 1986).

84. Hoffman, *The Twenties*, p. 181.
85. Ibid., p. 181. See also Benedict Anderson, 'The South of the Agrarians', in Michael Kreyling (ed.), *Inventing Southern Literature* (Jackson, MS: University Press of Mississippi, 1998), p. 5. The critical historiography of the Southern Renaissance is outlined by John M. Grammer, 'Reconstructing Southern Literature', *American Literary History* 13.1 (Spring 2001), pp. 126–40.
86. Donaldson, *I'll Take My Stand*, p. xxiv.
87. Clifford E. Wulfman, 'Sighting/siting/citing the Scar: Trauma and Homecoming in Faulkner's Soldiers' Pay', *Studies in American Fiction* 31.1 (2003), p. 29. Faulkner had volunteered but had not been able to serve in the war.
88. Gray, *A History of American Literature*, p. 448.
89. William Faulkner, *The Sound and the Fury and As I Lay Dying* (New York: Modern Library, 1946), p. 19.
90. Faulkner, *The Sound and the Fury*, p. 95. For a discussion of Faulkner's modernism see Daniel J. Singal, *William Faulkner: The Making of a Modernist* (Chapel Hill, NC: University of North Carolina Press, 1997). See also Doreen Fowler and Ann J. Abadie (eds), *Faulkner and the Southern Renaissance* (Jackson, MS: University of Mississippi Press, 1982).
91. Adams, *The Education of Henry Adams*, p. 382.
92. See John R. Cooley, *Savages and Naturals: Black Portraits by White Writers in Modern American Literature* (Newark, DE: University of Delaware Press, 1982); Susan Gubar, *Racechanges: White Skin, Black Face in American Culture* (New York: Oxford University Press, 1997); Michael North, *Dialect of Modernism: Race, Language, and Twentieth-Century Literature* (New York: Oxford University Press, 1998).
93. T. S. Stribling, *Birthright* (New York: Century, 1922).
94. Lynn Moss Sanders, *Howard W. Odum's Folklore Odyssey: Transformation to Tolerance through African American Folk Studies* (Athens: University of Georgia Press, 2004), p. 438; see also Singal, *The War Within*, pp. 115–53. See excerpt of *Black Ulysses* at: http://www.africanaheritage.com/OdumRainbowRound.asp.
95. Sigmund Freud, *Civilization and Its Discontents*, ed. James Strachey (New York: Norton, 1961), p. 33.
96. See, for example, Elazar Barkan and Ronald Bush (eds), *Prehistories of the Future: The Primitivist Project and the Culture of Modernism* (Stanford, CA: Stanford University Press, 1995); Susan Hegeman, *Patterns for America: Modernism and the Concept of Culture* (Princeton, NJ: Princeton University Press, 1999).
97. Houston A. Baker, *Modernism and the Harlem Renaissance* (Chicago: University of Chicago Press, 1987).
98. Charles T. Davis, 'Jean Toomer and the South: Region and Race as Elements Within a Literary Imagination', Victor A. Kramer and Robert A. Russ (eds), *Harlem Renaissance Re-Examined* (Troy, New York: Whitston Publishing Co., 1997), p. 217.
99. Jean Toomer, *Cane: An Authoritative Text, Backgrounds, Criticism*, ed. Darwin T. Turner (New York: Norton, 1988), p. 121.
100. Ibid., p. 136.
101. Ibid., p. 4.
102. Ibid., p. 6.

103. Ibid., p. 14.

104. Davis, 'Jean Toomer and the South', p. 222.

105. Gorham B. Munson, *Destinations: A Canvass of American Literature since 1900* (New York: J. H. Sears & Co., 1928), p. 181.

106. Toomer, *Cane*, p. 7.

107. Ibid., *Cane*, p. 42.

108. Barbara Foley, '"In the Land of Cotton": Economics and Violence in Jean Toomer's *Cane*', *African American Review* 32.2 (1998), p. 181.

109. Toomer, *Cane*, p. 109.

110. Mark Helbling, *The Harlem Renaissance: The One and the Many* (Westport, CT: Greenwood Press, 1999), pp. 131, 130.

111. Ibid., p. 131.

112. Arthur A. Schomburg, 'The Negro Digs Up His Past', *Survey Graphic* (March 1925), 670. Available online at http://etext.virginia.edu/harlem/SchNegrF.html.

113. The full text of James Weldon Johnson's *God's Trombones*, with illustrations by Aaron Douglas, is available online at http://docsouth.unc.edu/southlit/johnson/johnson.html.

114. Sociologist Robert E. Park reviewed all of these in one extended review in *The American Journal of Sociology* 33.6 (May 1928), pp. 988–95.

115. Jordan Miller and Winifred Frazer, *American Drama Between the Wars: A Critical History* (Boston: Twayne Publishers 1991), p. 252.

116. Alain Locke, 'Negro Youth Speaks', in *The New Negro*, p. 49.

117. W. E. B. Du Bois, 'Criteria of Negro Art', *The Crisis* 32 (October 1926), pp. 290–7. Available online at: http://www.webdubois.org/dbCriteriaNArt.html.

118. George S. Schuyler, 'The Negro-Art Hokum', *Nation* 122 (16 June 1926), pp. 662–3. Available online at: http://www.westga.edu/~sboyd/George%20Schuyler%20negro%20art%20hokum.pdf.

119. Hughes, 'The Negro Artist and the Racial Mountain', p. 693.

120. Bruce Nugent, 'Smoke, Lilies, Jade', available online at http://www.brucenugent.com/Assets/Text/Smoke.htm.

121. Zora Neale Hurston, 'How It Feels to Be Colored Me', *World Tomorrow* 11 (May 1928), pp. 215–16. Available online at: http://xroads.virginia.edu/~MA01/Grand-Jean/Hurston/Chapters/how.html.

122. David Krasner, 'Migration, Fragmentation, and Identity: Zora Neale Hurston's *Color Struck* and the Geography of the Harlem Renaissance', *Theatre Journal* 53 (2001), p. 534.

123. Some of her unpublished plays are available at the Zora Neale Hurston digital archive online at http://memory.loc.gov/ammem/znhhtml/znhhome.html. *Color Struck* is available at: http://xroads.virginia.edu/~MA01/Grand-Jean/Hurston/Chapters/supporting/color.html.

124. Published in *Crisis*, 1925; see Heather E. Spahr, 'Marita Bonner (1898–1971)', in Emmanuel S. Nelson (ed.), *African American Authors, 1745–1945 A Bio-Bibliographical Critical Sourcebook* (Westport, CT: Greenwood Press, 2000), p. 31.

125. Joyce Flynn and Joyce Occomy Stricklin (eds), *Frye Street and Environs: The Collected Works of Marita Bonner* (Boston: Beacon Press, 1987).

126. Shafer, *American Women Playwrights*, p. 431.

127. Deborah Parsons, *Djuna Barnes* (Tavistock: Northcote House, 2003), p. 29.

128. Karen Jackson Ford, *Gender and the Poetics of Excess: Moments of Brocade* (Jackson, MS: University Press of Mississippi, 1997), p. 96. See also Ford's 'Essay on Patriarchal Poetry' at the *Modern American Poetry* archive online at http://www.english.uiuc.edu/maps/poets/s_z/stein/ford.htm.
129. Dorothy Parker, *The Collected Dorothy Parker* (London: Penguin Books, 2001), p. 201.
130. Anita Loos, *Gentlemen Prefer Blondes: The Illuminating Diary of a Professional Lady* (New York: Penguin Books, [1926] 1998), p. 90.

2. Music and Performance

1. Paul Whiteman quoted in Isaac Goldberg, *Tin Pan Alley: A Chronicle of the American Popular Music Racket* (New York: John Day, 1930), p. 291. Most of the original recordings mentioned in this chapter can be heard at the *Red Hot Jazz Archive* at http://www.redhotjazz.com.
2. Kathy Ogren, *The Jazz Revolution: Twenties America and the Meaning of Jazz* (New York: Oxford University Press, 1989), pp. 5–6.
3. Sigmund Spaeth quoted in Lawrence Levine, *The Unpredictable Past*, p. 182.
4. Anne Shaw Faulkner, 'Does Jazz Put the Sin in Syncopation?', *Ladies Home Journal* (August 1921), pp. 16–34. Online at http://faculty.pittstate.edu/~knichols/syncopate.html.
5. Paul Whiteman quoted in Goldberg, *Tin Pan Alley*, p. 291.
6. Okeh Records Advert reproduced in Derrick Stewart-Baxter's *Ma Rainey and the Classic Blues Singers* (London: Studio Vista, 1970), p. 60.
7. J. A. Rogers, 'Jazz at Home', *Survey Graphic* (March 1925), p. 665, online at http://etext.virginia.edu/harlem/RogJazzF.html.
8. Ibid.
9. Ibid., p. 667.
10. F. Scott Fitzgerald, *The Great Gatsby* (London: Penguin Books, [1926] 2000), pp. 102, 51.
11. Quoted in Sascha Feinstein, *Jazz Poetry: From the 1920s to the Present* (Westport, CT: Praeger, 1997), p. 17.
12. Vachel Lindsay, *Collected Poems* revised ed. (New York: Macmillan, 1925), p. 401.
13. Joel Dinerstein, *Swinging the Machine: Modernity, Technology, and African American Culture between the World Wars* (Amherst, MA: University of Massachusetts Press, 2003), p. 112.
14. For a detailed history of the role of ethnicity and race in the early recording industry see William Howland Kenney, *Recorded Music in American Life: The Phonograph and Popular Memory, 1890–1945* (New York: Oxford University Press, 1999)
15. Stewart-Baxter, *Ma Rainey*, p. 12.
16. David Evans, 'The Development of the Blues', in Allan Moore (ed.), *The Cambridge Companion to Blues and Gospel Music*, (Cambridge: Cambridge University Press, 2002), p. 27.
17. Amiri Baraka, *Blues People: Negro Music in White America* (New York: W. Morrow, 1963), p. 129.
18. *Victor Records; Vocal Blues, Religious Spirituals, Red Hot Dance Tunes, Sermons,*

Novelties (1929) available online at http://memory.loc.gov/mbrs/amrlr/lr03/lr030001.jpg.

19. Gunter Schuller, *Early Jazz: Its Roots and Musical Development* (New York: Oxford University Press, 1968), pp. 176–81.

20. Ted Gioia, *The History of Jazz* (New York: Oxford University Press, 1999), p. 46.

21. For a discussion of white rebellion through jazz see Burton W. Peretti, *The Creation of Jazz: Music, Race and Culture in Urban America* (Chicago: University of Illinois Press, 1992), pp. 76–99; Neil Leonard, *Jazz and the White Americans: The Acceptance of a New Art Form* (Chicago: University of Chicago Press, 1962).

22. William Ruhlmann, *Breaking Records: 100 Years of Hits* (New York: Routledge, 2004), p. 40; Leonard, *Jazz and the White Americans*, p. 92.

23. Dinerstein, *Swinging the Machine*, p. 111.

24. Douglas, *Terrible Honesty*, p. 410.

25. On the diverse origins and development of early classic blues and jazz see Baraka, *Blues People*, pp. 81–141.

26. Richard Hadlock, *Jazz Masters of the 20s* (New York: Da Capo Press, 1988), p. 221.

27. John W. Parker, 'Lemon, Jelly, and All That Jazz', in Lawrence R. Broer and John D. Walther (eds), *Dancing Fools and Weary Blues: The Great Escape of the Twenties*, (Bowling Green, OH: Bowling Green State University Popular Press, 1990), p. 149.

28. Dick Weissman, *Blues: The Basics* (New York: Routledge, 2004), p. 34.

29. Angela Davis, *Blues Legacies and Black Feminism: Gertrude "Ma" Rainey, Bessie Smith, and Billie Holiday* (New York: Pantheon Books, 1998), p. xiii.

30. Bessie Smith, 'Young Woman's Blues', in Rose (ed.), *American Decades: Primary Sources*, p. 29.

31. Chris Albertson, *Bessie: A Biography* (London: Barrie and Jenkins, 1972), p. 107.

32. Ibid., pp. 142–4.

33. Hadlock, *Jazz Masters*, p. 236.

34. Ruhlmann, *Breaking Records*, p. 44. To hear examples of popular recordings from the 20s that were jazzed-up popular songs rather than authentic jazz go to *1920s Dance Music Recordings* at http://www.besmark.com/index.html.

35. Leonard, *Jazz and the White Americans*, p. 92.

36. Marshall W. Stearns, *The Story of Jazz* (London: Oxford University Press, 1970), p. 165.

37. Gilbert Seldes, *The Seven Lively Arts* (New York: Harper & Brothers, 1924), p. 83.

38. George Gershwin, 'The Composer in the Machine Age', in Sayler, *Revolt in the Arts*, p. 266.

39. Lawrence W. Levine, 'Jazz and American Culture', *The Journal of American Folklore* 102.403 (1989), p. 7.

40. Faulkner, 'Does Jazz Put the Sin in Syncopation?'.

41. Ibid.

42. Ibid. Further examples of such opposition to jazz are in Levine, 'Jazz and American Culture' and Leonard, *Jazz and the White Americans*, pp. 29–46.

43. For an analysis and explanation of the lyrics and how they changed over the 20s to accommodate commercial and social imperatives see Leonard, *Jazz and the White Americans*, pp. 108–19, 167–9.

44. Goldberg, *Tin Pan Alley*, p. 293.

45. Frank Tirro, *Jazz: A History* (New York: Norton, 1993), p. 142.

46. Carol J. Oja, *Making Music Modern: New York in the 1920s* (New York: Oxford University Press, 2000), p. 328.

47. See also Levine, 'Jazz and American Culture', p. 12.

48. Alan Locke, 'Harlem', *Survey Graphic* (March 1925), p. 629.

49. Langston Hughes, 'The Negro Artist and the Racial Mountain', *Nation* 72 (23 June 1926), 693. Available online at: http://www.hartford-hwp.com/archives/45a/360.html.

50. Peretti, *The Creation of Jazz*, p. 61.

51. Samuel A. Floyd Jr, 'Music in the Harlem Renaissance: An Overview', in Samuel A. Floyd Jr (ed.), *Black Music in the Harlem Renaissance* (Westport, CT: Greenwood Press, 1990), p. 7.

52. Jeffrey Magee, *The Uncrowned King of Swing: Fletcher Henderson and Big Band Jazz* (New York: Oxford University Press, 2005).

53. Mark Tucker, *Ellington: The Early Years* (Champaign, IL: University of Illinois Press, 1995).

54. Stearns, *The Story of Jazz*, pp. 184–5. Arnold Shaw, *The Jazz Age: Popular Music in the 1920s* (New York: Oxford University Press, 1990), p. 62.

55. Harvey G. Cohen, 'The Marketing of Duke Ellington: Setting the Strategy for an African American Maestro', *The Journal of African American History* 89.4 (2004), p. 291.

56. Dinerstein, *Swinging the Machine*, p. 115. See also Floyd (ed.), *Black Music in the Harlem Renaissance*, p. 8.

57. Peretti, *The Creation of Jazz*, p. 118.

58. Paul Burgett, 'The Writings of Alain Locke', in Samuel A. Floyd Jr (ed.), *Black Music in the Harlem Renaissance* (Westport, CT: Greenwood Press, 1990), p. 36.

59. Mark Tucker, 'The Renaissance Education of Duke Ellington', in Floyd (ed.), *Black Music in the Harlem Renaissance*, p. 123.

60. Dinerstein, *Swinging the Machine*, p. 58.

61. Quote by Noble Sissle in Constance Valis Hill, *Brotherhood in Rhythm: The Jazz Tap Dancing of the Nicholas Brothers* (New York: Oxford University Press, 2000), p. 11.

62. George Gershwin, 'The Composer in the Machine Age', in Sayler, *Revolt in the Arts*, p. 264.

63. Goldberg, *Tin Pan Alley*, p. 268.

64. For examples of his performances go to the website http://www.antheil.org/.

65. Dinerstein, *Swinging the Machine*, p. 112.

66. Oja, *Making Music Modern*, p. 356.

67. Ibid., p. 72.

68. Felix Borowski, 'John Alden Carpenter', *The Musical Quarterly* 16.4 (1930), 449–68.

69. Nicholas E. Tawa, *Mainstream Music of Early Twentieth Century America: The Composers, Their Times, and Their Works* (Westport, CT: Greenwood Press, 1992), p. 177.

70. Oja, *Making Music Modern*, pp. 337–40.

71. Aaron Copland, 'Jazz Structure and Influence', in *Modern Music* (January–February 1927), quoted in Goldberg, *Tin Pan Alley*, p. 296.

72. Marion Bauer, *Twentieth Century Music: How it Developed, How to Listen to It* (New York: G. P. Putnam's Sons, 1933), p. 273.

73. Oja, *Making Music Modern*, p. 342.

74. Floyd, *Black Music in the Harlem Renaissance*, p. 15.

75. Ibid., p. 13.

76. Oja, *Making Music Modern*, p. 331; Peretti, *The Creation of Jazz*, p. 73.

77. Floyd, *Black Music in the Harlem Renaissance*, p. 22.

78. 'William Grant Still and Verna Avey Papers', *University of Arkansas Library Special Collections*, at http://libinfo.uark.edu/SpecialCollections/findingaids/still/still4aid.html.

79. Whiteman quoted in Leonard, *Jazz and the White Americans*, p. 80.

80. Ibid., p. 79.

81. Oja, *Making Music Modern*, p. 318.

82. Henry O. Osgood, *So This Is Jazz* (Boston: Little, Brown, 1926), p. 180.

83. Leonard, *Jazz and the White Americans*, pp. 80–2.

84. Oja, *Making Music Modern*, p. 327.

85. Rogers, 'Jazz at Home', p. 712.

86. Seldes, *The Seven Lively Arts*, p. 97.

87. Paul Whiteman and Mary Margaret McBride, *Jazz* (New York: J. H. Sears & Co., 1926), p. 155, cited in Leonard, *Jazz and the White Americans*, p. 77.

88. Stearns, *The Story of Jazz*, p. 167.

89. Goldberg, *Tin Pan Alley*, p. 259.

90. Paul Rosenfield, *An Hour with American Music* (Philadelphia, PA: J. B. Lippincott Co., 1929), pp. 11, 13.

91. Leonard, *Jazz and the White Americans*, p. 88.

92. Jacqui Malone, 'Jazz Music in Motion: Dancers and Big Bands', in Robert G. O'Meally (ed.), *The Jazz Cadence of American Culture* (New York: Columbia University Press, 1998), p. 278.

93. Dinerstein, *Swinging the Machine*, pp. 29–39.

94. Ibid., pp. 58–9.

95. Sterns, *The Story of Jazz*, p. 95. See Hill, *Brotherhood in Rhythm*, p. 25 for origins of jazz dance in ragtime and minstrel shows.

96. Langston Hughes, 'When the Negro Was in Vogue' [1940], in Alexander Klein (ed.), *Empire City: A Treasury of New York* (New York: Ayer Publishing, 1971) p. 265.

97. Rae Linda Brown, 'William Grant Still, Florence Price, and William Dawson: Echoes of the Harlem Renaissance', in Floyd (ed.), *Black Music in the Harlem Renaissance*, p. 72.

98. Marshall Stearns and Jean Stearns, *Jazz Dance: The Story of American Vernacular Dance* (New York: Macmillan, 1968), pp. 132–48.

99. On Josephine Baker see Sieglinde Lemke, *Primitivist Modernism: Black Culture and the Origins of Transatlantic Modernism* (Oxford: Oxford University Press, 1998), p. 96.

100. 'Charleston', in Rose (ed.), *American Decades*, p. 209.

101. Stearns and Stearns, *Jazz Dance*, p. 29.

102. Ibid., pp. 111–12.
103. Constance Valis Hill, *Brotherhood in Rhythm: The Jazz Tap Dancing of the Nicholas Brothers* (New York: Oxford University Press, 2000), p. 27.
104. Stearns and Stearns, *Jazz Dance*, p. 145.
105. Dinerstein, *Swinging the Machine*, p. 253.
106. Seldes quoted in Gary Dean Best, *The Dollar Decade: Mammon and the Machine in 1920s America* (Westport, CT: Praeger, 2003), p. 14.
107. Constance Valis Hill, *Brotherhood in Rhythm: The Jazz Tap Dancing of the Nicholas Brothers* (New York: Oxford University Press, 2000), p. 27.
108. Jane Grant, 'Charleston', *New York Times* (30 August 1925), SM2.
109. Seldes in Best, *The Dollar Decade*, p. 14.
110. Stearns and Stearns, *Jazz Dance*, p. 112.
111. Paul R. Gorman, *Left Intellectuals and Popular Culture in Twentieth-Century America* (Chapel Hill, NC: University of North Carolina Press, 1996), p. 92.
112. 'Charleston? Heart Shimmy? Health Director Blames Strenuous Dance for Prevalence of Organic Troubles Among Young People', *Los Angeles Times* (7 April 1926), p. 9.
113. This story was in the *Los Angeles Times*, the *Washington Post* and the *New York Times*. See 'Girl Dead From Charleston; Doctor Calls Dance Dangerous', *New York Times* (16 February 1926), p. 27.
114. 'Charleston Causes Death; Strain of Prize Dance Affects Heart of Cincinnati Girl', *New York Times* (6 June 1926), p. 15.
115. 'Charleston in Rowboat Costs Lives of Six; Boy Demonstrating Dance Capsizes Craft', *New York Times* (21 June 1926), p. 2.
116. Stearns and Stearns, *Jazz Dance*, p. 315.
117. Dinerstein, *Swinging the Machine*, pp. 250–82.
118. Amritjit Singh and Daniel M. Scott (eds), *The Collected Writings of Wallace Thurman: A Harlem Renaissance Reader* (New Brunswick, NJ: Rutgers University Press, 2003), p. 49.
119. Stuart Chase, 'Play', in Charles A. Beard (ed.), *Whither Mankind: A Panorama of Modern Civilization* (New York: Longmans, Green & Co., 1928), p. 347.
120. Dinerstein, *Swinging the Machine*, p. 29.
121. 'Dance Teachers Hold "Henry Ford Night"; Continue Efforts to Discourage Charleston by Illustrating Old-Fashioned Steps', *New York Times* (26 August 1926), p. 10.
122. Julia L. Foulkes, *Modern Bodies: Dance and American Modernism from Martha Graham to Alvin Ailey* (Chapel Hill, NC: University of North Carolina Press, 2002), p. 13.
123. Ibid., p. 17.
124. Helen Thomas, *Dance, Modernity, and Culture: Explorations in the Sociology of Dance* (New York: Routledge, 1995), p. 108.
125. Ibid., p. 91. Martha Graham, 'Seeking an American Art of the Dance', in Sayler (ed.), *Revolt in the Arts*, p. 254.
126. Malcolm Cowley, *Exile's Return: A Literary Odyssey of the 1920s* ed. Donald Faulkner (New York: Penguin Books, 1994), p. 279.
127. Stearns and Stearns, *Jazz Dance*, p. 148.
128. Singh and Scott (eds), *The Collected Writings of Wallace Thurman*, p. 37.
129. Langston Hughes, 'When the Negro Was in Vogue', p. 266.

130. Walter White, 'Color Lines', *Survey Graphic* (March 1925), pp. 680–2, online at http://etext.virginia.edu/harlem/WhiColoF.html.
131. Claude McKay, *Harlem: Negro Metropolis* (New York: E. P. Dutton, 1968), pp. 118–19.
132. Leonard, *Jazz and the White Americans*, pp. 109–11.
133. Osgood, *So This Is Jazz*, p. 103.
134. Ann Douglas, *Terrible Honesty*, p. 395.
135. William Ruhlmann, *Breaking Records: 100 Years of Hits* (New York: Routledge, 2004), p. 42.

3. Film and Radio

1. See Lary May, *Screening Out the Past: The Birth of Mass Culture and the Motion Picture Industry* (Chicago: University of Chicago Press, [1980] 1983), pp. 60–95.
2. Lewis Jacobs, *The Rise of the American Film: A Critical History* (New York: Harcourt, Brace, 1939), p. 397.
3. Richard Wood and David Culbert (eds), *Film and Propaganda in America: A Documentary History: World War I* (New York: Greenwood Press, 1990). See also H. D. Lasswell, *Propaganda Technique in the World War* (New York: Knopf, 1927).
4. Charles Merz, 'When the Movies Go Abroad', *Harper's Magazine* (January 1926), reprinted in W. Brooke Graves (ed.), *Readings in Public Opinion: Its Formation and Control* (New York: D. Appleton, 1928), p. 372.
5. Richard Maltby, '"To Prevent the Prevalent Type of Book": Censorship and Adaptation in Hollywood, 1924–1934', *American Quarterly* 44.4 (December 1992), p. 557.
6. Will H. Hays, *See and Hear: A Brief History of Motion Pictures and the Development of Sound* (New York: Motion Picture Producers and Distributors of America, 1929), p. 4.
7. Merz, 'When the Movies Go Abroad', p. 375.
8. Jesse L. Lasky, 'Art on A Manufacturing Basis', in Oliver Sayler (ed.), *Revolt in the Arts*, pp. 215–21.
9. Ibid., p. 216.
10. Kristin Thompson and David Bordwell, *Film History: An Introduction* (Boston: McGraw-Hill, 2003), p. 144.
11. Steven J. Ross, 'Fantasy and Politics: Movie-Going and Movies in the 1920s', in Steven J. Ross (ed.), *Movies and American Society* (Oxford: Blackwell, 2002), pp. 64–97.
12. Richard Koszarski, *An Evening's Entertainment: The Age of the Silent Feature Picture, 1915–1928* (Berkeley, CA: University of California Press, [1990] 1994), pp. 45–53.
13. Ibid., p. 9.
14. Odegard, *The American Public Mind*, p. 218.
15. Lewis Jacobs, *The Rise of the American Film: A Critical History* (New York: Harcourt, Brace, 1939), p. 288.
16. Jacobs, *The Rise of the American Film*, p. 291. See also Benjamin Hampton, *History of the American Film Industry From Its Beginnings to 1931* (New York: Dover Publications, [1931] 1970), p. 318; and May, *Screening Out the Past*, p. 177.

17. Koszarski, *An Evening's Entertainment*, p. 104 and May, *Screening Out the Past*, pp. 214, 257.
18. Peter Odegard, *The American Public Mind* (New York: Columbia University Press, 1930), p. 199.
19. Steven Alan Carr, *Hollywood and Anti-Semitism: A Cultural History up to World War II* (Cambridge: Cambridge University Press, 2001), p. 98.
20. Odegard, *The American Public Mind*, p. 199.
21. Lynd and Lynd, *Middletown*, p. 266.
22. Ibid., p. 265.
23. Jim Heiman (ed.), *All-American Ads of the 20s* (New York: Taschen, 2004), p. 348.
24. Images and essays on these are available at 'Some Enchanted Evenings: American Picture Palaces', online at http://xroads.virginia.edu/~CAP/PALACE/. On the different types of establishments outside of the deluxe, see Koszarski, *An Evening's Entertainment*, p. 10.
25. Hampton, *History of the American Film Industry*, p. 326.
26. Lloyd Lewis, 'The Deluxe Picture Palace', *The New Republic* (27 March 1929), p. 175, reprinted in Steven J. Ross (ed.), *Movies and American Society*, p. 91. See also David Nasaw, *Going Out: The Rise and Fall of Public Amusements* (New York: Basic Books, 1993), pp. 221–40.
27. Gaylyn Studlar, *This Mad Masquerade: Stardom and Masculinity in the Jazz Age* (New York: Columbia University Press, 1996), p. 153.
28. Koszarski, *An Evening's Entertainment*, p. 30. See also Gaylyn Studlar, 'The Perils of Pleasure? Fan Magazine Discourse as Women's Commodified Culture in the 1920s', in Richard Abel (ed.), *Silent Film* (New Brunswick, NJ: Rutgers University Press, 1996), p. 263.
29. May, *Screening Out the Past*, pp. 233–4.
30. Odegard, *The American Public Mind*, pp. 200–1. Also discussed in Carr, *Hollywood and Anti-Semitism*, p. 63. Ross, *Movies and Mass Culture*, p. 77.
31. May, *Screening Out the Past*, p. 305.
32. See Richard Griffith and Arthur Mayer, *The Movies* (Feltham: Spring Books, 1971), pp. 121–37.
33. Mary P. Ryan, 'The Projection of a New Womanhood: The Movie Moderns in the 1920s', in Lois Scharf and Joan M. Jensen (eds), *Decades of Discontent: The Women's Movement, 1920–1940* (Boston: Northeastern University Press, 1987), p. 119.
34. See Sumiko Higashi, *Cecil B. DeMille and American Culture: The Silent Era* (Berkeley, CA: University of California Press, 1994), p. 143.
35. Higashi, *Cecil B. DeMille*, p. 144.
36. Odegard, *The American Public Mind*, p. 205.
37. Lori Landay, 'The Flapper Film: Comedy, Dance and Jazz Age Kinaesthetics', in Jennifer M. Bean and Diane Negra (eds), *A Feminist Reader in Early Cinema* (Durham, NC: Duke University Press, 2002), pp. 221–48.
38. Diane Negra, *Off-White Hollywood: American Culture and Ethnic Female Stardom* (London: Routledge, 2001), p. 29.
39. Marsha Orgeron, 'Making *It* in Hollywood: Clara Bow, Fandom, and Consumer Culture', *Cinema Journal* 42.4 (Summer 2003), p. 78.
40. Orgeron, 'Making *It* in Hollywood', p. 82.

41. Cleveland Amory and Frederick Bradlee, *Cavalcade of the 1920s and 1930s: Selections from America's Most Memorable Magazine 'Vanity Fair'* (London: The Bodley Head, 1960), p. 153.

42. David Stenn, *Clara Bow: Runnin' Wild* (New York: Cooper Square Press [1988] 2000).

43. Orgeron, 'Making *It* in Hollywood', p. 96.

44. Landay, 'The Flapper Film', p. 238.

45. Stenn, *Clara Bow*, p. 87. See also Lottie Da and Jan Alexander, *Bad Girls of the Silver Screen* (London: Pandora, 1990), p. 40.

46. Ryan, 'The Projection of a New Womanhood', p. 118. Georganne Scheiner, *Signifying Female Adolescence: Film Representations and Fans, 1920–1950* (Westport, CT: Praeger Publishers, 2000), p. 49.

47. Orgeron, 'Making *It* in Hollywood', p. 81.

48. Cynthia Felando, 'Clara Bow is It', in Andrew Willis (ed.), *Film Stars: Hollywood and Beyond* (Manchester University Press, 2004), pp. 8–23.

49. Landay, 'The Flapper Film', pp. 221–48. See also Felando, 'Clara Bow is It', p. 21.

50. Ryan, 'The Projection of a New Womanhood', pp. 120–6.

51. Ibid., p. 117.

52. Orgeron, 'Making *It* in Hollywood', p. 80.

53. Heather Addison, *Hollywood and the Rise of Physical Culture* (New York: Routledge, 2003), pp. 103–8.

54. Gaylyn Studlar, 'Valentino, "Optic Intoxication" and Dance Madness', in Steven Cohan and Ina Rae Hark (eds), *Screening the Male: Exploring Masculinities in Hollywood Cinema* (London: Routledge, 1993), p. 28.

55. See Miriam Hansen, *Babel and Babylon: Spectatorship in American Silent Film* (Cambridge, MA: Harvard University Press, 1991), p. 254.

56. George N. Fenin and William K. Everson, *The Western, from Silents to Cinerama* (New York: Bonanza Books, 1962), p. 115.

57. See Molly Haskell, 'The Twenties', in Richard Dyer MacCann, *Films of the Twenties* (London: The Scarecrow Press, 1996), pp. 63–71, 107–10.

58. Koszarski, *An Evening's Entertainment*, p. 137.

59. Ibid., p. 137.

60. William Lyon Phelps, 'Speed and the Essayist', in Sayler (ed.), *Revolt in the Arts*, p. 305.

61. Kozsarski, *An Evening's Entertainment*, pp. 56–7.

62. Zora Neale Hurston, for example, shot fieldwork footage in 1928 as part of her ethnographic research on Southern culture.

63. Robert J. Christopher, *Robert and Frances Flaherty: A Documentary Life, 1883–1922* (Montreal: McGill-Queen's University, 2005).

64. Eric Barnouw, *Documentary: A History of the Non-Fiction Film* (New York: Oxford University Press, 1993), pp. 32–51. See also Jeffrey Geiger, 'Nanook of the North: Fiction, Truth and the Documentary Contract', in Jeffrey Geiger and R. L. Rutsky (eds), *Film Analysis: A Norton Reader* (New York: Norton, 2005), pp. 118–38.

65. See Geiger, 'Nanook of the North' for a discussion of these various criticisms.

66. Barnouw, *Documentary*, p. 42.

67. Fatimah Tobing Rony, *The Third Eye: Race, Cinema, and Ethnographic Spectacle* (Durham, NC: Duke University Press, 1996).

68. Geiger, 'Nanook of the North', pp. 121–2.
69. Barnouw, *Documentary*, p. 43. See also Rony, *The Third Eye*, p. 99.
70. Rony, *The Third Eye*, p. 132. Barnouw, *Documentary*, p. 48.
71. Hampton, *History of the American Film Industry*, p. 422.
72. William K. Everson, *American Silent Film* (New York: Oxford University Press, 1978), p. 235. This trend is examined in Thomas Doherty, *Pre-Code Hollywood: Sex, Immorality, and Insurrection in American Cinema, 1930–1934* (New York: Columbia University Press, 1999).
73. Odegard, *The American Public Mind*, p. 208.
74. Lee Grieveson, *Policing Cinema: Movies and Censorship in Early-Twentieth-Century America* (Berkeley, CA: University of California Press, 2004), p. 211.
75. Lynd and Lynd, *Middletown*, pp. 267–8.
76. Miriam Van Waters, *Youth in Conflict* (New York: Republic, 1925), p. 61.
77. Hays, *See and Hear*, p. 26.
78. Carr, *Hollywood and Anti-Semitism* pp. 57–66. William Aylott Orton, *America in Search of Culture* (Boston: Little, Brown, 1933), pp. 218–19.
79. Richard Butsch, *The Making of American Audiences: From Stage to Television, 1750–1990* (Cambridge: Cambridge University Press, 2000), p. 167.
80. Garth Jowett et al., *Children and the Movies: Media Influence and the Payne Fund Controversy* (New York: Cambridge University Press, 1996).
81. W. Brooke Graves (ed.), *Readings in Public Opinion: Its Formation and Control* (New York: D. Appleton, 1928), p. 386.
82. Jowett et al., *Children and the Movies*, p. 17.
83. Odegard, *The American Public Mind*, p. 207.
84. Graves (ed.), *Readings in Public Opinion*, p. 399.
85. Hays, *See and Hear*, p. 4.
86. Butsch, *The Making of American Audiences*, p. 164.
87. See Perley Poore Sheehan, *Hollywood as a World Center* (Hollywood, CA: Hollywood Citizen Press, c.1924), cited in Koszarski, *An Evening's Entertainment*, p. 100.
88. Thomas Cripps, *Slow Fade to Black: The Negro in American Film, 1900–1942* (New York: Oxford University Press, 1993), p. 174.
89. Ibid., p. 84.
90. Ibid., pp. 176–8.
91. Ibid., p. 180.
92. Charlene Regester, 'The African-American Press and Race Movies, 1909–1929', in Pearl Bowser, Jane Gaines and Charles Musser (eds), *Oscar Micheaux and His Circle: African-American Filmmaking and Race Cinema of the Silent Era* (Bloomington, IN: Indiana University Press, 2001), pp. 34–52.
93. Donald Bogle, *Toms, Coons, Mulattoes, Mammies, and Bucks: An Interpretive History of Blacks in American Films* (New York: Continuum Publishing, [1973] 2001), pp. 101–16. See also Pearl Bowser and Louise Spence, 'Identity and Betrayal: The *Symbol of the Unconquered* and Oscar Micheax's "Biographical Legend"', in Daniel Bernardi (ed.), *The Birth of Whiteness: Race and the Emergence of U.S. Cinema* (New Brunswick, NJ: Rutgers University Press, 1996), pp. 56–80.
94. Regester, 'The African-American Press', p. 44.
95. Bowser and Spence, 'Identity and Betrayal', p. 86.

96. Michele Wallace, 'Within our Gates: From Race Melodrama to Opportunity Narrative', in Bowser et al. (eds), *Oscar Micheaux and His Circle*, p. 60. Bowser and Spence, 'Identity and Betrayal', p. 85.

97. Cripps, *Slow Fade to Black*, p. 181.

98. Donald Crafton, *The Talkies: American Cinema's Transition to Sound, 1926–1931* (New York: Simon and Schuster, 1997).

99. Everson, *American Silent Film*, p. 339.

100. Lasky, 'Art on A Manufacturing Basis', p. 221.

101. Everson, *American Silent Film*, p. 338.

102. Edward Bowes, 'Radio as an Independent Art', in Sayler (ed.), *Revolt in the Arts*, p. 281.

103. Phyllis Blanchard, *The Child and Society: An Introduction to the Social Psychology of the Child* (New York: Longmans, Green, 1928), p. 213.

104. Ray Barfield, *Listening to Radio, 1920–1950* (Westport, CT: Praeger Publishers, 1996), p. 3. John Dunning, *On the Air: The Encyclopedia of Old-Time Radio* (New York: Oxford University Press, 1998), p. 628.

105. Dunning, *On the Air*, p. 628.

106. Eric Barnouw, *A Tower in Babel: A History of Broadcasting in the United States to 1933* (New York: Oxford University Press, 1966), p. 72.

107. Odegard, *The American Public Mind*, p. 224.

108. Bowes, 'Radio as an Independent Art', p. 280.

109. Susan Douglas, *Listening in: Radio and the American Imagination* (Minneapolis: University of Minnesota Press, 2004), p. 70.

110. Butsch, *The Making of American Audiences*, p. 185.

111. Barnouw, *A Tower in Babel*, pp. 126–7. Dunning, *On the Air*, p. 61.

112. Butsch, *The Making of American Audiences*, p. 187.

113. David Kyvig, *Daily Life in the United States, 1920–1939: Decades of Promise and Pain* (Westport, CT: Greenwood, 2002), p. 75.

114. On the 'hillbilly' craze and country recording hits see William Ruhlmann, *Breaking Records: 100 Years of Hits* (New York: Routledge, 2004), p. 47.

115. Kyvig, *Daily Life*, p. 80.

116. Kathleen Morgan Drowne and Patrick Huber (eds), *The 1920s* (Westport, CT: Greenwood Press, 2004), pp. 210–12.

117. William Howland Kenney, *Recorded Music in American Life: The Phonograph and Popular Memory, 1890–1945* (New York: Oxford University Press, 1999), p. 135. Kenney sees this period as inventing 'hillybilly' music.

118. Kyvig, *Daily Life*, p. 83.

119. Mitchell (ed.), *Recent Social Trends*, p. 214.

120. Graves, *Readings in Public Opinion*, p. 563.

121. Mitchell, *Recent Social Trends*, p. 216.

122. Ibid.

123. Graves, *Readings in Public Opinion*, pp. 532, 550.

124. Ibid., p. 564.

125. Dunning, *On the Air*, p. 485.

126. Mitchell (ed.), *Recent Social Trends*, p. 215.

127. Barnouw, *A Tower In Babel*, p. 173.

128. Odegard, *The American Public Mind*, p. 226.

129. Graves, *Readings in Public Opinion*, p. 533.

130. Ibid., p. 535.
131. Tona J. Hangen, *Redeeming the Dial: Radio, Religion and Popular Culture in America* (Chapel Hill, NC: University of North Carolina Press, 2002), p. 22.
132. Ibid., p. 77.
133. Graves, *Readings in Public Opinion*, p. 560.
134. Odegard, *The American Public Mind*, p. 227.
135. Susan J. Douglas, *Listening In: Radio and the American Imagination* (Minneapolis: University of Minnesota Press, 2004), p. 59.
136. John Dunning, *On the Air*, p. 1.
137. See Drowne and Huber, *The 1920s*, p. 68.
138. Graves, *Readings*, p. 535.
139. Barnouw, *A Tower in Babel*, p. 191.
140. Michele Hilmes, *Hollywood and Broadcasting: From Radio to Cable* (Chicago: University of Illinois Press, 1990), p. 34.
141. Ibid., pp. 35–6.
142. Ibid., p. 36.
143. Edward L. Bernays, 'Typescript on Publicizing the New Dodge Cars, 1927–1928', in *Prosperity and Thrift: The Coolidge Era and the Consumer Economy, 1921–29*, available online at http://memory.loc.gov/cgi-bin/query/r?ammem/coolbib:@field(NUMBER+@band(amrlm+me06))::.
144. Hilmes, pp. 53–54.
145. Graves, *Readings*, p. 565.
146. David Sarnoff, "A New Art in Birth-Throes", in Sayler (ed.), *Revolt in the Arts*, p. 284.
147. Jesse L. Lasky, 'Art on A Manufacturing Basis', in *Revolt in the Arts*, p. 219.
148. Graves, *Readings*, p. 571.
149. David Sarnoff, 'A New Art in Birth-Throes', in *Revolt in the Arts*, p. 287.

4. Visual Art and Design

1. Lewis Mumford, 'The City', in Harold Evans Stearns (ed.), *Civilization in the United States* (New York: Harcourt, Brace & Co., 1922), p. 12.
2. Richard F. Bach, 'Art in the Market Place: The Industrial Arts in the Machine Age', in Charles A. Beard (ed.), *Toward Civilization* (London: Longmans, Green & Co., 1930), p. 200.
3. Abraham A. Davidson, *Early American Modernist Painting, 1910–1935* (New York: Harper and Row, 1981), p. 10.
4. Wanda Corn, *The Great American Thing: Modern Art and National Identity 1915–1935* (Berkeley: University of California Press, 2000), p. 54.
5. See Corn, *The Great American Thing*, p. 56. On 'Américanisme' see pp. 43–89.
6. Ibid., p. 43.
7. Ibid., pp. 43–6.
8. Joshua C. Taylor, *America As Art* (New York: Harper and Row, 1976), pp. 187–215.
9. Sheldon Cheney and Martha Cheney, *Art and the Machine: An Account of Industrial Design in 20th-Century America* (New York: McGraw-Hill, 1936), p. x.
10. Corn, *The Great American Thing*, p. 4.

11. Sophie Levy, *A Transatlantic Avant-Garde: American Artists in Paris, 1918–1939* (Berkeley, CA: University of California Press, 2003).
12. Park, *New Backgrounds*, p. 62.
13. Edwin Avery Park, *New Backgrounds for a New Age* (New York: Harcourt, Brace & Co., 1927), p. 41.
14. Henry M. Sayre, 'American Vernacular: Objectivism, Precisionism, and the Aesthetics of the Machine', *Twentieth Century Literature* 35.3 (Autumn 1989), p. 324. Barbara Haskell, *The American Century: Art and Culture, 1900–1950* (New York: Norton, 1999), pp. 145–7.
15. Holger Cahill and Alfred H. Barr, *Art in America: A Complete Survey* (New York: Reynal and Hitchcock, 1935), p. 95.
16. Martin L. Friedman, *The Precisionist View in American Art: An Exhibition* (Minneapolis, MN: Walker Art Center, 1960).
17. John Baur, *Revolution and Tradition in Modern American Art* (Cambridge, MA: Harvard University Press, 1951).
18. *Manifesto of the Futurist Painters*, online at http://www.unknown.nu/futurism/painters.html.
19. Karal Ann Marling, 'My Egypt: The Irony of the American Dream', *Winterthur Portfolio* 15.1 (Spring 1980), pp. 25–39.
20. Ibid., p. 34.
21. Cecilia Tichi, *Shifting Gears: Technology, Literature, Culture in Modernist America* (Chapel Hill, NC: University of North Carolina Press, 1987), p. 267. Bram Dijkstra (ed.), *A Recognizable Image: William Carlos Williams on Art and Artists* (New York: New Directions, 1978), p. 2.
22. Dickran Tashjian, *William Carlos Williams and the American Scene, 1920–1940* (New York: Whitney Museum of American Art, 1978). See also Bram Dijkstra, *The Hieroglyphics of a New Speech: Cubism, Stieglitz, and the Early Poetry of William Carlos Williams* (Princeton, NJ: Princeton University Press, 1969).
23. John Dewey, in Albert Einstein et al., *Living Philosophies* (New York: Simon and Schuster, 1931), p. 24.
24. John Dewey, 'Experience, Nature and Art' (1925), in Louis Menand (ed.), *Pragmatism: A Reader* (New York: Vintage Books, 1997), p. 236.
25. John Dewey, in Albert Einstein et al., *Living Philosophies*, p. 25.
26. Karen Tsujimoto, *Images of America: Precisionist Painting and Modern Photography* (Seattle: University of Washington Press, 1982).
27. Sarah Whitaker Peters, *Becoming O'Keeffe: The Early Years* (New York: Abbeville Press, 1991), pp. 216–21. See also Jessica Murphy, 'Precisionism', *Timeline of Art History* (New York: The Metropolitan Museum of Art, 2007), online at http://www.metmuseum.org/toah/hd/prec/hd_prec.htm as well as her essay on Paul Strand at: http://www.metmuseum.org/toah/hd/pstd/hd_pstd.htm.
28. Barbara Zabel, *Assembling Art: The Machine and the American Avant-Garde* (Jackson, MS: University Press of Mississippi, 2004), p. xvii.
29. Ibid., p. 60.
30. Charles Sheeler, *Charles Sheeler: Paintings, Drawings, Photographs* (New York: The Museum of Modern Art, 1939), p. 11.
31. Sayre, 'American Vernacular', p. 323.
32. Zabel, 'Louis Lozowick and Urban Optimism of the 1920s', p. 19.

33. Maria Morris Hambourg, 'Photography between the Wars: Selections from the Ford Motor Company Collection', *The Metropolitan Museum of Art Bulletin* 45.4 (Spring 1988), 5–56.
34. Richard Guy Wilson, Dianne Pilgrim and Dickran Tashjian, *The Machine Age in America, 1918–1941* (New York: The Brooklyn Museum, 1986), p. 23. See also Haskell, *The American Century*, pp. 160, 176.
35. Terry Smith, *Making the Modern: Industry, Art, and Design in America* (Chicago: University of Chicago Press, 1993), pp. 111–35. See also Karen Lucic, *Charles Sheeler and the Cult of the Machine* (Cambridge, MA: Harvard University Press, 1991).
36. Lucic, *Charles Sheeler and the Cult of the Machine*, p. 66.
37. Smith, *Making the Modern*, pp. 111–12.
38. Mary Jane Jacob and Linda Downs, *The Rouge: The Image of Industry in the Art of Charles Sheeler and Diego Rivera* (Detroit: Detroit Institute of Arts, 1978), p. 7.
39. Ibid., p. 13.
40. Ibid., p. 14.
41. Smith, *Making the Modern*, p. 113.
42. Haskell, *The American Century*, p. 155.
43. Robert A. M. Stern, Gregory Gilmartin and Thomas Mellins, *New York 1930: Architecture and Urbanism between the Two World Wars* (New York: Rizzoli, 1987), p. 29.
44. Zabel, *Assembling Art*, p. xii. See also her essay 'Louis Lozowick and Urban Optimism of the 1920s', *Archives of American Art Journal* 14.2 (1974), pp. 17–21.
45. Margaret C. Anderson (ed.), *The Little Review Anthology* (New York: Hermitage House, 1953), p. 341.
46. Zabel, *Assembling Art*, p.xiii.
47. Ibid., p.xxi.
48. See *Hugh Ferris: Delineator of Gotham*, a collection of Ferris's futuristic online at http://thenonist.com/index.php/thenonist/permalink/hugh_ferriss_delineator_of_gotham/.
49. See digital images at the Hirshorn Museum, online at http://hirshhorn.si.edu/search.asp?search=Lozowick.
50. Cheney and Cheney, *Art and the Machine*, p. 14.
51. Louis Lozowick, 'The Americanization of Art', reprinted in Janet Flint (ed.), *The Prints of Louis Lozowick* (New York: Hudson Hills Press, 1982), pp. 18–19. See also Virginia Hagelstein Marquardt, 'Louis Lozowick: From "Machine Ornaments" to Applied Design, 1923–1930', *The Journal of Decorative and Propaganda Arts* 8 (Spring 1988), pp. 40–57.
52. Louis Lozowick, 'The Americanization of Art', pp. 18–19.
53. Genevieve Taggard, 'The Ruskinian Boys See Red', *New Masses* (July 1927), 18.
54. Cheney and Cheney, *Art and the Machine*, p. 14.
55. Norman Bel Geddes, 'The Challenge of Industrial Design', in Sayler (ed.), *Revolt in the Arts*, p. 334.
56. Susan Noyes Platt, *Modernism in the 1920s: Interpretations of Modern Art in New York from Expressionism to Constructivism* (Ann Arbor, MI: UMI Research Press, [1981] 1985), p. 131.

57. Katherine Solomon, *The Chicago Tribune Tower Competition: Skyscraper Design and Cultural Change in the 1920s* (Chicago: University of Chicago Press, 2001).

58. For a discussion of the transition from old New York to new and the impact of new ideas concerning vision, time and space, see Douglas Tallack, *New York Sights: Visualizing Old and New New York* (New York: Berg, 2006).

59. See, for example, Anna C. Chave, '"Who Will Paint New York?": "The World's New Art Center" and the Skyscraper Paintings of Georgia O'Keeffe', *American Art* 5 (Winter–Spring 1991), p. 87. See also Corn, *The Great American Thing*.

60. Solomon, *The Chicago Tribune Tower Competition*, p. 178.

61. Jeffrey L. Meikle, *Twentieth Century Limited: Industrial Design in America, 1925–1939* (Philadelphia: Temple University Press, 2001), p. 31.

62. On the design goals of these buildings see Park, *New Backgrounds*, pp. 147–53.

63. See Emily Zimmerman, *Building the Chrysler Building: The Social Construction of the Skyscraper*, online at http://xroads.virginia.edu/~1930s/display/chrysler/Frame-1.html.

64. Merrill Schleier, 'The Skyscraper, Gender and Mental Life: Sophie Treadwell's Play *Machinal* of 1928', in Roberta Moudry (ed.), *The American Skyscraper: Cultural Histories* (New York: Cambridge University Press, 2005), p. 234.

65. Douglas, *Terrible Honesty*, p. 434.

66. See Corn, *The Great American Thing*, pp. 135–56.

67. Stern et al., *New York 1930*, p. 61.

68. Jan-Christopher Horak, 'Paul Strand's and Charles Sheeler's *Manhatta*', in Jan-Christopher Horak (ed.), *Lovers of Cinema: The First American Film Avant-garde, 1919–1945* (Madison, WI: University of Madison Press, 1995), pp. 267–86.

69. Lewis Jacobs, 'Experimental Cinema in America: (Part One: 1921–1941)', *Hollywood Quarterly* 3.2 (Winter 1947–8), pp. 111–24.

70. All editions are available at *The Whitman Archive* online at http://www.whitmanarchive.org/published/LG/index.html.

71. Heather Hole and Barbara Buhler Lynes, *Marsden Hartley and the West: The Search for an American Modernism* (New Haven, CT: Yale University Press: 2007), p. 48.

72. Wall Street was not the only photo of the city from the 1910s that the film replicated; see Horak, 'Paul Strand's and Charles Sheeler's *Manhatta*', pp. 273–4.

73. Ibid., p. 267.

74. Martin F. Norden claimed it 'shows no human beings' in 'The Avant-Garde Cinema of the 1920s: Connections to Futurism, Precisionism, and Suprematism', *Leonardo* 17.2 (1984), 108–112. See also Lucic, *Charles Sheeler and the Cult of the Machine*, pp. 55–66.

75. Juan A. Suarez, Pop Modernism: Noise and the Reinvention of the Everyday (Chicago: University of Illinois Press), p. 74. See also Tallack, *New York Sights*, pp. 147–8.

76. Lucic, *Charles Sheeler and the Cult of the Machine*, p. 48.

77. Jacobs, 'Experimental Cinema in America', p. 113.

78. Ibid.

79. Stuart Chase, *Men and Machines* (New York: Macmillan, 1929), p. 245.

80. Lewis Mumford, *Sticks and Stones, a Study of American Architecture and Civilization* (New York: Boni and Liveright, 1924), p. 188.

81. 'Neglect of Worship and "Machine Age Spirit" Are Causes of Anti-Religion', *New York Times* (18 July 1927), p. 20.

82. Stern et al., *New York 1930*, p. 152.

83. Rolf Lundén, *Business and Religion in the American 1920s* (New York: Greenwood Press, 1988), pp. 80, 82.

84. Mumford, *Sticks and Stones*, p. 176.

85. Ibid., p. 174.

86. Chase, *Men and Machines*, p. 246.

87. Willis T. Lee, *The Face of the Earth as Seen from the Air: A Study in the Application of Airplane Photography to Geography* (New York: American Geographical Society, 1922). For a history of the development of special cameras and the use of aerial photography during World War I, see Theodore Macfarlane Knappen, *Wings of War: An Account of the Important Contribution of the United States to Aircraft Invention, Engineering, Development and Production during the World War* (New York: G. P. Putnam's Sons, 1920). The first aerial mosaic photograph for military use was created in 1915; see Herbert A. Johnson, *Wingless Eagle: U.S. Army Aviation through World War I* (Chapel Hill, NC: University of North Carolina Press, 2001), p. 68.

88. Paul K. Saint-Amour, 'Modernist Reconnaissance', *Modernism/Modernity* 10.2 (April 2003), pp. 349–80.

89. Ibid., p. 355.

90. Ibid., p. 356.

91. Marcel Duchamp, Man Ray and Francis Picabia, *New York Dada: Duchamp, Man Ray, Picabia*, ed. A. Zweite (Munchen: Prestel-Verlag, 1973), p. 84.

92. Haskell, *The American Century*, p. 147.

93. Sarah Whitaker Peters, *Becoming O'Keeffe: The Early Years* (New York: Abbeville Press, 1991), p. 277; Park, *New Backgrounds*, p. 153.

94. Georgia O'Keeffe, *Georgia O'Keeffe* (New York: Penguin Books, [1976] 1983), p. 20.

95. Ibid., p. 17.

96. Images of some of these are embedded in the essay 'Skyscrapers and Cityscapes', online at http://xroads.virginia.edu/~MA02/freed/okeeffe/skyscrapers.html.

97. O'Keeffe, *Georgia O'Keeffe*, pp. 12–13.

98. Corn, *The Great American Thing*, p. 241.

99. Vivien Green Fryd, 'Georgia O'Keeffe's "Radiator Building": Gender, Sexuality, Modernism, and Urban Imagery', *Winterthur Portfolio*, 35.4 (Winter 2000), pp. 269–89.

100. Ibid.

101. Georgia O'Keeffe, *Georgia O'Keeffe*, pp. 18–19.

102. Abraham A. Davidson, *Early American Modernist Painting, 1910–1935* (New York: Harper and Row, 1981), p. 204.

103. Haskell, *The American Century*, p. 142.

104. Park, *New Backgrounds*, p. 162.

105. Charlotte Benton, Tim Benton and Ghislaine Wood (eds), *Art Deco 1910-1939* (London: V&A Publications, 2003), p. 13.

106. For the dissemination of art deco in America after the expo and a discussion of the influence over Hollywood style, see Wendy Kaplan, '"The Filter of American Taste": Design in the USA in the 1920s', in Benton et al. (eds), *Art*

Deco 1910–1939, pp. 335–43. Anne Massey, *Hollywood Beyond the Screen: Design and Material Culture* (New York: Berg, 2000), pp. 44–57. See also Lucy Fischer, *Designing Women: Cinema, Art Deco, and the Female Form* (New York: Columbia University Press, 2003).

107. Cheney and Cheney, *Art and the Machine*, p. 41

108. Bonnie L. Grad, 'Stuart Davis and Contemporary Culture', *Artibus et Historiae* 12.24 (1991), pp. 165–91.

109. Ibid., p. 177.

110. Mark Helbling, *The Harlem Renaissance: The One and the Many* (Westport, CT: Greenwood Press, 1999), p. 133.

111. John A. Kouwenhoven, *Made in America: The Arts in Modern Civilization* (New York: Farrar, Straus and Giroux, 1975), p. 266.

112. Viewable at the Museum of Modern Art online collection at http://www.moma. org/collection/search.php.

113. Donna M. Cassidy, *Painting the Musical City: Jazz and Cultural Identity in American Art 1910–1940* (Washington, DC: Smithsonian Institution, 1997), p. 54.

114. Ibid., p. 86.

115. Martha Jane Nadell, *Enter the New Negroes: Images of Race in American Culture* (Cambridge, MA: Harvard University Press, 2004), pp. 12–33.

116. Locke, *Enter the New Negro*, p. 631.

117. Online at http://etext.virginia.edu/harlem/ReiHarlF.html. For a discussion of Reiss and his role in creating the Harlem Renaissance aesthetic, see Sieglinde Lemke, *Primitivist Modernism: Black Culture and the Origins of Transatlantic Modernism* (Oxford: Oxford University Press, 1998), pp. 124–9.

118. Anne Elizabeth Carroll, *Word, Image, and the New Negro: Representation and Identity in the Harlem Renaissance* (Bloomington, IN: Indiana University Press, 2005), p. 118.

119. Caroline Goeser, *Picturing the New Negro: Harlem Renaissance Print Culture and Modern Black Identity* (Lawrence, KA: University Press of Kansas, 2007).

120. Alain Locke, 'The Art of the Ancestors', *Survey Graphic*, special edn, *Harlem: Mecca of the New Negro* (March 1925), 673. Available online at http://etext. virginia.edu/harlem/LocArtaF.html.

121. On Aaron Douglas see Mary Schmidt Campbell, *Harlem Renaissance: Art of Black America* (New York: Harry N. Abrams, for the Studio Museum in Harlem, 1987). See also Joanna Skipwith (ed.), *Rhapsodies in Black: Art of the Harlem Renaissance* (Berkeley: University of California Press, 1997). For an online exhibition of black art from the period see *Rhapsodies in Black* online at http://www.iniva.org/harlem/intro.html.

122. Benjamin Brawley quoted in Campbell, *Harlem Renaissance*, p. 77.

123. Stuart Chase, *Men and Machines*, p. 251.

124. Shelley Armitage, *John Held, Jr. Illustrator of the Jazz Age* (Syracuse, NY: Syracuse University Press, 1987). Richard Merkin, *The Jazz Age As Seen Through the Eyes of Ralph Barton, Miguel Covarrubias, and John Held* (Providence, RI: Rhode Island School of Design, 1968). To see some of Held's flapper illustrations go to http://www.animationarchive.org/2007/02/pinups-john-held-jr.html.

125. Benton et al., *Art Deco 1910–1939*, p. 288; Haskell, *The American Century*, p. 177.

126. Roland Marchand, *Advertising the American Dream: Making Way for Modernity, 1920–1940* (Berkeley, CA: University of California Press, 1985), p. 140. See also Jackson Lears, *Fables of Abundance: A Cultural History of Advertising in the United States* (New York: Basic Books, 1994), p. 325.

127. Graham Howe and G. Ray Hawkins, *Paul Outerbridge Jr: Photographs 1921–39* (London: Thames and Hudson, 1980).

128. Paul R. Gorman, *Left Intellectuals and Popular Culture in Twentieth-Century America* (Chapel Hill, NC: University of North Carolina Press, 1996), p. 71. See also Lears, *Fables*, pp. 305–6.

129. Lears, *Fables*, p. 313.

130. Zabel, *Assembling Art*, p. xx.

131. Clock Wheels available online at http://artgallery.yale.edu/pages/collection/popups/pc_prints/enlarge03.html.

132. Zabel, *Assembling Art*, p. 98.

133. Ibid., p. 59.

134. Grad, 'Stuart Davis and Contemporary Culture', p. 169.

135. Zabel, *Assembling Art*, p. 14. For *Miss Woolworth* see Corn, *The Great American Thing*, p. 18.

136. Haskell, *The American Century*, p. 182.

137. Park, *New Backgrounds*, p. 132.

5. Consumption and Leisure

1. Stuart Chase, *Prosperity: Fact or Myth* (New York: C. Boni, 1929), p. 22.

2. Glen Jeansonne, *Transformation and Reaction: America 1921–1945* (New York: HarperCollins, 1994), p. 63. On business ideology in the era, see James W. Prothro, *The Dollar Decade: Business Ideas in the 1920s* (Baton Rouge, LA: Louisiana State University Press, 1954).

3. Michael E. Parrish, *Anxious Decades: America in Prosperity and Depression 1920–1941* (New York: Norton, 1993), p. 54.

4. Ibid., p. 66.

5. Leo Wolman, 'Consumption and the Standard of Living', in *Recent Economic Changes in the United States* (New York: McGraw-Hill, 1929), available online at http://www.nber.org/books/comm29-1.

6. Robert Lynd, 'The People as Consumers', in Mitchell (ed.), *Recent Social Trends*, p. 857.

7. Wolman, 'Consumption', p. 58.

8. Chase, *Prosperity*, p. 37.

9. Ibid., p. 43.

10. Wolman, 'Consumption', p. 59.

11. Lendol Calder, *Financing the American Dream: A Cultural History of Consumer Credit* (Princeton, NJ: Princeton University Press, 1999), p. 18. See also Martha Olney, *Buy Now, Pay Later: Advertising, Credit, and Consumer Demand in the 1920s* (Chapel Hill, NC: University of North Carolina Press, 1991).

12. Robert and Helen Lynd, *Middletown: A Study in Contemporary American Culture* (New York: Harcourt, Brace/Harvest Books, [1929] 1957), pp. 254–5.

13. Calder, *Financing the American Dream*, p. 21.

14. Adams, *Our Business Civilization*, p. 35.

15. Herbert Hoover, 'Rugged Individualism' (1928), reprinted in Rose (ed.), *American Decades*, p. 315.

16. Ibid., p. 316.

17. Adams, *Our Business Civilization*, p. 36.

18. Robert S. McElvaine, *The Great Depression: America 1929–41* (New York: Times Books, 1993), p. 16.

19. Cited in Simone Weil Davis, *Living Up to the Ads: Gender Fictions of the 1920s* (Durham, NC: Duke University Press, 2000), p. 55. See also Lundén, *Business and Religion in the American 1920s*, pp. 15–17.

20. Chase, *Prosperity*, p. 40.

21. Adams, *Our Business Civilization*, p. 10

22. F. Scott Fitzgerald, 'My Lost City' (1932), in *The Crack Up* (New York: New Directions [1945] 1962), p. 30.

23. Lewis, *Babbitt*, p. 212.

24. Jackson Lears, *Fables of Abundance: A Cultural History of Advertising in the United States* (New York: Basic Books, 1994), pp. 318–19, p. 305.

25. Edward Bernays, *Propaganda* (New York: Ig Publishing, [1928] 2004), p. 37. See also John C. Burnham, 'The New Psychology: From Narcissism to Social Control', in John Braeman et al., *Change and Continuity in Twentieth-Century America: The 1920s* (Columbus: Ohio State University Press, 1968), pp. 351–98.

26. Ibid., pp. 75–6.

27. Walter Lippmann, *Public Opinion* (New York: Courier Dover Publications, [1920] 2004), p. 135.

28. Stuart Chase, *The Tragedy of Waste* (New York: Macmillan, 1925), p. 108.

29. The entire text of *Your Money's Worth* is online at the Library of Congress website, http://hdl.loc.gov/loc.gdc/amrlg.lg07.

30. On fear of crowds and their easy manipulation, see Lears, *Fables of Abundance*, pp. 222–34.

31. See Niall Palmer, *The Twenties in America: Politics and History* (Edinburgh: Edinburgh University Press, 2006), pp. 97–8.

32. W. F. Wamsley, 'How Financial "Speakeasies" Net Suckers', *New York Times* (25 August 1929), XX3.

33. Andrew Sinclair, *Prohibition: The Era of Excess* (Boston: Little, Brown, 1962), p. 47.

34. David E. Kyvig (ed.), *Law, Alcohol, and Order: Perspectives on National Prohibition* (Westport, CT: Greenwood Press, 1985), p. 7.

35. John J. Rumbarger, *Profits, Power, and Prohibition: Alcohol Reform and the Industrializing of America, 1800–1930* (Albany, NY: State University of New York Press, 1989), p. 184.

36. Harry S. Warner, *Prohibition, an Adventure in Freedom* (Westerville, OH: World League Against Alcoholism, 1928), p. 221.

37. Sinclair, *Prohibition*, p. 222.

38. Ibid., pp. 187–8.

39. Ibid., p. 220.

40. Ibid., p. 222.

41. Stuart A. Rice (ed.), *Methods in Social Science: A Case Book* (Chicago: University of Chicago Press, 1931), p. 511.

42. Kyvig, *Law, Alcohol, and Order*, p. 4.
43. Preston William Slosson, *The Great Crusade and After, 1914–1928* (New York: Macmillan, 1930), p. 128.
44. Parrish, *Anxious Decades*, p. 82.
45. Chase, *Prosperity*, p. 24.
46. Wolman, 'Consumption', p. 78.
47. For working conditions and wages for blue- and white-collar workers in this period see Dumenil, *The Modern Temper*, pp. 56–76.
48. William Trufant Foster and Waddill Catchings, *The Road to Plenty* (Boston: Houghton Mifflin, 1928), p. 194.
49. Lynd and Lynd, *Middletown*, p. 7.
50. Ibid., pp. 7–8.
51. Ibid., p. 6.
52. Ibid.. p. 6.
53. Mark C. Smith, *Social Science in the Crucible: The American Debate over Objectivity and Purpose, 1918–1941* (Durham, NC: Duke University Press, 1994), p. 136.
54. Richard Wightman Fox, 'Epitaph for Middletown: Robert S. Lynd and the Analysis of Consumer Culture', in Richard Wightman Fox and Jackson Lears (eds), *The Culture of Consumption: Essays in American History, 1880–1980* (New York: Pantheon Books, 1983), p. 113.
55. Ibid., p. 122.
56. Conference on Unemployment, *Recent Economic Changes in the United States* (New York: McGraw-Hill Book Co. Inc., 1929), available online at National Bureau of Economic Research Website, http://www.nber.org/books/comm29-1.
57. Adams, *Our Business Civilization*, p. 306.
58. Cindy S. Aron, *Working at Play: A History of Vacations in the United States* (New York: Oxford University Press, 1999), p. 203.
59. Adams, *Our Business Civilization*, p. 19.
60. Ibid., p. 58.
61. Ibid., p. 32.
62. Mary K. Coffey, 'The American Adonis: A Natural History of the Average American (Man), 1921–32', in Susan Currell and Christina Cogdell (eds), *Popular Eugenics: National Efficiency and American Mass Culture in the 1930s* (Athens, OH: Ohio University Press, 2006), p. 200.
63. William Fielding Ogburn, *Social Change with Respect to Culture and Original Nature* (Gloucester, MA: Peter Smith, [1922] 1964), p. 313.
64. Raymond B. Fosdick, *The Old Savage in the New Civilization* (New York: Doubleday, Doran & Co., Inc., 1928), p. 21.
65. Lucy T. Benjamin Jr and William H. M. Bryant, 'A History of Popular Psychology Magazines in America', in Wolfgang G. Bringmann et al. (eds), *A Pictorial History of Psychology* (Chicago: Quintessence, 1997), p. 585.
66. Chip Rhodes, *Structures of the Jazz Age: Mass Culture, Progressive Education, and Racial Discourse in American Modernism* (London: Verso, 1998), p. 109.
67. George E. Mowry (ed.), *The Twenties: Fords, Flappers, and Fanatics* (Englewood Cliffs, NJ: Prentice-Hall, 1963), p. 157.
68. Frederick Lewis Allen, *Only Yesterday. An Informal History of the Nineteen-Twenties* (New York City: Blue Ribbon Books, 1931), p. 180.

69. Parrish, *Anxious Decades*, p. 78.

70. Joseph F. Kett, *The Pursuit of Knowledge Under Difficulties: From Self-Improvement to Adult Education in America, 1750–1990* (CA: Stanford University Press, 1994), p. 348. Joan Shelley Rubin, *The Making of Middlebrow Culture* (Chapel Hill, NC: University of North Carolina Press, 1992), p. 232.

71. See Rubin, *The Making of Middlebrow Culture*, p. 94, and Megan Benton, '"Too Many Books": Book Ownership and Cultural Identity in the 1920s', *American Quarterly* 49.2 (1997), pp. 268–97.

72. B. Stolberg, 'Degradation of American Psychology', *The Nation*, 113 (15 October 1930), pp. 395–8.

73. Lorine Pruette and Harry Elmer Barnes, *Women and Leisure: A Study of Social Waste* (New York: E. P. Dutton & Co., 1924), p. xi.

74. Elizabeth Ellis Hoyt, *The Consumption of Wealth* (New York: Macmillan, 1928), p. 162.

75. Slosson, *The Great Crusade*, p. 155.

76. Catherine Manton, *Fed Up: Women and Food in America* (Westport, CT: Bergin and Garvey, 1999), p. 53. On the history of dieting, see Hillel Schwartz, *Never Satisfied: A Cultural History of Diets, Fantasies and Fat* (New York: Free Press, 1986).

77. Drowne, *The 1920s*, pp. 152–3.

78. Charles Panati, *Panati's Parade of Fads, Follies, and Manias: The Origins of Our Most Cherished Obsessions* (New York: HarperPerennial, 1991), pp. 120–1. See also Drowne, *The 1920s*, pp. 146–54.

79. Carol Martin, *Dance Marathons: Performing American Culture of the 1920s and 1930s* (Jackson, MS: University Press of Mississippi, 1994), pp. 5–21.

80. Ibid., pp. 10–11.

81. A. Scott Berg, *Lindbergh* (London: Pan Books, [1998] 1999), pp. 104, 116.

82. John W. Ward, 'The Meaning of Lindbergh's Flight', *American Quarterly* 10 (Spring 1958), pp. 3–16.

83. Berg, *Lindbergh*, pp. 161–2.

84. Ann Douglas, *Terrible Honesty*, p. 456.

85. F. Scott Fitzgerald, 'Echos of the Jazz Age' (1931), reprinted in Baritz (ed.), *The Culture of the Twenties*, p. 421.

86. Ward, 'The Meaning of Lindbergh's Flight', p. 7.

87. Ibid., p. 6.

88. Ibid., pp. 5, 10.

89. Ibid., p. 6.

90. Ibid.

91. Berg, *Lindbergh*, p. 141.

92. Ward, 'The Meaning of Lindbergh's Flight', p. 14.

93. Charles Lindbergh, *Autobiography of Values*, cited in Susan M. Gray, *Charles A. Lindbergh and the American Dilemma: The Conflict of Technology and Human Values* (Bowling Green, OH: Bowling Green State University Popular Press, 1988), p. 1.

94. Berg, *Lindbergh*, p. 8.

95. Lippmann quoted in Schlesinger, *The Crisis of the Old Order*, p. 147.

96. Chase, *Prosperity*, p. 12.

97. McElvaine, *The Great Depression*, pp. 43–44.

98. Schlesinger, *The Crisis of the Old Order*, p. 159.
99. On economic organisation leading up to the Crash, see Edwin F. Gay and Leo Wolman, 'Trends in Economic Organization', in Mitchell (ed.), *Recent Social Trends*, pp. 218–67.
100. Jeansonne, *Transformation and Reaction*, p. 112.
101. For the various arguments about the causes and consequences of the Great Depression, see McElvaine, *The Great Depression*, pp. 25–50.
102. Chase, *Prosperity*, p. 11.
103. John Dewey, *Individualism Old and New* (New York: Minton Balch & Co., 1930), p. 18.
104. Michael Szalay, *New Deal Modernism: American Literature and the Invention of the Welfare State* (Durham, NC and London: Duke University Press, 2000), p. 56.
105. Chase, *Prosperity*, p. 10.

Conclusion

1. Frederick Lewis Allen, *Only Yesterday. An Informal History of the Nineteen-Twenties* (New York City: Blue Ribbon Books, 1931), pp. 3–4.
2. F. Scott Fitzgerald, 'Echoes of the Jazz Age' (1931), reprinted in *The Crack Up*, (New York: New Directions, [1945] 1962), p. 21.
3. Jason Scott Smith, 'The Strange History of the Decade: Modernity, Nostalgia, and the Perils of Periodization', *Journal of Social History* 32.2 (1998), p. 277.
4. Ibid., p. 269.
5. Ibid., p. 272.
6. See Graham Thompson, *American Culture in the 1980s* (Edinburgh: Edinburgh University Press, 2007) pp. 1–6, 179–183; and David Eldridge, *American Culture in the 1930s* (Edinburgh: Edinburgh University Press, 2008).
7. Eldridge, *American Culture in the 1930s*, p. 189.
8. Smith, 'The Strange History of the Decade', p. 274.
9. Irene Taviss Thomson, 'The Transformation of the Social Bond: Images of Individualism in the 1920s versus the 1970s', *Social Forces* 67.4 (June 1989), pp. 851–70.
10. Gregory Bergman, 'The 1920s and the 1980s – a Comparison', *Monthly Review* 38.5 (October 1986), pp. 29–36.
11. McElvaine, *The Great Depression*, p. 14.
12. Bergman, 'The 1920s and the 1980s', p. 29.

Bibliography

General

Allen, Frederick Lewis, *Only Yesterday. An Informal History of the Nineteen-Twenties* (New York City: Blue Ribbon Books, 1931).

Alpers, Benjamin, *Dictators, Democracy, and American Public Culture: Envisioning the Totalitarian Enemy, 1920s–1950s* (Chapel Hill, NC: University of North Carolina Press, 2003).

Baritz, Loren (ed.), *The Culture of the Twenties* (New York: Bobbs-Merrill Co., Inc., 1970).

Beard, Charles A. (ed.), *Whither Mankind: A Panorama of Modern Civilization* (New York: Longmans, Green & Co., 1928).

Best, Gary Dean, *The Dollar Decade: Mammon and the Machine in 1920s America* (Westport, CT: Praeger, 2003).

Bilton, Alan and Philip Melling (eds), *America in the 1920s: Literary Sources and Documents*, 3 Vols (Robertsbridge, UK: Helm Information, 2004).

Broer, Lawrence R. and John D. Walther (eds), *Dancing Fools and Weary Blues: The Great Escape of the Twenties* (Bowling Green, OH: Bowling Green State University Popular Press, 1990).

Brown, Dorothy M., *Setting a Course: American Women in the 1920s* (Boston: Twayne, 1987).

Bulmer, Martin, *The Chicago School of Sociology: Institutionalization, Diversity and the Rise of Sociological Research* (Chicago: University of Chicago Press, 1984).

Carter, Paul A., *The Uncertain World of Normalcy: The 1920s* (New York: Pitman, 1971).

Carter, Paul A., *Another Part of the Twenties* (New York: Columbia University Press, 1977).

Cashman, Sean Dennis, *America in the Twenties and Thirties: The Olympian Age of Franklin Delano Roosevelt* (New York: New York University Press, 1989).

Cayton, Mary Kupiec and Peter W. Williams (eds), *Encyclopedia of American Cultural and Intellectual History*, Vol. 1 (New York; London: Charles Scribner, 2001).

Ciment, James (ed.), *Encyclopedia of the Jazz Age: From the End of World War I to the Great Crash* (New York: M. E. Sharpe Inc., 2007).

Cobden, Stanley, *Rebellion Against Victorianism: The Impetus for Cultural Change in 1920s America* (New York: Oxford University Press, 1991).

Davis, Simone Weil, *Living Up to the Ads: Gender Fictions of the 1920* (Durham, NC: Duke University Press, 2000).

Douglas, Ann, *Terrible Honesty: Mongrel Manhattan in the 1920s* (New York: Farrar, Straus and Giroux, 1995).

Drowne, Kathleen Morgan and Patrick Huber (eds), *The 1920s* (Westport, CT: Greenwood Press, 2004).

Dumenil, Lynn, *The Modern Temper: American Culture and Society in the 1920s* (New York: Hill and Wang, 1995).

English, Daylanne K., *Unnatural Selections: Eugenics in American Modernism and the Harlem Renaissance* (Chapel Hill, NC: University of North Carolina Press, 2004).

Fabre, Genevieve and Michael Feith (eds), *Temples for Tomorrow: Looking Back at the Harlem Renaissance* (Bloomington, IN: Indiana University Press, 2001).

Faris, Robert, *Chicago Sociology, 1920–1932* (San Francisco, CA: Chandler Publishing Co., 1967).

Gatewood, Willard B., *Preachers, Pedagogues and Politicians: The Evolution Controversy in North Carolina, 1920–1927* (Chapel Hill, NC: University of North Carolina, 1966).

Goldberg, David J., *Discontented America: The United States in the 1920s* (Baltimore, MD: Johns Hopkins University Press, 1999).

Goodman, Paul and Frank Gatell, *America in the Twenties: The Beginnings of Contemporary America* (New York: Holt, Rinehart and Winston, Inc., 1972).

Gorman, Paul R., *Left Intellectuals and Popular Culture in Twentieth-Century America* (Chapel Hill, NC: University of North Carolina Press, 1996).

Grebstein, Sheldon Norman (ed.), *Monkey Trial: The State of Tennessee vs. John Thomas Scopes* (Boston: Houghton Mifflin, 1960).

Green, Harvey, *The Uncertainty of Everyday Life: 1915–1945* (New York: HarperCollins, 1992).

Hale, Nathan, *The Rise and Crisis of Psychoanalysis in the United States: Freud and the Americans, 1917–1985* (New York: Oxford University Press, 1995).

Hegeman, Susan, *Patterns for America: Modernism and the Concept of Culture* (Princeton, NJ: Princeton University Press, 1999).

Helbling, Mark, *The Harlem Renaissance: The One and the Many* (Westport, CT: Greenwood Press, 1999).

Hill, Laban Carrick, *Harlem Stomp: A Cultural History of the Harlem Renaissance* (New York: Little, Brown, 2003).

Hoffman, Frederick, *Freudianism and the Literary Mind* (Baton Rouge, LA: Louisiana State University Press, 1957).

Hooker, Clarence, *Life in the Shadows of the Crystal Palace, 1910–1927: Ford Workers in the Model T Era* (Bowling Green, OH: Bowling Green State University Popular Press, 1997).

Hutchinson, George, *The Harlem Renaissance in Black and White* (Cambridge, MA: Harvard University Press, 1995).

Kramer, Victor A. and Robert A. Russ (eds), *Harlem Renaissance Re-Examined* (Troy, NY: Whitston Publishing Co., 1997).

Kyvig, David, *Daily Life in the United States, 1920–1939: Decades of Promise and Pain* (Westport, CT: Greenwood, 2002).

Larson, Edward J., *Summer for the Gods: The Scopes Trial and America's Continuing Debate over Science and Religion* (New York: Basic Books, 1997).

Leinwand, Gerald, *1927: High Tide of the 1920s* (New York: Four Walls Eight Windows, 2001).

Lemke, Sieglinde, *Primitivist Modernism: Black Culture and the Origins of Transatlantic Modernism* (Oxford: Oxford University Press, 1998).

Leuchtenburg, William E., *The Perils of Prosperity: 1914–32* (Chicago: University of Chicago Press, 1993).

Levine, Lawrence W., *The Unpredictable Past: Explorations in American Cultural History* (New York: Oxford University Press, 1993).

Locke, Alain, *The New Negro: Voices from the Harlem Renaissance* (New York: Simon and Schuster, [1925] 1997).

Louria, Margot, *Triumph and Downfall: America's Pursuit of Peace and Prosperity, 1921–1933* (Westport, CT: Greenwood, 2001).

Merz, Charles, *The Dry Decade* (New York: Doubleday, Doran, 1931).

Michaels, Walter Benn, *Our America: Nativism, Modernism, and Pluralism* (Durham, NC: Duke University Press, 1995).

Miller, Nathan, *New World Coming: The 1920s and the Making of Modern America* (Cambridge, MA: Da Capo Press, 2004).

Moore, R. Laurence, *Selling God: American Religion in the Marketplace of Culture* (New York: Oxford University Press, 1995).

Mowry, George E. (ed.), *The Twenties: Fords, Flappers, and Fanatics* (Englewood Cliffs, NJ: Prentice-Hall, 1963).

Nash, Roderick, *The Nervous Generation: American Thought, 1917–1930* (Chicago: Rand-McNally & Co., 1970).

North, Michael, *Reading 1922: A Return to the Scene of the Modern* (Oxford: Oxford University Press, 1999).

Palmer, Niall, *America in the 1920s* (Edinburgh: Edinburgh University Press, 2003).

Parrish, Michael E., *Anxious Decades: America in Prosperity and Depression 1920–1941* (New York: Norton, 1993).

Paschen, Stephen H. and Leonard Schlup (eds), *The United States in the 1920s as Observed in Contemporary Documents: The Ballyhoo Years* (Lewiston, NY: Edwin Mellen Press, 2007).

Perrett, Geoffrey, *America in the Twenties: A History* (New York: Simon and Schuster, 1982).

Rose, Cynthia (ed.), *American Decades Primary Sources: 1920–1929* (Detroit, MI: Gale Publishing, 2004).

Scharf, Lois and Joan M. Jensen (eds), *Decades of Discontent: The Women's Movement, 1920–1940* (Boston: Northeastern University Press, 1987).

Schlesinger, Arthur M. Jr, *The Crisis of the Old Order, 1919–1933* (Boston: Houghton Mifflin, 1957).

Segal, Howard P., *Recasting the Machine Age: Henry Ford's Village Industries* (Amherst, MA: University of Massachusetts Press, 2005).

Seldes, Gilbert, *The Seven Lively Arts* (New York: Harper & Brothers, 1924).

Sinclair, Andrew, *Prohibition: The Era of Excess* (Boston: Little, Brown, 1962).

Sklar, Robert (ed.), *The Plastic Age: 1917–30* (New York: George Braziller, 1971).

Slosson, Preston William, *The Great Crusade and After: 1914–1928* (New York: Macmillan, 1930).

Smith, Mark C., *Social Science in the Crucible: The American Debate over Objectivity and Purpose, 1918–1941* (Durham, NC: Duke University Press, 1994).

Soule, George, *Prosperity Decade, from War to Depression: 1917–1929* (New York: Rinehart & Co., 1947).

Starr, Kevin (ed.), *Material Dreams: Southern California through the 1920s* (New York: Oxford University Press, 1996).

Stearns, Harold Evans (ed.), *Civilization in the United States* (New York: Harcourt, Brace & Co., 1922).

Stein, Judith M., *The World of Marcus Garvey: Race and Class in Modern*

Society (Baton Rouge, LA: Louisiana State University Press, 1986).

Stephens, Michelle, *Black Empire: The Masculine Global Imaginary of Caribbean Intellectuals in the United States 1914–1962* (Durham, NC: Duke University Press, 2005).

Stevenson, Elizabeth, *Babbitts and Bohemians: From the Great War to the Great Depression* (New Brunswick, NJ: Transaction Publishers, 1998).

Ward, Steven C., *Modernizing the Mind: Psychological Knowledge and the Remaking of Society* (Westport, CT: Praeger, 2002).

Wilson, Edmund, *The American Earthquake: A Documentary of the Twenties and Thirties* (New York: Doubleday, 1958).

Fiction, Poetry and Drama

Baker, Houston A., *Modernism and the Harlem Renaissance* (Chicago: University of Chicago Press, 1987).

Balshaw, Maria, *Looking for Harlem: Urban Aesthetics in African-American Literature* (London: Pluto, 2000).

Barkan, Elazar and Ronald Bush (eds), *Prehistories of the Future: The Primitivist Project and the Culture of Modernism* (Stanford, CA: Stanford University Press, 1995).

Bercovitch, Sacvan, *The Cambridge History of American Literature: Volume 6, Prose Writing 1910–1950* (Cambridge: Cambridge University Press, 2002).

Berman, Ronald, *The Great Gatsby and Modern Times* (Urbana, IL: University of Illinois Press, 1994).

Berman, Ronald, *The Great Gatsby and Fitzgerald's World of Ideas* (Tuscaloosa, AL: University of Alabama Press, 1997).

Berman, Ronald, *Fitzgerald, Hemingway, and the Twenties* (Tuscaloosa, AL: University of Alabama Press, 2002).

Botshon, Lisa and Meredith Goldsmith (eds), *Middlebrow Moderns: Popular American Women Writers of the 1920s* (Boston: Northeastern University Press, 2003).

Bzowski, Frances, *American Women Playwrights, 1900–1930: A Checklist* (Westport, CT: Greenwood Press, 1992).

Carpenter, Humphrey, *Geniuses Together: American Writers in Paris in the 1920s* (Boston: Houghton Mifflin, 1987).

Cooley, John R., *Savages and Naturals: Black Portraits by White Writers in Modern American Literature* (Newark, DE: University of Delaware Press, 1982).

Cowley, Malcolm, *Exile's Return: A Literary Odyssey of the 1920s* (New York: Penguin Books, [1934] 1994).

Curnutt, Kirk, *The Cambridge Introduction to F. Scott Fitzgerald* (Cambridge: Cambridge University Press, 2007).

Favor, Martin J., *Authentic Blackness: The Folk in the New Negro Renaissance* (Durham, NC: Duke University Press, 1999).

Feinstein, Sascha, *Jazz Poetry: From the 1920s to the Present* (Westport, CT: Praeger Publishers, 1997).

Fitzgerald, F. Scott, *The Crack Up* (New York: New Directions, [1945] 1962).

Gerwitz, Arthur and James J. Kolb (eds), *Art, Glitter and Glitz: Mainstream Playwrights and Popular Theatre in 1920s America* (Westport, CT: Praeger Publishers, 2004).

Goody, Alex, *Modernist Articulations: A Cultural Reading of Djuna Barnes, Mina Loy and Gertrude Stein* (London: Palgrave Macmillan, 2007).

Gray, Richard, *A History of American Literature* (Malden, MA: Blackwell Publishing, 2004).

Gubar, Susan, *Racechanges: White Skin, Black Face in American Culture* (New York: Oxford University Press, 1997).

Hegeman, Susan, *Patterns for America: Modernism and the Concept of Culture* (Princeton, NJ: Princeton University Press, 1999).

Hobson, Fred C., *Serpent in Eden: H. L. Mencken and the South* (Chapel Hill, NC: University of North Carolina Press, 1974).

Hoffman, Frederick, *The Twenties: American Writing in the Postwar Decade* (New York: Free Press, 1965).

Jones, Sharon L., *Rereading the Harlem Renaissance: Race, Class, and Gender in the Fiction of Jessie Fauset, Zora Neale Hurston, and Dorothy West* (Westport, CT: Greenwood Press, 2002).

Kelly, Katherine (ed.), *Modern Drama by Women, 1880s–1930s: An International Anthology* (New York: Routledge, 1996).

Kramer, Victor A. and Robert A. Russ (eds), *Harlem Renaissance Re-Examined* (Troy, NY: Whitston Publishing Co., 1997).

MacDonald, Gail, *American Literature and Culture, 1900–1960: An Introduction* (Malden, MA: Blackwell Publishing, 2008).

Martin, Ronald E., *American Literature and the Destruction of Knowledge: Innovative Writing in the Age of Epistemology* (Durham, NC: Duke University Press, 1991).

Miller, Jordan and Winifred Frazer, *American Drama Between the Wars: A Critical History* (Boston: Twayne Publishers, 1991).

Miller, Nina, *Making Love Modern: The Intimate Public Worlds of New York's Literary Women* (New York: Oxford University Press, 1999).

Murphy, Paul V., *The Rebuke of History: The Southern Agrarians and American Conservative Thought* (Chapel Hill, NC: University of North Carolina Press, 2001).

North, Michael, *The Dialect of Modernism: Race, Language and Twentieth-Century Literature* (New York: Oxford University Press, 1994).

Parsons, Deborah, *Djuna Barnes* (Tavistock: Northcote House, 2003).

Pfeiffer, Kathleen, *Race Passing and American Individualism* (Amherst, MA: University of Massachusetts Press, 2002).

Pfister, Joel, *Eugene O'Neill and the Politics of Psychological Discourse* (Chapel Hill, NC: University of North Carolina Press, 1995).

Prigozy, Ruth (ed.), *Cambridge Companion to F. Scott Fitzgerald* (Cambridge: Cambridge University Press, 2002).

Raub, Patricia, *Yesterday's Stories: Popular Women's Novels of the Twenties and Thirties* (Westport, CT: Greenwood Press, 1994).

Rhodes, Chip, *Structures of the Jazz Age: Mass Culture, Progressive Education, and Racial Discourse in American Modernism* (London: Verso, 1998).

Schwarz, A. B. Christa, *Gay Voices of the Harlem Renaissance* (Bloomington, IN: Indiana University Press, 2003).

Shafer, Yvonne, *American Women Playwrights, 1900–1950* (New York: Peter Lang, 1997).

Sievers, W. David, *Freud on Broadway: A History of Psychoanalysis and the American Drama* (New York: Hermitage House, 1955).

Singal, Daniel J., *William Faulkner: The Making of a Modernist* (Chapel Hill, NC: University of North Carolina Press, 1997).

Singh, Amritjit and Daniel M. Scott (eds), *The Collected Writings of Wallace Thurman: A Harlem Renaissance Reader* (New Brunswick, NJ: Rutgers University Press, 2003).

Singh, Amritjit, *Twelve Black Writers, 1923–1933* (University Park, PA: Pennsylvania State University Press, 1976).

Valgemae, Mardi, *Accelerated Grimace: Expressionism in the American Drama of the 1920s* (Carbondale, IL: Southern Illinois University Press, 1972).

Wald, Gayle, *Crossing the Line: Racial Passing in Twentieth-Century U.S. Literature and Culture* (Durham, NC: Duke University Press, 2000).

Watson, Steven, *The Harlem Renaissance: Hub of African-American Culture, 1920–1930* (New York: Pantheon, 1995).

Wilson, Edmund, *The Twenties: From Notebooks and Diaries of the Period* (New York: Macmillan, 1975).

Wintz, Cary D., *Black Culture and the Harlem Renaissance* (Houston, TX: Rice University Press, 1988).

Witemeyer, Hugh (ed.), *Pound / Williams: Selected Letters of Ezra Pound and William Carlos Williams* (New York: New Directions, 1996).

Music and Performance

Albertson, Chris, *Bessie: A Biography* (London: Barrie and Jenkins, 1972).

Baraka, Amiri, *Blues People: Negro Music in White America* (New York: W. Morrow, 1963).

Crunden, Robert, *Body and Soul: The Making of American Modernism* (New York: Basic Books, 2000).

Davis, Angela, *Blues Legacies and Black Feminism: Gertrude 'Ma' Rainey, Bessie Smith, and Billie Holiday* (New York: Pantheon Books, 1998).

Dinerstein, Joel, *Swinging the Machine: Modernity, Technology, and African American Culture between the World Wars* (Amherst, MA: University of Massachusetts Press, 2003).

Dunning, John, *On the Air: The Encyclopedia of Old-Time Radio* (New York: Oxford University Press, 1998).

Foulkes, Julia L., *Modern Bodies: Dance and American Modernism from Martha Graham to Alvin Ailey* (Chapel Hill, NC: University of North Carolina Press, 2002).

Gioia, Ted, *The History of Jazz* (New York: Oxford University Press, 1999).

Goldberg, Isaac, *Tin Pan Alley: A Chronicle of the American Popular Music Racket* (New York: John Day, 1930).

Hadlock, Richard, *Jazz Masters of the 20s* (New York: Da Capo Press, 1988).

Harrison, Daphne Duval, *Black Pearls: Blues Queens of the 1920s* (New Brunswick, NJ: Rutgers University Press, 1990).

Hazzard-Gordon, Katrina, *Jookin': The Rise of Social Dance Formations in African American Culture* (Philadelphia: Temple University Press, 1990).

Hill, Constance Valis, *Brotherhood in Rhythm: The Jazz Tap Dancing of the Nicholas Brothers* (New York: Oxford University Press, 2000).

Jackson, Buzzy, *A Bad Woman Feeling Good: Blues and the Women Who Sing Them* (New York: Norton, 2005).

Jasen, David A., *Tin Pan Alley: An Encyclopedia of the Golden Age of American Song* (New York: Routledge, 2003).

Kay, Jackie, *Bessie Smith* (Bath: Absolute Press, 1997).

Kenney, William Howland, *Recorded Music in American Life: The Phonograph and Popular Memory, 1890–1945* (New York: Oxford University Press, 1999).

Latham, Angela J., *Posing a Threat: Flappers, Chorus Girls, and Other Brazen Performers of the American 1920s* (Hanover, NH: University Press of New England, 2000).

Lemke, Sieglinde, *Primitivist Modernism: Black Culture and the Origins of Transatlantic Modernism* (Oxford: Oxford University Press, 1998).

Leonard, Neil, *Jazz and the White Americans: The Acceptance of a New Art Form* (Chicago: University of Chicago Press, 1962).

Locke, Alain, *The Negro and His Music: Negro Art, Past and Present* (New York: Arno Press, 1969).

Ogren, Kathy, *The Jazz Revolution: Twenties America and the Meaning of Jazz* (New York: Oxford University Press, 1989).

Oja, Carol J., *Making Music Modern: New York in the 1920s* (New York: Oxford University Press, 2000).

Oliver, Paul, *Bessie Smith* (London: Cassell, 1959).

O'Meally, Robert G. (ed.), *The Jazz Cadence of American Culture* (New York: Columbia University Press, 1998).

Overton, Grant, *American Nights Entertainment* (New York: D. Appleton & Co., 1923).

Peretti, Burton W., *The Creation of Jazz: Music, Race and Culture in Urban America* (Chicago: University of Illinois Press, 1992).

Rosenfield, Paul, *An Hour with American Music* (Philadelphia: J. B. Lippincott, 1929).

Ruhlmann, William, *Breaking Records: 100 Years of Hits* (New York: Routledge, 2004).

Schuller, Gunter, *Early Jazz: Its Roots and Musical Development* (New York: Oxford University Press, 1968).

Shaw, Arnold, *The Jazz Age: Popular Music in the 1920s* (New York: Oxford University Press, 1990).

Stearns, Marshall W., *The Story of Jazz* (London: Oxford University Press, 1970).

Stewart-Baxter, Derrick, *Ma Rainey and the Classic Blues Singers* (London: Studio Vista, 1970).

Suskin, Steven, *Show Tunes: The Songs, Shows, and Careers of Broadway's Major Composers* (New York: Oxford University Press, 2000).

Thomas, Helen, *Dance, Modernity, and Culture: Explorations in the Sociology of Dance* (New York: Routledge, 1995).

Tirro, Frank, *Jazz: A History* (New York: Norton, 1993).

Weissman, Dick, *Blues: The Basics* (New York: Routledge, 2004).

Film and Radio

Abel, Richard (ed.), *Silent Film* (New Brunswick, NJ: Rutgers University Press, 1996).

Addison, Heather, *Hollywood and the Rise of Physical Culture* (New York: Routledge, 2003).

Bachman, Gregg and Thomas Slater (eds), *American Silent Film: Discovering Marginalized Voices* (Carbondale, IL: Southern Illinois University Press, 2002).

Barfield, Ray, *Listening to Radio, 1920–1950* (Westport, CT: Praeger Publishers, 1996).

Barnouw, Eric, *A Tower in Babel: A History of Broadcasting in the United States to 1933* (New York: Oxford University Press, 1966).

Barrios, Richard, *A Song in the Dark: The Birth of the Musical Film* (New York: Oxford University Press, 1995).

Bernardi, Daniel (ed.), *The Birth of Whiteness: Race and the Emergence of U.S. Cinema* (New Brunswick, NJ: Rutgers University Press, 1996).

Bogle, Donald, *Toms, Coons, Mulattoes, Mammies, and Bucks: An Interpretive History of Blacks in American Films* (New York: Continuum Publishing, [1973] 2001).

Bordwell, David, Janet Staiger and Kristin Thompson, *The Classical Hollywood Cinema: Film Style and Mode of Production to 1960* (London: Routledge, 1988).

Bowser, Pearl, Jane Gaines and Charles Musser (eds), *Oscar Micheaux and His Circle: African-American Filmmaking and Race Cinema of the Silent Era* (Bloomington, IN: Indiana University Press, 2001).

Butsch, Richard, *The Making of American Audiences: From Stage to Television, 1750–1990* (Cambridge: Cambridge University Press, 2000).

Carr, Steven Alan, *Hollywood and Anti-Semitism: A Cultural History up to World War II* (Cambridge: Cambridge University Press, 2001).

Cohan, Steven and Ina Rae Hark, *Screening the Male: Exploring Masculinities in Hollywood Cinema* (London: Routledge, 1993).

Cohen, Paula, *Silent Film and the Triumph of the American Myth* (New York: Oxford University Press, 2001).

Crafton, Donald, *The Talkies: American Cinema's Transition to Sound, 1926–1931* (New York: Simon and Schuster, 1997).

Cripps, Thomas, *Slow Fade to Black: The Negro in American Film, 1900–1942* (New York: Oxford University Press, 1993).

Douglas, Susan J., *Listening in: Radio and the American Imagination* (Minneapolis: University of Minnesota Press, 2004).

Dunning, John, *On the Air: The Encyclopedia of Old-Time Radio* (New York: Oxford University Press, 1998).

Everson, William K., *American Silent Film* (New York: Oxford University Press, 1978).

Fuller, Kathryn H., *At the Picture Show: Small-Town Audiences and the Creation of Movie Fan Culture* (Charlottesville, VA: University Press of Virginia, 2001).

Gomery, Douglas, *Shared Pleasures: A History of Movie Presentation in the United States* (Madison, WI: University of Wisconsin Press, 1992).

Gomery, Douglas, *The Coming of Sound: A History* (New York: Routledge, 2004).

Green, Ronald, *With a Crooked Stick: The Films of Oscar Micheaux* (Bloomington, IN: Indiana University Press, 2004).

Guerrero, Ed, *Framing Blackness: The African American Image in Film* (Philadelphia: Temple University Press, 1993).

Hall, Ben, *The Best Remaining Seats: The Golden Age of the Movie Palace* (New York: Clarkson N. Potter, 1961).

Hampton, Benjamin, *History of the American Film Industry from its Beginnings to 1931* (New York: Dover Publications, [1931] 1970).

Hangen, Tona J., *Redeeming the Dial: Radio, Religion and Popular Culture in America* (Chapel Hill, NC: University of North Carolina Press, 2002).

Hansen, Miriam, *Babel and Babylon: Spectatorship in American Silent Film* (Cambridge, MA: Harvard University Press, 1991).

Higashi, Sumiko, *Virgins, Vamps and Flappers: The American Silent Movie Heroine* (Montreal, Quebec: Eden Press, 1978).

Higashi, Sumiko, *Cecil B. DeMille and American Culture: The Silent Era* (Berkeley, CA: University of California Press, 1994).

Hilmes, Michele, *Hollywood and Broadcasting: From Radio to Cable* (Chicago: University of Illinois Press, 1990).

Jacobs, Lea, *The Decline of Sentiment: American Film in the 1920s* (Berkeley, CA: University of California Press, 2008).

Jacobs, Lewis, *The Rise of the American Film: A Critical History* (New York: Harcourt, Brace, 1939).

Kaplan, E. Ann, *Women and Film: Both Sides of the Camera* (London: Methuen, 1983).

Koszarski, Richard, *An Evening's Entertainment: The Age of the Silent Feature Picture, 1915–1928* (Berkeley, CA: University of California Press, [1990] 1994).

Leab, Daniel J., (ed.), *From Sambo to Superspade: The Black Experience in Motion Pictures* (London: Secker and Warburg, 1975).

MacCann, Richard Dyer, *Films of the Twenties* (London: The Scarecrow Press, 1996).

Markovitz, Jonathan, *Legacies of Lynching: Racial Violence and Memory* (Minneapolis: University of Minnesota Press, 2004).

Margolies, John and Emily Gwathmey, *Ticket to Paradise: American Movie Theaters and How We Had Fun* (Boston: Little, Brown, 1991).

May, Lary, *Screening Out the Past: The Birth of Mass Culture and the Motion Picture Industry* (Chicago: University of Chicago Press, [1980] 1983).

Mayne, Judith, *The Women at the Keyhole: Feminism and Women's Cinema* (Bloomington, IN: Indiana University Press, 1990).

McCaffrey, Donald W. and Christopher P. Jacobs, *Guide to the Silent Years of American Cinema* (Westport, CT: Greenwood Press, 1999).

Menefee, David W., *The First Female Stars: Women of the Silent Era* (Westport, CT: Praeger, 2004.

Naylor, David, *American Picture Palaces: The Architecture of Fantasy* (New York: Prentice Hall Editions, 1981).

Negra, Diane, *Off-White Hollywood: American Culture and Ethnic Female Stardom* (London: Routledge, 2001).

Pizzitola, Louis, *Hearst over Hollywood: Power, Passion, and Propaganda in the Movies* (New York: Columbia University Press, 2002).

Rony, Fatimah Tobing, *The Third Eye: Race, Cinema, and Ethnographic Spectacle* (Durham, NC: Duke University Press, 1996).

Sarris, Andrew, *You Ain't Heard Nothin' Yet: The American Talking Film: History and Memory, 1927–1949* (New York: Oxford University Press, 1998).

Scheiner, Georganne, *Signifying Female Adolescence: Film Representations and Fans, 1920–1950* (Westport, CT: Praeger Publishers, 2000).

Starr, Kevin (ed.), *Material Dreams: Southern California through the 1920's* (New York: Oxford University Press, 1996).

Studlar, Gaylyn, *This Mad Masquerade: Stardom and Masculinity in the Jazz Age* (New York: Columbia University Press, 1996).

Thompson, Kristin, *Herr Lubitsch Goes to Hollywood: German and American Film after World War I* (Amsterdam: Amsterdam University Press, 2005).

Waller, Gregory A., *Main Street Amusements: Movies and Commercial Entertainment in a Southern City, 1896–1930* (Washington, DC: Smithsonian Institution, 1995).

Visual Art and Design

Armitage, Shelley, *John Held, Jr. Illustrator of the Jazz Age* (Syracuse, NY: Syracuse University Press, 1987).

Barr, Alfred Hamilton, *American Art of the 20s and 30s* (New York: Arno Press, 1969).

Baur, John, *Revolution and Tradition in Modern American Art* (Cambridge, MA: Harvard University Press, 1951).

Brown, Milton W., *American Painting: From the Armory Show to the Depression* (Princeton, NJ: Princeton University Press, 1955).

Bry, Doris and Nicholas Callaway (eds), *Georgia O'Keeffe: The New York Years* (New York: Knopf, 1991).

Cahill, Holger and Alfred H. Barr, *Art in America: A Complete Survey* (New York: Reynal and Hitchcock, 1935).

Carroll, Anne Elizabeth, *Word, Image, and the New Negro: Representation and Identity in the Harlem Renaissance* (Bloomington, IN: Indiana University Press, 2005).

Cassidy, Donna M., *Painting the Musical City: Jazz and Cultural Identity in American Art 1910–1940* (Washington, DC: Smithsonian Institution, 1997).

Chase, Stuart, *Men and Machines* (New York: Macmillan, 1929).

Driskell, David et al., *Harlem Renaissance: Art of Black America* (New York: Studio Museum in Harlem, 1987).

Cheney, Sheldon and Martha Cheney, *Art and the Machine: An Account of Industrial Design in 20th-Century America* (New York: McGraw-Hill, 1936).

Corn, Wanda, *The Great American Thing: Modern Art and National Identity 1915–1935* (Berkeley, CA: University of California Press, 2000).

Davidson, Abraham A., *Early American Modernist Painting, 1910–1935* (New York: Harper and Row, 1981).

Dijkstra, Bram, *The Hieroglyphics of a New Speech: Cubism, Stieglitz, and the Early Poetry of William Carlos Williams* (Princeton, NJ: Princeton University Press, 1969).

Dijkstra, Bram (ed.), *A Recognizable Image: William Carlos Williams on Art and Artists* (New York: New Directions, 1978).

Eldredge, Charles C., *Georgia O'Keeffe: American and Modern* (New Haven, CT: Yale University Press, 1993).

Fischer, Lucy, *Designing Women: Cinema, Art Deco, and the Female Form* (New York: Columbia University Press, 2003).

Flint, Janet (ed.), *The Prints of Louis Lozowick* (New York: Hudson Hills Press, 1982).

Friedman, Martin L., *The Precisionist View in American Art: An Exhibition* (Minneapolis, MN: Walker Art Center, 1960).

Goeser, Caroline, *Picturing the New Negro: Harlem Renaissance Print Culture and Modern Black Identity* (Lawrence, KA: University Press of Kansas, 2007).

Goodrich, Lloyd and John I. H. Baur, *American Art of Our Century* (New York: Praeger, 1961).

Haskell, Barbara, *The American Century: Art and Culture, 1900–1950* (New York: Norton, 1999).

Howe, Graham and G. Ray Hawkins, *Paul Outerbridge Jr: Photographs 1921–39* (London: Thames and Hudson, 1980).

Jacob, Mary Jane and Linda Downs, *The Rouge: The Image of Industry in the Art of Charles Sheeler and Diego Rivera* (Detroit: Detroit Institute of Arts, 1978).

Lemke, Sieglinde, *Primitivist Modernism: Black Culture and the Origins of Transatlantic Modernism* (Oxford: Oxford University Press, 1998).

Levy, Sophie (ed.), *A Transatlantic Avant-Garde: American Artists in Paris, 1918–1939* (Berkeley, CA: University of California Press, 2003).

Lucic, Karen, *Charles Sheeler and the Cult of the Machine* (Cambridge, MA: Harvard University Press, 1991).

Massey, Anne, *Hollywood Beyond the Screen: Design and Material Culture* (New York: Berg, 2000).

Merkin, Richard, *The Jazz Age As Seen Through the Eyes of Ralph Barton, Miguel Covarrubias, and John Held* (Providence, RI: Rhode Island School of Design, 1968).

Mumford, Lewis, *Sticks and Stones, a Study of American Architecture and Civilization* (New York: Boni and Liveright, 1924).

Nadell, Martha Jane, *Enter the New Negroes: Images of Race in American Culture* (Cambridge, MA: Harvard University Press, 2004).

Park, Edwin Avery, *New Backgrounds for a New Age* (New York: Harcourt, Brace & Co., 1927).

Peters, Sarah Whitaker, *Becoming O'Keeffe: The Early Years* (New York: Abbeville Press, 1991).

Platt, Susan Noyes, *Modernism in the 1920s: Interpretations of Modern Art in New York from Expressionism to Constructivism* (Ann Arbor, MI: UMI Research Press, [1981] 1985).

Pyne, Kathleen, *Modernism and the Feminine Voice: O'Keeffe and the Women of the Stieglitz Circle* (Berkeley, CA: University of California Press, 2007).

Robinson, Cervin and Rosemarie Haag Bletter, *Skyscraper Style: Art Deco New York* (New York: Oxford University Press, 1975).

Robinson, Jontyle Theresa and Wendy Greenhouse, *The Art of Archibald J. Motley, Jr.* (Chicago: Chicago Historical Society, 1991).

Sayler, Oliver M., *Revolt in the Arts: A Survey of the Creation, Distribution and Appreciation of Art in America* (New York: Brentano's, 1930).

Sheeler, Charles, *Charles Sheeler: Paintings, Drawings, Photographs* (New York: The Museum of Modern Art, 1939).

Skipwith, Joanna (ed.), *Rhapsodies in Black: Art of the Harlem Renaissance* (Berkeley, CA: University of California Press, 1997).

Smith, Terry, *Making the Modern: Industry, Art, and Design in America* (Chicago: University of Chicago Press, 1993).

Solomon, Katherine, *The Chicago Tribune Tower Competition: Skyscraper Design and Cultural Change in the 1920s* (Chicago: University of Chicago Press, 2001).

Stern, Robert A. M., Gregory Gilmartin and Thomas Mellins, *New York 1930: Architecture and Urbanism between the Two World Wars* (New York: Rizzoli, 1987).

Tashjian, Dickran, *Skyscraper Primitives: Dada and the American Avant Garde, 1910–1925* (Middletown, CT: Wesleyan University Press, 1975).

Tashjian, Dickran, *William Carlos Williams and the American Scene, 1920–1940* (New York: Whitney Museum of American Art, 1978).

Taylor, Joshua C., *America As Art* (New York: Harper and Row, 1976).

Tichi, Cecilia, *Shifting Gears: Technology, Literature, Culture in Modernist America* (Chapel Hill, NC: University of North Carolina Press, 1987).

Tsujimoto, Karen, *Images of America: Precisionist Painting and Modern Photography* (Seattle: University of Washington Press, 1982).

Vlack, Don, *Art Deco Architecture in New York* (New York: Harper and Row, 1974).

Wilson, Richard Guy, Dianne Pilgrim and Dickran Tashjian, *The Machine Age in America, 1918–1941* (New York: The Brooklyn Museum, 1986).

Zabel, Barbara, *Assembling Art: The Machine and the American Avant-Garde* (Jackson, MS: University Press of Mississippi, 2004).

Consumption and Leisure

Adams, James Truslow, *Our Business Civilization: Some Aspects of American Culture* (New York: A. and C. Boni, 1929).

Aron, Cindy S., *Working at Play: A History of Vacations in the United States* (New York: Oxford University Press, 1999).

Calder, Lendol, *Financing the American Dream: A Cultural History of Consumer Credit* (Princeton, NJ: Princeton University Press, 1999).

Cohen, Lizabeth, *Making a New Deal: Industrial Workers in Chicago, 1919–1939* (Cambridge, MA: Cambridge University Press, 1990).

Fass, Paula, *The Damned and the Beautiful: American Youth in the 1920s* (New York: Oxford University Press, 1979).

Fox, Richard Wightman and Jackson Lears (eds), *The Culture of Consumption: Essays in American History, 1880–1980* (New York: Pantheon Books, 1983).

Heiman, Jim (ed.), *All-American Ads of the 20s* (New York: Taschen, 2004).

Jeansonne, Glen, *Transformation and Reaction: America 1921–1945* (New York: HarperCollins, 1994).

Kyvig, David E. (ed.), *Law, Alcohol, and Order: Perspectives on National Prohibition* (Westport, CT: Greenwood Press, 1985).

Jackson Lears, *Fables of Abundance: A Cultural History of Advertising in the United States* (New York: Basic Books, 1994).

Lundén, Rolf, *Business and Religion in the American 1920s* (Westport, CT: Greenwood Press, 1988).

Lynd, Robert and Helen, *Middletown: A Study in Contemporary American Culture* (New York: Harcourt, Brace, 1929).

Marchand, Roland, *Advertising the American Dream: Making Way for Modernity, 1920–1940* (Berkeley, CA: University of California Press, 1985).

Martin, Carol, *Dance Marathons: Performing American Culture of the 1920s and 1930s* (Jackson, MS: University Press of Mississippi, 1994).

Nasaw, David, *Going Out: The Rise and Fall of Public Amusements* (New York: Basic Books, 1993).

Olney, Martha, *Buy Now, Pay Later: Advertising, Credit, and Consumer Demand in the 1920s* (Chapel Hill, NC: University of North Carolina Press, 1991).

Prothro, James W., *The Dollar Decade: Business Ideas in the 1920s* (Baton Rouge, LA: Louisiana State University Press, 1954).

Pruette, Lorine and Harry Elmer Barnes, *Women and Leisure: A Study of Social Waste* (New York: E. P. Dutton & Co., 1924).

Rumbarger, John J., *Profits, Power, and Prohibition: Alcohol Reform and the Industrializing of America, 1800–1930* (Albany, NY: State University of New York Press, 1989).

Sinclair, Andrew, *Prohibition: The Era of Excess* 1st ed. (Boston: Little, Brown, 1962).

Susman, Warren, 'Culture and Civilization: The Nineteen-Twenties' and 'Culture Heroes: Ford, Barton, Ruth', in *Culture as History* (Washington, DC: Smithsonian Institution, 2003).

Tucker, David M., *The Decline of Thrift in America: Our Cultural Shift from Saving to Spending* (New York: Praeger Publishers, 1991).

Ward, John W., 'The Meaning of Lindbergh's Flight', *American Quarterly*, 10 (Spring 1958).

Index